D0988979

Recipes with a Spice

Indian Cuisine for Balanced Nutrition

Kusum L. Gupta

© 2002 by Kusum L. Gupta. All rights reserved.

No part of this book may be reproduced, stored in a retrieval system, or transmitted by any means, electronic, mechanical, photocopying, recording, or otherwise, without written permission from the author.

ISBN: 0-7596-9552-0 (e-book)
ISBN: 0-7596-9553-9 (Paperback)

This book is printed on acid free paper.

1stBooks - rev. 9/24/02

To perpetuate the art of cooking from generation to generation.

Contents

Preface

The trial edition of this cookbook was so well received that all copies were gone within a few months. Encouraged by the response, I decided to bring out this version, containing not only additional recipes but also guidelines for nutritive cooking and eating. The chapter called *Healthful Eating* describes various foods and some cooking techniques required for balanced nutrition. This is to help those making a life–style change or switching to vegetarian food for health or other reasons. Many ideas are based on the guidelines followed in our family for all–round health. Thanks to my friend, Chandra Balusu, MS, CDN, diet and nutrition consultant who reviewed the information and guided me in including the nutritive analysis.

I have collected recipes for this book mostly from friends and family. I have included some of my mother's specialties as I lovingly remember her cooking in our kitchen next to the open courtyard. The chapter *Cooking by Children* is largely motivated by my grandchildren and is an example of globalization of ingredients and cooking techniques.

My major objective is to present diverse regional foods of India, focusing on healthy alternatives, and allowing for flexibility and ease in the use of seasonings. The recipes have been tried out in several homes. I hope you will enjoy the delicious results trying them out for yourself.

I thank and express my sincere appreciation to my family and friends in USA, Canada, and India, who so generously shared their recipes with me. Without their help and valuable suggestions, this book would not have been possible. My special thanks to my husband, children, and grandchildren, who not only helped in putting the book together but also supported me in my endless hours of work.

Kusum Gupta
Always experimenting with food

Fred Dahl, Ashvini Mahajan, and Anjali Nandedkar helped in artwork and production. Some of the pictures are taken from nutrition.about.com. Recipes have been contributed by:

Agarwal, Meera
Agrawal, Promila
Balusu, Chandra
Basi, Gurdeep
Bhatia, Anu
Bhutani, Mala
Chander,Anuradha
Desai, Madhuri
Garg, Nina
Goel, Puja
Gupta, Abha
Gupta, Satwant
Kapur, Shukla
Khurana, Pushpa
Kumar, Anu
Kumar, Poonam

Kumar, Suman
Malhotra, Asha
Manocha, Renu
Mirchandani, Vasanti
Mittal, Usha
Naik, Sudha
Parashar, Girjesh
Rao, Sharda
Satyendra, Uma
Shah, Kusum
Shah, Manisha
Shah, Vilas
Sharma, Pushpa
Srivastava,Sheela
Uppal, Sashi
Varma, Madhu

Introduction

The purpose of this book is to provide selected recipes from different parts of India that can be easily prepared and relished by those interested in Indian cuisine or those making a life-style change to healthy cooking and eating. It includes breads from the wheat growing regions of north India, rice dishes from the coastal areas, spicy snacks from western India, and delicious milk and cheese desserts from eastern India. It addresses the needs of the most experienced as well as the adventurous beginner to explore the wonderful world of cooking.

Recipes are described step by step so that they can be tried by anybody wishing to enjoy healthy and delicious dishes full of aromatic seasonings. Many meatless dishes are included. A special effort has been made to include recipes that help produce well-balanced and heart-healthy meals.

Organization of the Book

This book is comprised of:

- Introduction that gives an overview of the book, describes how ingredients can be tailored, and gives helpful hints to facilitate cooking.
- A chapter called *Healthful Eating* that describes the nutritive value of foods in different Food Groups[1] and how they can be incorporated in your cooking.
- Chapters for general preparation techniques, ingredients and terms used in Indian cuisine, and sample menus.
- Recipes in alphabetical order in separate chapters, starting with appetizers and ending with desserts, and a chapter on foods that children like to eat and cook. Besides a list of main ingredients and preparation steps, each recipe includes storage information, number of persons served, nutritive analysis, and a list of seasonings (garlic, ginger, spices, etc.) that can be modified per taste. Variations and healthy alternatives are included in some cases.
- Appendices describing major nutrients and vitamins, and nutritive facts of some foods.

Ingredients Can Be Tailored

Readily available ingredients are used in the recipes whenever possible. There are some ingredients that are unique to Indian cuisine and can be purchased from health food stores or Indian grocery stores. You, however, can substitute or omit ingredients to suit your taste and needs. Cooking should be creative and fun, and satisfy your passion and need for food. Experimentation is the best guide.

Flexibility of ingredients allows you to:

- Use any oil that you prefer for cooking. Canola or olive oil or a mixture of the two is recommended instead of butter or

---

[1]Food Groups, based on the Food Guide Pyramid recommended by the United States Department of Agriculture, are: Grain, Fruit, Vegetable, Legumes/Meat, Dairy, Fat, and Sugar.

clarified butter. You may reduce the amount of oil used by following some of the suggestions in *Making the Change* on page 24.

- Use any grade of milk that you prefer unless specified.
- Change quantities of sugar, salt, and other seasonings to your taste. You may be one of those experts who just 'pour' the right amount of seasoning without ever measuring.
- Omit or adjust red chili powder and green chilies based on your level of tolerance for hot spicy food. You can also opt to use milder green chilies for taste and aroma.
- Modify quantities of onions, garlic, tomatoes, and ginger which are added for flavor and thickening of the gravy. These are considered healthy additives to Indian foods.
- Use fresh, frozen, or canned vegetables, beans, and condiments. Researchers suggest that frozen vegetables that are picked at their peak and frozen immediately may be as nutritious as many of the fresh vegetables. Sometimes canned ingredients are specified for ease.

Substitution of Ingredients

At times a particular ingredient may not be available. The guidelines for substitution include:

1 teaspoon baking powder	= ½ teaspoon cream of tartar mixed with ¼ teaspoon baking soda
1 cup dry beans, soaked	= 2 cups canned beans
1 medium whole egg	= ¼ cup egg substitute
1 cup self-rising flour	= 1 cup all-purpose flour mixed with ½ teaspoon baking powder and ¼ teaspoon salt
1 teaspoon dry herbs	= 1 tablespoon fresh herbs
1 teaspoon mango powder	= 1½ teaspoons lemon juice
1 cup fresh milk	= ½ cup evaporated milk plus ½ cup water or 4 tablespoons nonfat dry milk mixed with 1

		tablespoon butter and 1 cup water
14 oz sweetened condensed milk	=	3 cups nonfat dry milk mixed with 2 cups sugar and 1½ cups milk
1 cup uncooked rice	=	3 cups cooked rice
1 teaspoon tamarind paste	=	3 teaspoons lemon juice
1 large tomato	=	1/3 cup canned tomato.

Helpful Hints

Listed below are some suggestions for:

> ➢ Cooking and handling of food
> ➢ Food safety and storage
> ➢ Cutting down food preparation time.

Cooking and Handling of Food

To prevent some of the errors and to facilitate cooking:

- ◆ If **brown sugar** hardens, place the open box of sugar and 1 cup of hot water in the microwave oven; microwave at high for 2–5 minutes until the sugar can be crumbled.
- ◆ If you are **chopping fruit** or making desserts while working with onions, garlic, and chilies, take care to keep the knives and cutting boards separate so that smells do not travel from one food to another.
- ◆ A few teaspoons of sugar and cinnamon slowly browned in a pan or in the oven will hide unpleasant **cooking odors** in the house.
- ◆ When cooking or **heating in a microwave oven**, cover the dishes leaving a small opening for steam to get out. This ensures faster heating and avoids splatter. For uniform cooking of vegetables, cut them before putting them in the microwave. If using whole vegetables, poke them and arrange them in spoke fashion in a microwave container.
- ◆ To make it easier to extract **juice from limes or lemons**, put them in water for about an hour; or microwave on high for 20–30 seconds.

- Never cover a pot completely when cooking with **milk** because it can easily boil over.
- Peel **onions** under cold running water, then freeze them for 5 minutes before chopping them. This will keep your eyes from being irritated while working with them. Also keep the root intact which prevents the onion from falling apart when chopping.
- Add a few drops of lemon juice to **rice** when it is almost cooked to keep the grains from sticking together.
- To prevent **scorching** when boiling milk, first rinse the pan with hot water.
- If a dish becomes **too salty**, add a little lemon juice, vinegar, yogurt, chopped tomatoes, or any crushed vegetable. Another way is to add some raw potato pieces and cook a little. Potatoes absorb extra salt and can be removed before serving, if desired.

Food Safety and Storage

To ensure that food stays fresh and free from contamination:

- Refrigerate opened **cooking oil, shelled nuts**, and flour to keep them from turning rancid.
- Let **hot foods** cool off so that they can be refrigerated as soon as possible. For faster cooling, divide large amounts into smaller containers or add some ice cubes to hot liquids. Use refrigerated cooked foods within one to two weeks.
- Allow **fruits** to ripen at room temperature before refrigerating them.
- Keep a box of baking soda next to the stove to dump on any **grease fire** that might occur. To deprive the fire of oxygen, cover a pan or close the oven door.
- Squeeze out all the air from plastic bags when you close them for storing food in the freezer. This prevents **ice crystals** from forming on food,
- **Don't jam** too much food in your refrigerator; let the cold air flow over, under, and around the food.
- Don't **refreeze** cooked thawed food.
- Use cooked **frozen foods** within a few months.

- Clean the **inside of the refrigerator** with a clean sponge soaked in a solution of warm water and baking soda.
- If there are any **green spots on a potato,** simply pare off the area before cooking to avoid bitterness.
- Wrap **high–moisture vegetables,** such as asparagus, green onions, mushrooms, and cucumber, in paper before putting in a plastic bag to store in the refrigerator.
- Never **soak vegetables** for too long after slicing; they will lose much of the nutritional value.
- When using a **pressure cooker,** follow the following safety tips:
  - Put enough water for cooking.
  - Ensure the hole in the lid is not blocked.
  - Let the pressure cooker cool down, and then remove the pressure regulator before opening the lid.
  - Check and oil the rubber ring occasionally.

Reducing Food Preparation Time

Cooking is one of the very nurturing rhythms of life that should be fun and not all time consuming. To put meals on the table in a short time:

- Use a food processor to **crush large quantities** of ginger, onions, garlic, and green chilies in advance and freeze them in separate bags for use as needed. Double bag so that smells do not travel to other foods.
- Make a large quantity of **dough** and keep it covered in the refrigerator (4–6 days) or freezer. Thaw the frozen dough in the refrigerator (takes about 12 hours) or in the microwave, before using.
- Make instant **herb cubes** to be used whenever needed. Puree fresh leaves and tender stems of coriander, mint, basil, or parsley with little water in a blender. Freeze in an ice cube tray. Store the cubes in a freezer bag for use in prepared dishes.
- Use a pressure cooker for **fast cooking of legumes** (dry beans, lentils and 'dal' or Indian lentils). Do a quick soak of dry beans (see page 30). If you are able to plan ahead, use

a slow cooker for cooking while away. Food started with cold water takes 7–8 hours in a slow cooker. Start with hot water to reduce cooking time. Cook enough to freeze some for the next time.

♦ Make a **list of ingredients** that you use while cooking. Keep your pantry, refrigerator, and freezer well stocked so that you do not have to do a last–minute shopping run.

♦ Start cooking lentils, 'dal', and beans first because they take **longer to cook**. While they are simmering, sauté the vegetables and prepare salads and yogurt dishes.

♦ Use the **microwave to cook vegetables** such as potatoes, carrots, and squash, while you sauté the condiments. Then cook the vegetables and the condiments together to prepare delicious dishes in very short time.

♦ Make **one–pot dishes** like 'Bulgur Pulao', 'Tahiri' (Vegetable Rice), and 'Vegetable Noodle Soup' that are liked by almost everybody. Serve yogurt and salad on the side.

♦ **Start cooking** before everything is ready. Sauté the garlic and onions while you prepare the remaining ingredients to be added.

♦ Set a **timer** when something is cooking while you go to do something else. This prevents burning of food that you start with so much care and love.

♦ Prepare a dish in **two or more steps**. Usually it is possible to do one step at one time and postpone the next step to another day or time.

♦ Wash and cut large quantities of **vegetables** in advance. Refrigerate or freeze them in convenient size bags, ready to be used when needed.

♦ Keep prepared spice mixtures such as **'Onion and garlic masala'** (page 33) and **'Tomato–yogurt curry'** (page 27) in the refrigerator or freezer to be used when needed.

♦ Make larger quantity of **yogurt and fresh cheese (paneer)**. Yogurt easily keeps in the refrigerator for 5–7 days. 'Paneer' can be frozen.

Weights and Measures

Some standard measures include:

3 teaspoons	=	1 tablespoon
4 tablespoons	=	¼ cup or 2 fluid oz. or 60 ml.
1 cup	=	8 fluid oz. or 240 ml.
2 cups	=	1 pint
2 pints (4 cups)	=	1 quart or almost 1 liter
4 quarts (16 cups)	=	1 gallon
1 oz. (weight)	=	28.4 grams (g)
16 oz. (weight)	=	1 pound or 454 g
2.2 pounds	=	1 kilogram or 1000 g

A standard cup of liquid is the same volume for any type of liquid. However a standard cup measure of a dry or solid ingredient will vary in weight depending on the type of ingredient. Some of the approximate weights are:

1 cup chopped carrots	=	128 g
1 cup shredded cheese	=	114 g
1 cup fine flour	=	140 g
1 cup legumes, rice or nuts	=	150 g
1 cup green peas	=	145 g
1 cup sugar	=	190 g
1 cup chopped tomatoes	=	180 g
1 cup chopped vegetables like cabbage and mushrooms	=	70 – 100 g

Healthful Eating

Nutritionists have always advised eating healthy and doing exercise for the well–being of mind and body. Based on many studies, there are several recommendations about what to eat and what to avoid in order to reduce the risk of disease. The recommendations include:

- ♦ Eat high-fiber foods, using fat and sugar sparingly.
- ♦ Enjoy a wide variety of foods in balance and moderation.
- ♦ Focus on the right ingredients.

Fruits, vegetables, and whole grains are high in fiber, supply nutrients that protect and maintain your health, and neutralize the effect of fat you consume. Add minimum possible fat, especially saturated animal fat contained in butter, hard cheese, and fatty meats. Use nonfat and lean products as much as possible. Minimize extra sugar because milk and fruits like bananas and oranges supply plenty of natural sugar.

Eating many different foods, including spices and herbs, will ensure that you get all the required nutrients. The body needs many nutrients in varying quantities to maintain optimum health. Make sure that your plate looks pretty with something green, yellow, red, and orange. Expand your culinary horizons by trying new foods and international dishes you have not had before; you just might find some new favorites. Now you can find a variety of products, vegetables, and exotic seasonings almost everywhere because a healthy fusion of foods has occurred along with the mixing of cultures practically all over the world.

Using the freshest ingredients ensures wholesome and delicious meals. Pay attention to the quality of foods you buy. Use plenty of fruits and vegetables. Consider growing your own vegetables or buying organic produce, grown without the use of synthetic fertilizers and pesticides. The toxic level caused by the pesticides can be more harmful to young children.

Check nutrition facts label on all processed or canned foods to find out what you are eating. Avoid the products that contain hydrogenated oil, a cheap fat used to extend the shelf life of foods.

Food Groups

You may be familiar with the Food Guide Pyramid recommended by the United States Department of Agriculture (USDA) and endorsed by many other organizations for nutrition and dietetics. The figure shows the relative proportions in which the various Food Groups should be consumed. The nutritionists have found that if you eat the recommended number of servings from each of the five major Food Groups — Grain, Fruit, Vegetable, Legumes/Meat, and Dairy, you should be getting all the vitamins and minerals you need.

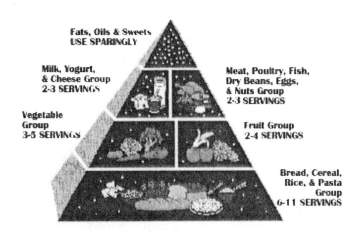

USDA Food Guide Pyramid

Treat the Food Groups as a guide, not an exact classification of nutrients. You will get most of your fat and sugar requirements when you pick foods like milk, cheese, eggs, nuts, and meat from the five major Food Groups. Some fruits such as bananas and oranges provide enough sugar. Choose low-fat foods and minimize added fat and sugar.

Number of Servings

A range of daily servings from different Food Groups is given in the Pyramid. It allows for different requirements of calorie intake for different people. **For a 2000-calorie diet for people with active life-style, you may take the middle number of servings in the range, i.e., 8 servings of Grain, 3 of Fruit, 4 of Vegetable, 2½ each of Legumes/Meat and Dairy, and minimum possible of added Fat and Sugar.** Balance your food intake according to your chemistry profile and metabolism. The dietitians believe nutrition should be calibrated to take on the health concerns that crop up with every decade of life.

Recipes with a Spice

Suggested range of daily servings is:

Grain
6–11 servings of whole grain products, rice, and pasta that provide complex carbohydrates (starch and fiber). Potatoes are also in this group because they are high in carbohydrates.

Fruit and Vegetable
2–4 servings of fruits and **3–5 servings** of vegetables. It is recommended to take the maximum possible number of fruits and vegetables.

Legumes/Meat
2–3 servings of legumes[1] (dried beans, lentils, and 'dal' or Indian lentils), tofu, nuts, eggs, and meat.

Dairy
2–3 servings of dairy products (preferably low-fat), for calcium and protein.

Fat and Sugar
Sparing use of fat and sugar. (If using fat, use olive, canola, or sunflower oil.)

Serving Size
A few standard size servings of various foods, as defined by the USDA, are given below. Estimated serving sizes for some of the Indian dishes are also included.

Grain: 1 slice of bread, ½ of 'Nan', 1 medium size 'Chapati', 'Roti', 'Parantha', or tortilla, 1 cup cereal flakes, ½ cup cooked cereal, rice, grain or pasta, ¼ cup flour.

Fruit: 1 medium size fruit, ½ cup cooked or canned

---

[1]Combine legumes and grains so that amino acids missing from one are made up by the other to supply complete protein.

fruit, ¾ cup berries, 1 cup chopped melon or other fruit, ¼ cup dried fruit, ¾ cup juice.

Vegetable: ½ cup cooked vegetables, ¾ cup soup or juice.

Legumes/Meat: ½ cup cooked legumes (without liquid), ¾ cup cooked legumes (like 'dal' or chunky soup), 3 oz. tofu or soy product, 3 oz. cooked lean meat, poultry or fish, 1 egg, 2 tablespoons peanut butter, 1/3 cup nuts or seeds.

Dairy: 1 cup milk or yogurt, ½ cup cottage cheese, ¼ cup grated or 2 thin slices (1 oz) processed cheese, 1/3 cup dry milk.

Fat: 1 tablespoon butter or oil, 1 tablespoon heavy cream, 2 tablespoons half-and-half or sour cream.

Sugar: 1 tablespoon sugar or honey.

Food Group Exchange

Strict diets are generally too restrictive and burdensome. This book recommends a flexible, easy to follow general plan to incorporate foods from all Food Groups. An estimate at the end of each recipe gives Food Group Exchange for a standard helping of the dish. Use it as a guideline to determine which dishes to relish, adjust the size of the helping taken, or modify the proportions in which different ingredients are used in a recipe. For example, if you do not want the extra fat in a recipe, cook without oil or heavy cream. The aim is to eat the recommended number of servings from each of the Food Groups.

See *Food Group Servings* in the appendix for the basis of estimating Food Group Exchange in a standard helping of a dish.

Nutritive Value

This book also gives nutritive analysis of a serving to help track intake of calories, protein, carbohydrates, fat, cholesterol, and fiber. The total nutritional value of all the ingredients in a recipe is divided by the estimated number of servings to derive the value per serving. A change in the size of serving affects the nutritive value. Numbers are rounded off for ease of understanding. Data is based largely on the USDA nutritional information database. Optional ingredients, garnishes, and small quantities of seasonings in the recipes are not included. For calculation, it is assumed that:

- Low-fat milk or yogurt is used.
- Medium size fruits and vegetables are used.
- About 200 grams (1.3 cups) of 'paneer' (fresh cheese) is derived from ½ gallon milk.
- When marinade or syrup are used and then discarded, about ¾ of the ingredients are used.
- Canola oil is used for cooking.
- About ¾ tablespoon oil per piece is used when deep–frying and about 1 teaspoon when pan–frying.

See *Nutrition Table* in the appendix for nutritive analysis of some of the commonly used foods. To maintain the ideal weight, take the recommended number of calories depending on your weight and level of exercise. Taking more calories than you burn leads to increase in weight.

Foods for Health

Our bodies need all kinds of nutrients. No nutrient acts completely independent of other nutrients. They work in harmonious concert with one another. See *Major Nutrients and Vitamins* in the appendix for a list of different nutrients and how you can include them in your diet. The chapter *Sample Menus* helps you to plan meals that provide balanced nutrition.

Fruits and vegetables have many nutritional benefits. They provide fiber, and necessary vitamins and minerals. Only a few years ago, hardly anyone knew about **antioxidants**— food chemicals that help keep the immune system at peak performance and block damaging chemical changes or oxidation caused by substances called free radicals. Antioxidants include vitamin A or beta-carotene, vitamin C and E, and selenium found in leafy dark greens and red, yellow and orange vegetables and fruits.

Another word that is catching attention is **'phytochemicals'**, (or phytonutrients) referring to the literally thousands of chemicals that are contained in plants and have cancer-fighting potential. Their weapon against disease appears to be in their antioxidant abilities. Research suggests that, in addition to beta-carotene, many other phytochemicals such as isoflavones, limonene, flavonoids and allylic sulfides may also protect against cancer and other diseases.

Vegetarian Food

The Indian cuisine is inherently vegetarian–friendly as it includes a number of dishes containing lentils, beans, whole grains, and vegetables. The American Dietetic Association (ADA) agrees "that appropriately planned vegetarian diets are healthful, are nutritionally adequate, and provide health benefits in the prevention and treatment of certain diseases." It is recommended that the vegetarians rely heavily on whole grains and beans and take the required servings from Fruit and Vegetable group.

If you do not take dairy products, supplement with other foods rich in calcium. If you do not take eggs, get protein from soy products and legumes. Another concern for vegetarians can be to get enough iron (especially for young adults) and vitamin B12. See *Major Nutrients and Vitamins* in the appendix for sources of these nutrients.

Super Foods

Based on research, some foods are regarded as super foods that supply the required minerals and vitamins. Some of the super foods are:

Food Group: Grain
1. Different types of whole grains and flour.

Food Group: Fruit, Vegetable
2. Red/orange fruits and vegetables such as strawberries, red grapes, carrots, and sweet potatoes

3. Cruciferous vegetables such as broccoli, cauliflower, brussel sprouts, and cabbage
4. Greens such as raw spinach and cooked collard, mustard, and broccoli rabe
5. Citrus fruits
6. Tomatoes, onions, and garlic.

Food Group: Legumes/Meat

7. Legumes (dry beans and different lentils including 'dal' or Indian lentils)
8. Nuts and seeds
9. Soy products
10. Seafood.

Advantages known to be derived from some of the foods are listed below. Use the information as a guideline to improve your eating habits, but not in place of your own doctor's advice who knows your medical history. See *Nutrition Table* in the appendix for calories and other nutrients in some of the foods.

Whole Grains and Flour

Whole grains such as barley, buckwheat, millet, oats, and wheat, break down slowly and provide sustained level of energy. Bran, the outer covering of the grains, is the highest source of dietary fiber. Germ or embryo is rich in vitamin E and minerals.

Barley ('jon' in Hindi) is high in selenium and vitamin E. Pearl barley is stripped of the healthful bran layer. Hulled barley or flour is more nutritious. Hulled barley has to be soaked overnight before cooking.

Buckwheat is known to prevent the spread of cancer. It is a source of high–quality protein and nutrients. It is toasted before use. Kasha is the roasted form of the grain and is available in health food stores.

Millet ('bajra' in Hindi) is a nutritious, mild tasting grain that looks like a tiny yellow bead. It is high in protein and magnesium. Millet flour is widely used in India to make bread.

Oats are known to lower the cholesterol and blood sugar. Unlike other grains, processed oats such as oatmeal and quick oats retain the bran and germ layers where most of the nutrients reside.

Wheat, a versatile grain, besides being used as flour, is used in the form of:

bulgur — wheat kernels that have been parboiled and dried; cracked wheat — broken form of whole grain;

semolina (suji) or cream of wheat — coarsely ground wheat flour;

wheat germ — the embryo or sprouting part of the grain. It is a very concentrated source of vitamin E;

couscous — processed from wheat.

All–purpose flour loses all fiber and many minerals due to processing.

Fruits

Full of minerals and vitamins, fruits are an excellent source of antioxidants and bioflavonoids. Bananas and citrus fruits contain potassium that can lower blood pressure. The health benefits of citrus fruits are greatest when they are eaten whole, rather than as juice. Melons and kiwi are also excellent sources of vitamin C. Apple skin and pulp are known as excellent blood vessel dilators. Mangoes, guavas and papayas, the tropical fruits widely available in India, are becoming popular all over the world. Mangoes have  been farmed in India for more than 4000 years. Papayas top in antioxidant content and are considered to be therapeutic for stomach ailments.

Some fruits, though rich in carbohydrates and other nutrients, are high in calories, e.g., **avocados** (4 oz. serving = 200 calories), **raisins** (3½ oz = 297.7 calories), **dates** (3½ oz = 272.9 calories).

Low calorie fruits include **grapefruit** (½ average = 32 calories), **strawberries** (3½ oz serving = 29.8 calories), **melon** (¼ average = 34.7 calories), **papaya** (1/3 average = 39 calories), **mango** (½ average = 65 calories), **apple** (1 average = 81 calories), **orange** (1 average = 92 calories), and **banana** (1 average = 105 calories).

Vegetables

Study after study shows that people who eat vegetables have the lowest rate of heart disease and cancer. Vegetables are high in fiber, calcium, potassium, and vitamins that can lower blood pressure. They also contain carotenoids, a group of antioxidants proven to help prevent your cells from being damaged by pollutants.

Fresh and frozen vegetables are said to contain similar nutritive value because frozen vegetables are processed and packaged as soon as they are picked. In general, lightly cooked vegetables can have more anti-cancer properties than raw ones because chopping and heating break down plant cell walls, releasing anti-cancer carotenoids. Overcooking destroys anti-cancer action and vitamin C. Some of the nutritious vegetables are:

- *Beans*— good source of protein (½ cup = 7gr)
- *Bitter Melon or Karela*— of the gourd family, also called bitter gourd, it is a fruit of a climbing vine and is available in Asian stores. This vegetable is known to lower blood sugar and improve glucose tolerance; its effects are gradual and cumulative.
- *Broccoli*— an excellent source of vitamin C and contains significant amount of vitamins A and E, protein, calcium, iron and other minerals.
- *Carrots*— known to be used by doctors long before cooks did. They are prized especially for the vitamin A they provide. Carrot juice has been used as a cure-all in cases of bronchitis and various stomach ailments.
- *Cucumbers*— called one of the calorie–free foods that you can eat whenever you like, generally as much as you like, it is mostly water and provides minerals like calcium and potassium. Radishes, lettuce, parsley, and some raw vegetables are also regarded as free foods.
- *Greens*— different types (beets, kale, mustard, turnip, collard, and broccoli rabe) are rich in vitamin A and C. They contain more iron than beefsteak, and nearly as much calcium as milk. Choose greens like arugula, baby spinach and watercress in salads.

- **Potatoes**— one medium size potato contains only 85 calories, less than an apple, and contains plenty of vitamins, minerals and fiber. A potato's healing properties start in the peel. (Rich in complex carbohydrates, potatoes are classified under the Food Group 'Grain' in this book.)
- **Red bell peppers**— have more vitamin C than green bell peppers (also known as capsicums) and four times more vitamin C than oranges. They are high in Vitamin A too.
- **Spinach**— the best vegetable in terms of overall nutrition, spinach is number one in hemoglobin boosting iron, and number two in calcium and riboflavin. It is best taken fresh and uncooked.
- **Tomatoes**— have been strongly linked to a reduced risk of cancers of the prostate and digestive tract. They are rich in lycopene (one of the carotenoids which makes tomatoes red and is known to be effective in enhancing health), vitamin C, potassium, and folic acid. Some studies have proved that cooking tomatoes enhances available lycopene by breaking down fibrous cell walls that inhibit its release from the raw food.

Herbs, Spices, and Tea

Herbs and spices have long been known as flavor enhancers with insignificant calories. However flavor enhancement is not the top quality; ancient people regarded them as gifts from the gods that contribute to fundamental enjoyment of life. What better way to feel comfort than through the aroma of fresh herbs filling warm kitchens. Many of the seasonings, used in small quantities, enhance digestion, help preserve food, and can kill or stop the growth of dozens of species of bacteria. According to studies by food microbiologists, some of the herbs and spices, especially garlic, onion, allspice, cinnamon, cumin, cloves, and chilies, can inhibit 75 to 100 percent of the bacteria species against which they were tested. You could however be allergic to any of the herbs and spices, and should check with your doctor if you notice any adverse effect.

Some of the herbs and spices and their benefits are:

- *Asafetida* (Hing): A member of the carrot family, it is used in very small quantity. It is known to combat flatulence (intestinal gas). Some researchers have suggested that it may help lower blood pressure.
- *Caraway* (Ajwain): These tiny pungent seeds are prescribed for reducing stomach pain. They are often taken after meals to help in digestion.
- *Chilies:* Generally long and thin, they range from mild to very hot. The varieties include habanero, cayenne, serrano, and jalapeno. Generally, the smaller and thinner the chili, the hotter it is. Chilies' fire is primarily in the white tissue the seeds are attached to; so you can moderate the heat by removing the tissue and seeds. They can be used fresh, dried whole, or dried crushed. The chemical responsible for the hotness of chilies is **capsaicin** that is also known to contain the pain relieving properties when used in an emollient. Eating foods spiced with moderate amount of green chili or red chili powder may be helpful for headaches and sinus problems. They are also a good source of beta-carotene. However, for some people, hotness of chilies may irritate the lining of their mouth or stomach.
- *Cinnamon*: A proven antiseptic and digestive aid, it enhances the activity of trypsin, an enzyme that breaks down proteins in the small intestine. Also accelerates the breakdown of fats.
- *Cloves:* Have long been used to treat indigestion, diarrhea, and intestinal parasites. Oil of cloves is a popular perfume used in a variety of cosmetics including toothpaste, soaps and body lotions. In India, it is customary to put one whole clove in your mouth to relieve toothache and mask bad breath.
- *Coriander (or cilantro):* A member of the carrot family, it is known for its unique aroma. Both seeds and leaves are used in cooking. Crushed seeds are used for making curry and help in digestion. Fresh green leaves and tender stems are a good source of vitamin C.

- *Cumin:* Used extensively in Indian cuisine, it is known to help in digestion. In India, it is often recommended for nursing mothers.
- *Dill:* Useful as a vegetable preservative and digestive aid. An infusion of the seeds, known as dill water is often used for childhood digestive complaints. You may also chew the seeds. Leaves, best when used fresh, are added as a garnish.
- *Fennel* (Sonf): It is prized as a digestive aid and mouth freshener, and is often chewed after a meal. An infusion of fennel seeds is said to help reduce hot flashes.
- *Fenugreek* (Methi): Used as seeds or as fresh leaves, it is known to improve glucose tolerance. It is a source of fiber and protein. Seeds are also used in some pickles as a preservative.
- *Garlic:* A super–food that has blood–thinning properties and packs a lot of antibacterial punch. It is known to reduce blood pressure, relieve arthritis pain, reduce cholesterol level, and kill the bacteria that cause food poisoning, colds and flu, women's bladder infections, and tuberculosis. Garlic is most effective if eaten fresh, but chopped, lightly sautéed garlic is also beneficial. **Note**: More than 3 raw cloves of garlic a day can cause diarrhea or other problems to some.
- *Ginger:* Has been used in cooking and healing since the dawn of history. It is recommended for colds, fever, chills, and menstrual cramps. Ginger's anti-nausea action is known to relieve motion sickness better than some drugs. In India, many people use pickled ginger or chew on dry ginger after meals or have ginger tea to help in digestion. Refrigerate fresh ginger in a paper bag. You may store peeled ginger in a jar of sherry or freeze crushed ginger for use in cooking. Tastes of fresh ginger and ginger powder are different and cannot always be substituted one for the other.
- *Mint:* The oils and flavonoids found in mint leaves relieve gas in the digestive tract by stimulating bile production, which improves the digestion of fats. Mint tea is widely used as a digestive aid and for treatment of colds, cough, and fever.

- ◆ **Mustard:** Seeds are used in cooking for nutty flavor. Crushed seeds are used in some pickles as a preservative.
- ◆ **Onions**: Neutralize the ability of saturated fat in meats and dairy products to clog the arteries. They are said to improve kidney function. Shallots, chives and leeks belong to the same family.
- ◆ **Turmeric:** Besides adding color to a dish, it is an antiseptic. Many people make it into a paste and use it as a poultice to relieve pain and swelling.

Tea: It has been found that one cup of green or black tea brewed for 3-5 minutes, contains about the same amount of cancer fighting antioxidants as one serving of vegetables. It also contains folic acid that helps to reduce homocysteine known to encourage blood clots. Green tea is 1/3 better than black tea. However, take caffeinated tea in moderate amount (2–3 cups a day) because caffeine can be harmful and is known to raise heart disease risk.

It is advisable to take herbal or de–caffeinated tea. In India and many other countries, it is customary to add different herbs such as cardamom, sacred basil (tulsi), or ginger to tea to make 'masala tea' or 'chai'.

Legumes and Nuts

Legumes include dry beans and different types of lentils including 'dal' or Indian lentils. A mainstay of the vegetarian diet, they are amazing, full of soluble fiber, essential vitamins and minerals that strike down cholesterol; help fight against cancer; and let the body use insulin. They are a good source of protein, providing about 7 grams per half-cup serving. One cup of cooked legumes can replace a 3-ounce serving of meat, poultry or fish. Combine legumes and grains (or legumes and nuts) so that the amino acids missing from one are made up by the other to supply complete protein.

Gram flour (besan) and other flours derived from 'dal', are also used in many Indian dishes. Some of the beans and seeds such as Mung beans, soybean, black chickpeas, and sunflower seeds can be used for sprouting. (See *Sprouting* on page 34.) They are potent with energy, nutrition, and flavor. Use them in salads and sandwiches.

Soybeans contain anti-cancer elements, reduce the risk of heart disease by lowering cholesterol, and relieve symptoms of menopause. Studies indicate that eating soy can mimic estrogen and to some extent fill in for it. Soybeans and its products— bean curd or tofu, soy milk, and soy flour, contain just as much protein as meat; and no fat. Mix soybeans with other beans to make a stew; soy flour with other flour when making bread; and soy milk with regular milk for drinking. Also use Textured Vegetable Protein (TVP) in stews and soups. *Note*: Soy milk tends to curdle when boiled or used in cooking.

Fresh tofu (bean curd), available as firm, soft, and silken, can be kept in the refrigerator for about a week; change its water every other day to keep it fresh. Or use prepackaged tofu, which can be kept for several days. Drain the tofu and use in salads and vegetables. It can be eaten hot, cold, cooked or uncooked. It can also be frozen. A 3-ounce serving of tofu can replace a 3-ounce serving of meat, poultry or fish.

Nuts and Seeds contain antioxidants and are packed with vitamins and minerals. Grind them to add to desserts and breads. Peanuts (technically legumes), particularly with red skin, are blood vessel dilators. Walnuts are known to help reduce cholesterol level. In India, almonds are considered as brain food and very nourishing. Ounce for ounce, many nuts and seeds provide as much protein as red meat, yet without any cholesterol. **Flaxseeds** provide more omega-3 fatty acids than any other seed or grain. They also contain lignans, one of the phytochemicals with powerful antioxidant properties. Lightly roast and grind the flaxseeds or soak them overnight to soften them before using.

Seafood

Seafood is high in Omega-3 fat and is known to lower risk of heart disease. This fat is usually found in the fattiest fish from the coldest deep seas. Richest sources include mackerel, anchovies, sardines, and herring. Studies show that eating moderate amounts of fish oil reduces symptoms of arthritis and many other ailments.

Seafood can easily get bacterial contamination if not properly stored. Do not eat fish skin that is a prime depository of toxic chemicals.

Making the Change

Generally, it becomes a habit cooking and eating a certain way. For example, you may be accustomed to adding extra salt to food, eating butter, enjoying different types of animal products, or relishing sweet creamy desserts that seem to dissolve in your mouth. You may believe that only loads of fat spruces up the taste of a dish. It requires a lifestyle change to focus on the super foods listed in the previous section. It is a choice for better health, breaking some old habits and adopting agreeable ways to cook and eat. A meal minus the grease is healthy, tasty, and easy on the stomach. Suggestions to reduce fat and sugar, and to increase the intake of fiber, vitamins and minerals, are given below.

Brown Rice: Use brown rice that is wrapped in a nutritive outer skin high in fiber and minerals. They take little longer than white rice to cook.

Butter Spread: To keep butter taste and to reduce saturated fat, blend the butter and canola or olive oil (½ cup oil and ½ cup butter) in a blender until thoroughly combined. If desired, add herbs like sage, green coriander (cilantro), crushed garlic, onions, or ginger to the mixture. Store it in the refrigerator and use in place of butter.

Canola/Olive oil: When you use oil, select canola, olive, or sunflower oil. Avoid deep–fried or pan–fried foods; if you take them, blot on paper towel to absorb extra grease.

Cooking Method: Both extended heat and liquid can destroy or leach out valuable nutrients. Steam, roast, grill, bake, or sauté the vegetables instead of boiling. Cooking in the microwave is healthful because of short cooking time and usually no added water.

Cooking in the pressure cooker helps to preserve the nutrients because it is very fast.

Creamy Mix: Make a mixture by cooking together 12 oz. can of evaporated skim milk, 1 cup finely chopped mushrooms, and desired seasonings for 4–5 minutes, whisking until thick and bubbly. Use this creamy mix in soups or over pasta and vegetables. You shall not need butter or cream.

Eggs: They are an excellent source of protein, vitamin B12, and many other nutrients. Because egg yolks are high in cholesterol, limit their use to a maximum of 4 per week. You may however use egg whites (2 egg whites = 1 whole egg) and egg substitutes (¼ cup egg substitute = 1 medium whole egg). To make egg whites more palatable, whip 2 egg whites with 1 tablespoon nonfat dry milk, ½ teaspoon turmeric powder and 1 teaspoon oil. You may also substitute some of the eggs called for in a dessert by applesauce (1 egg = 3 tablespoons un–sweetened applesauce).
Eggs can be frozen. Whip them with little salt or sugar before freezing.

Fruit Desserts: Try desserts with fruit and less added sugar. Serve cakes with fruit sauce instead of frosting or whipped cream.

Fruit/Vegetable Peels: Generally, healing properties of many vegetables start in the peel. Do not peel vegetables and fruits such as carrots, squash, potatoes, and apples that have tender skin. However, always wash them carefully using a vegetable scrub brush and cut away bruised or damaged portions. Use clean peels and fibrous parts of vegetables like broccoli and cauliflower in vegetable stock (see page 34).

Fruit/Vegetable Puree: You just cannot lose by eating a lot of fruits and vegetables. Puree them and use in any stew or bread in place of water, milk, or cream. You may not even know that you are taking fruits or vegetables. Any fruit or vegetable such as carrots, apples, zucchini, and spinach can be easily pureed in a blender, adding little juice or vegetable stock as needed. You can also shred the vegetables if desired.

Honey: Substitute refined sugar by natural sugar or honey, wherever possible. Honey is said to contain special healing properties. Generally, brown sugar can be substituted for sugar, one to one, especially in baking. It helps to make the cakes more moist and tender. (If using baking soda, may increase the amount by ¼ teaspoon for every cup of brown sugar.)

Lemon Juice: Flavoring with lemon juice cuts down on salt and fat. Use it along with freshly ground black pepper on salads and crisp vegetables.

Milk: An excellent source of calcium, it also provides protein, but contains saturated fat. Use low–fat or no–fat milk whenever possible. To make the switch without shocking your taste buds, start by mixing reduced fat milk with full milk. You can also add 2–4 tablespoons of nonfat dry milk to thicken low-fat milk.

No-Fat Sauté: Use this technique to add herbs and spices without adding fat. Heat a non-stick pan on medium-high heat. Do not add oil; you may use a cooking spray or lightly grease the pan. Brown the seeds such as cumin and mustard first. (You may use them in powder form, if desired.) Then add chopped garlic, onions and salt; brown them on low heat, while stirring to avoid burning. Sprinkle water or vegetable stock as needed. Add ginger, tomatoes, chilies and other seasonings per taste. ***Note:*** You can make a large quantity and refrigerate or freeze for use when needed.

Reducing Fat in Baking: Substitute applesauce, mashed bananas, pureed prunes or dates, or yogurt cheese (page 27) for a third to one–half of the fat and eggs used in baking. Fruit enhances the flavor and ensures moistness. You can also substitute butter by oil — about 6 tablespoons oil for ½ cup (4 oz.) of butter.

Replacing Cream: Try to avoid cream that has more than 500 calories in a cup. Use an equal amount of milk or evaporated milk. If using skim milk, mix it with instant nonfat dry milk (1 cup milk to 1/3 cup dry milk). You can also use sour cream.

Salsas and Chutneys: Try different salsas and chutneys as accompaniment to vegetables, meat and poultry. Avoid heavy gravies and dressings.

Tomato-Yogurt Curry: Prepare and use this no–fat curry over steamed vegetables or seafood. Do a 'no-fat sauté' as described in this section, adding tomatoes and seasonings of your choice. When the sauté is almost done, blend in some yogurt gradually, while stirring to prevent yogurt from curdling. Add desired quantity of water and 1–2 teaspoons poppy seed powder to make the gravy thick; cook for a few minutes. **Note**: No-fat milk and yogurt tend to curdle more than regular milk and yogurt. Add a little bit of flour along with yogurt to prevent curdling.

Vegetable Stock: Use vegetable stock (see page 34) in place of water in soups and stews. It adds to the intake of vegetables.

Yogurt: Use low–fat yogurt, an excellent source of calcium and protein. It is an integral part of all Indian meals. The 'friendly' bacteria in yogurt is known to manufacture critical B-vitamins in the intestines and increase level of 'interferon', an immunity and longevity-enhancing hormone. **Buttermilk** is made from yogurt and is an excellent drink. **Yogurt cheese** that is made by draining yogurt, is used in desserts and can be substituted for fat and eggs.

Eat nothing that will prevent you from eating.
-Ibn Tibbon

Preparation Techniques

These are some general techniques that you may refer to as needed.

ALMONDS–Blanching:
Cover shelled un–skinned almonds with water. Bring the water to boil on top of the stove or in the microwave oven. Let the almonds soak for a couple of minutes. Drain; when cool enough to handle, press each almond between fingers to remove skin.
Note: If you are able to plan ahead, soak the almonds in water for 6–8 hours and then peel. This ensures whiter almonds.

COCONUT–Break and Use:
Coconuts are usually sold without the outer husk. Before buying a coconut, shake it to make sure it has liquid inside and the 'eyes' or soft spots are not moldy or wet.

Puncture 2 of the 3 dark 'eyes' by hammering in an ice pick or a screwdriver. Drain all the liquid that may be chilled for drinking.

Bake the empty coconut in the oven at 375°F for 15 minutes or in a microwave for 3–4 minutes. While the coconut is still warm, split the shell with the sharp blow of a hammer. The shell should fall away. If pieces of coconut are still sticking to the shell, use a small knife to remove them. You may peel the coconut skin before grating and using the coconut.

DEEP–FRY:

Heat 1–2 cups oil, enough to cover the delicacies to be fried, in a heavy deep skillet, wok, or deep fryer. When the oil is hot (about 375°F; it sizzles if you sprinkle a drop of water), add the snacks, vegetables or bread to be fried. Use a slotted spatula to turn making sure they are cooked on all sides. Regulate the heat as needed. The temperature is very important. When the oil is not hot enough, food cooks too slowly and becomes hard. If the oil is too hot, the food burns on the exterior before it has cooked through.

Remove and drain fried delicacies when done (may use a wire or metal strainer); then spread on paper towels or brown paper bag, lined with plastic underneath, to absorb extra oil.

DOUGH–Kneading:

Dough is generally made out of whole–wheat or all-purpose flour. Put the flour in a bowl; make a well in the center and pour water. (In general ¾ cup of water for 2 cups of flour is enough for soft dough. Use less water if stiffer dough is needed.)

Using your fingers (or a spatula), gradually draw the flour to the liquid. Continue mixing until all the flour is moistened. Knead the dough by folding it end to end and pushing it with your hand. (To make it easier to handle the dough, leave the dough to soften, covered, for about 5 minutes, before continuing.) Repeat 7–8 times, using flour or water as needed, until the dough takes on a smooth texture and a nice resiliency. Leave it covered for half-hour. Refrigerate the dough in a covered container, until ready to use.

Note: If using a food processor, follow manufacturer's directions.

DRY BEANS–Cooking:

It is more economical to use dry beans instead of canned or frozen beans. Moreover, beans long–simmered with herbs and spices absorb the flavor better and achieve a more complex taste. Two cups (16–oz bag) of dry beans equal almost 4 cups of frozen beans or two 15–oz. cans. Check and rinse beans until water runs clear. Soak in 3 times the water overnight or for minimum 6 hours. (For **quick soak**, bring the water and beans to a boil and cook for 2 minutes. Turn off the heat and let the beans soak for two hours before cooking them. Add more water as needed.)

Add some salt to the soaked beans and bring to boil in the same water. Simmer for 3–4 hours, covered, until the beans are soft. Add more water as needed. (You may use a slow cooker (takes 6–7 hours) or a pressure cooker (20–30 minutes) to cook soaked beans.)

Note: It is believed by some that water in which beans are soaked should be discarded because of gas–producing sugars. Traditionally the water is not discarded. Herbs and spices reduce beans' gas–producing effect.

GARLIC–Roasting:

Roasting makes the garlic cloves nutty-sweet and mild. Remove the papery outer layers of a garlic head. Cut off the top to expose the cloves slightly. Place the garlic head, covered, in the microwave oven for 2 minutes. Remove and put in aluminum foil, cut side up. Sprinkle a little olive oil and seasoning, if desired, on top. Wrap tightly in the foil and bake in the oven at 400°F for 10–15 minutes until the cloves feel soft when pressed. (If not using the microwave, it will take 30–35 minutes in the conventional oven to bake.) Squeeze the baked garlic out of its skin and use to make spreads or flavor a dish.

GHEE (Clarified Butter)–Making:

Cut un–sweetened butter (not margarine) into small pieces and melt in a saucepan over low heat. As it simmers, skim foam from the surface. Turn off the heat when the foam has subsided. Let it cool a little. Carefully pour off *ghee,* i.e., golden clarified butter

leaving milky residue in bottom of the pan. (May strain through a thin cloth.) Store *ghee* in a plastic or glass bottle; it will not go rancid as butter. However, it is better if you refrigerate it.
(One pound of butter gives about ¾ pound of *ghee*.) Some prefer to use *ghee* in cooking because it has a higher smoke point and wonderful aroma.

HERBS–Drying:
You may dry and store herbs such as mint and basil for future use, for upto one year. Wash them by standing them in water in a large bowl so that all dirt settles down. Rinse under running water and drain. Pat dry with paper towels. One traditional method is to tie a few stems together and hang them upside down. You may fasten several bunches to a coat hanger and let dry in a warm dry place.
Another method is to remove all hard stems and spread herbs in single layer, on a paper towel or cotton cloth, and dry them in a warm, sunny place, away from direct sunlight. Turn the leaves every other day. They take 5–7 days to dry and are ready for storage when brittle. Store in dark jars, away from heat and light. Normally ¼–1/3 teaspoon dried herbs are equal to 1 teaspoon fresh herbs.
You can also dry them in a food dehydrator per manufacturer's directions, or in a warm oven which has been turned off.
Note: Instead of drying, you may freeze chopped herbs or make herb cubes by freezing herbs crushed with little water.

PANEER (Fresh Cheese)–Making:
To make about a pound of 'paneer', heat 1 gallon of milk in a large pot that allows enough space for milk to boil. (Whole milk will produce little more and creamier cheese than that from 1% or 2% milk.) When milk is about to boil, immediately add 4–5 tablespoons of lemon juice and 1 tablespoon of vinegar (can substitute cream of tartar for lemon juice and vinegar). You may optionally add 1 cup of plain yogurt too. Be careful that milk does not boil over; lower heat if needed. Simmer until the milk curdles (cheese separates from clear liquid (whey)). Use more lemon juice or vinegar as needed. Turn off the heat.

Strain the cheese in a large sieve set over a bowl and lined with a thin muslin cloth or cheesecloth. Mash the cheese to make it smooth. Let it drain. **Note**: *Instead of discarding the "whey", you may use it as a substitute for water in soups, dough, or 'Besan Kadhi'.*

PANEER–(Fresh Cheese Pieces)–Frying:

Make 'paneer' as above and drain it as much as possible (couple of hours) till no liquid can be squeezed out. Blend the cheese with hand or in a food processor to make it smooth. Spread it evenly, about ½" thick on a cloth on flat board lined with paper towels. Fold the cloth over on four sides and cover the top. Put more paper towels on top. Put a large flat-bottomed skillet filled with water on top to put pressure to drain excess liquid. Change paper towels if they get wet. After 30-45 minutes, when paper towels appear dry, unwrap the cheese. Cut 'paneer' into ½-¾" cubes (or strips) and use without frying or fry as follows.

To fry, heat about 4 tablespoons of oil in a frying pan on medium heat. Lightly brown the cubes on all sides while turning with a slotted spatula. (Makes 30-40 pieces from a gallon of milk.)

ONIONS–Frying:

Cut one onion lengthwise into thin wedges. Heat 2–3 tablespoons oil in a wide skillet on medium–high heat. Add onion wedges and stir–fry, making sure they do not burn. Remove when golden brown and crispy. Use to garnish rice and 'dal' dishes.

SAUTÉ:

Sauté ('chhaunk' in Hindi) is the primary method to add different spices and cook vegetables, beans, and other dishes like 'dal'. There are a variety of spices and herbs that are used in Indian cooking. Cumin seeds, coriander powder, turmeric powder, and ginger are universally used. Tomatoes and yogurt are added for moistness and are good substitutes for fat. Green chilies or red chili powder are used to make the food hot.

A few methods to use different seasonings are given below. Measurements apply to 1–2 lb. of vegetables or 2–3 cups of cooked beans or 'dal'.

Cumin Seeds Sauté: Heat 2 teaspoons oil in a skillet or wok on medium-high heat. Add ½ teaspoon cumin seeds. As soon as they start to change color or splutter (5–10 seconds), stir in 1 teaspoon each of coriander powder and ginger. (If using cumin powder instead of cumin seeds, add everything together.)
After a few seconds, add the vegetables and other seasonings like ¼ teaspoon turmeric powder, ¼ teaspoon red chili powder (to taste) and salt (to taste). When the vegetables are almost done, add half chopped tomato and ½ teaspoon garam masala. Cook for a couple of minutes. (If using canned tomato, allow it to cook for 5–10 minutes to take away any metallic taste.) **Note:** For beans or 'dal', prepare the masala (sauté) and add to the cooked dish. Boil everything together for about 5 minutes to mix flavors.

Mustard Seeds Sauté: Heat 2 teaspoons oil in a skillet or wok on high heat. Add ½ teaspoon mustard seeds. Cover the pot because when the seeds splutter, they jump out of the pan. As soon as the seeds start to splutter (5–10 seconds), reduce the heat to medium, and add one whole red chili (optional) and ½ teaspoon cumin seeds. (Remove the skillet from heat if the spices start to burn.) After about 10 seconds, add ginger and 1/8 teaspoon asafetida powder. Add vegetables and other spices as above in *Cumin Seeds Sauté*.

Mustard Seeds and 'dal' Sauté: Heat about one tablespoon oil in a skillet or wok on high heat. Add ½ teaspoon mustard seeds. Cover the pot. As soon as the seeds start to splutter (5–10 seconds), reduce the heat, add 1 teaspoon split peeled 'Urad dal' and 1 teaspoon 'Chana dal'. As soon as 'dal' is light brown, add vegetables and other spices as above in *Cumin Seeds Sauté*.

Onions and Garlic Sauté: Heat one tablespoon oil in a skillet or wok on high heat. Add ½ teaspoon cumin seeds; as soon as they change color, add 1–2 teaspoons minced garlic and one chopped onion. Stir until the onions are light brown. Stir in ginger, coriander

33

powder, other spices, and vegetables, as above in *Cumin Seeds Sauté*. **Note:** You may make a large quantity of this sauté (onion and garlic masala). It is easier to process garlic, onions, ginger, and tomatoes in a food processor. Freeze the prepared 'masala' in an ice cube tray. Store the cubes in a freezer bag for use as needed. Double bag so that smell is not absorbed by other foods.

SPICES (or NUTS)–Roasting:

Bake spices (or nuts) in a 300°F oven, spread on a shallow baking pan, for 10-15 minutes until they are light brown and crisp. Check and stir them every few minutes as needed. (Cumin seeds need to be almost black; bake them at 400°F).
Another way is to roast them in a skillet on medium heat. Add a little bit of oil for nuts. You can also roast in microwave oven for a couple of minutes.
Grind roasted spices if needed; store when cold in a covered container in a cool, dry place.

SPROUTING:

Beans often used for sprouting include Mung beans, soybean and black chickpeas. Check, rinse and soak the beans for 6–8 hours. Rinse and drain the soaked beans. Tie them loosely in a cotton cloth, put in a wide shallow pan so that the beans are distributed evenly and get air circulation. Put in a warm dark place like oven for about 36 hours, checking in between to make sure there is enough moisture, no excess water, and sprouts start appearing. When ready, rinse and use. Sprouts must be refrigerated.

TOMATOES–Blanching:

Bring water to a boil in a saucepan. Immerse few tomatoes in the pan and boil for less than a minute. Remove tomatoes with a large slotted spoon and pick the peel with a pointed knife. The skin should come off easily. Use the tomatoes as desired.

VEGETABLE STOCK–Making:

Make your own vegetable stock, full of flavor and nutrition, and use it in place of water. For 1 quart stock, simmer for about one hour, any vegetables such as 2 stalks of celery, 2 unpeeled quartered onions, 4 unpeeled halved cloves of garlic, 1 scrubbed carrot, clean vegetable trimmings for example from broccoli, celery, cauliflower, in 2 quarts of water. Let it cool. Strain through a sieve, pressing the vegetables to extract all the juice. Store the stock in refrigerator or freezer for use in soups and 'dal'. **Note**: Do not use peels of waxed produce.

YOGURT–Making:

To make yogurt, bring the milk to boiling point. (You may heat the milk in a microwave oven; 4 cups take about 8 minutes at high setting.) Let the milk cool for some time (about 120°F). Blend in a touch of the starter or culture (½–1 teaspoon for 4 cups of milk, depending on the type of starter yogurt used). You may transfer the milk to a small plastic, glass or stainless steel container that can be used for serving. Cover and keep in a warm place, undisturbed, for 5–7 hours. (If yogurt does not appear to be setting after 5 hours, add another touch of starter yogurt.) Refrigerate the yogurt when ready. Use this yogurt as a starter next time you want to make yogurt.

You may condense yogurt like cheese by placing it in a muslin cloth wrapped from all sides, and hanging for 2–3 hours to drain excess liquid. **Yogurt cheese** is used in desserts and can be substituted for fat and eggs. The liquid can be used in soups.

Buttermilk is made from yogurt by whisking 1 part yogurt with ½ part water.

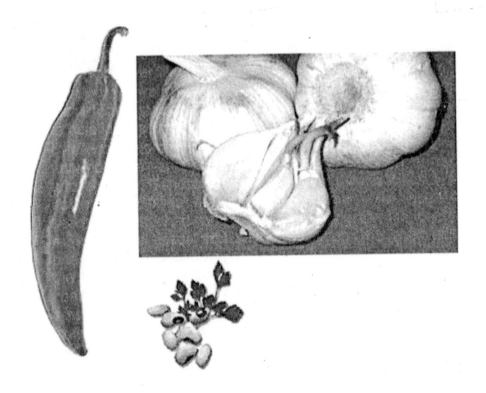

Ingredients and Terms

The secret of the taste of Indian cuisine lies in the variety of herbs, spices and legumes that are lavishly used. It is always better to buy whole spices that retain flavor longer than the ground ones. Grind the whole spices as needed every week or month. Tailor the type and amount of seasonings to suit your taste.

Some of the ingredients used in this cookbook are not available in all grocery stores; buy them from Indian or Pakistani grocery stores or health food stores existing at several locations. You can also order them on the Internet from sites geared to ethnic or Indian foods.

Ingredients and terminology (with alternative name in parentheses) include:

Asafetida (Hing)— dried gum resin that has a distinct strong flavor and smell, and is known for its digestive properties. Depending on its source, it may be reddish brown or pale yellow; intensity also varies. Available as powder or in lump form that has more powerful flavor and can be made into a powder. It is used in very small quantity and can be omitted from a recipe, if so desired.

Basmati— narrow, long grain aromatic rice grown originally in the foothills of the Himalayas in India. When cooked, it swells lengthwise, resulting in grains that can be easily separated.

Bay leaves (Tejpatta)— dried leaves used for flavor; remove them before serving a dish.

Bhel mix— a ready made mix used for "Bhel" (page 53).

Black–eye beans (Rongi)— kidney shaped, yellowish with black spot beans that are available dry, canned, or frozen.

Black salt (Kala namak)— type of rock salt used in small quantity for its unique flavor.

Black pepper— whole peppercorns hold their flavor better than ground pepper. Grind the peppers as needed. A black peppercorn is picked when still green and dried in the sun until it turns black. White and green peppercorns ripen on the vine. Black pepper has hotter flavor than green and white peppers.

Burfi— fudge like dessert which can be made from different ingredients such as flour, Ricotta cheese or nuts.

Caraway (Ajwain)— smaller than cumin seeds, these are more pungent and are used for flavor in some dishes only. Like fennel seeds, they are known for digestive properties.

Cardamom (Ilaychi)— a greenish pod which is peeled to get seeds. Freshly crushed seeds using a mortar and pestle have excellent aroma and are used in many desserts. Pods and seeds are also used as mouth fresheners. There are also large brown cardamoms that are used in 'garam masala' and some dishes.

Chaat Masala— a powdered mixture of equal parts of roasted and ground coriander seeds, red dry whole chilies, and cumin seeds. Also add equal part mango powder, salt to taste, 1/8 part black pepper and 1/8 part black salt.

Chickpeas (Chhole)— round yellowish legumes, also called garbanzos, that are available dry, canned, or frozen. Can also get black and green chickpeas that are smaller and considered more nutritious.

Chilies— range from mild to very hot. Generally large green chilies are mild and are used mostly for flavor. Small thin green chilies such as habareno, cayenne, serrano and jalapeno, are hot. Chilies' fire is primarily in the white tissue the seeds are attached to. You can moderate the heat by removing the tissue and seeds. Handle them carefully with gloved hands and do not touch your face or eyes while working with them. One safe way is to rinse them in cold water, break the stem, cut in 2–3 pieces, brush out the seeds if you do not want them too hot, and blend the chilies in a food processor. Store in a jar in refrigerator or freezer for use when needed. **Red dry chilies** are used whole, or crushed as flakes or powder. Whole chilies are put in a sauté to flavor the oil used in making a dish.

Chutney— a sweet, sour, and hot paste made from herbs and spices.

Coriander (Dhania)— seeds that are generally crushed as powder for use in a sauté. Fresh **green coriander**, also called **cilantro** or Chinese parsley, is the plant before it seeds. It is widely used for its texture, aroma, and color. Normally only the tender stems and leaves are chopped and used for garnishing. The harder stems can be used for chutney or chopped and added to a dish towards the end of cooking. Green coriander can be kept in the refrigerator for

1–2 weeks. Stand the stems, along with the roots, in a tall glass filled with about 1" of water. Cover the tops loosely with a perforated plastic bag. Or wrap the coriander along with stems in couple of paper towels. Put in a plastic bag and store.

Cumin (Jira)— seeds (or powder) used widely in a sauté. For roasted cumin powder, bake the seeds at 400°F for 5–10 minutes until almost black. Grind them when little cold.

Curry leaves (Curry patta or Mitha neem)— fresh or dried leaves that are added for aroma in some dishes.

Curry powder— a mixture of coriander, cumin, turmeric, and red chili powders.

Dal (Indian lentils)— generally available as dry, Indian lentils may be whole, or split with peel, or split without peel. Different types include:

> *Chana* (split yellow) made from brown chickpeas
> *Masoor* (whole dark brown or split reddish. The split dal becomes yellow when cooked.)
> *Moth* (whole brown)
> *Mung* (whole green, split green & yellow with peel, or peeled yellow)
> *Toor* (whole brownish, split dark yellow, or split with oil coating)
> *Urad* (whole black, split black & white with peel, or peeled light yellow).

Dosa— crepes made from rice and 'dal' or semolina (suji).

Fennel (Sonf)— seeds (or powder) used to give a semi-sweet flavor. Aniseeds (called patli sonf) also belong to the same family. Fennel and aniseeds are widely used to chew after meals to aid in digestion.

Fenugreek (Methi)— seeds used in some dishes for a unique flavor. The plant, before it seeds, is used as a green vegetable with delightful flavor and aroma. Dry leaves are also available for use in place of fresh greens.

Garam masala— a powdered mixture of roasted and ground spices—1 part cumin seeds, 1 part coriander seeds, 2 parts black peppercorns, 2 part cloves, 3 parts cinnamon, and 3 parts cardamom seeds (from large brown cardamom pods or small green pods). To make about 1 cup of garam masala, start with 1 tablespoon of cumin seeds and add everything else proportionally. Garam masala is sometimes called the grated Parmesan of India; it is added for aromatic flavor when a dish is almost cooked.

Gram (or Graham) flour (Besan)— flour derived from Chana dal that is high in protein. Due to its binding property, this flour is used to make several snacks.

Halva— sweet dessert made by reducing fruit, vegetable or flour mixed with butter and sugar.

Indian rice krispies (Murmura)— parboiled crisp rice.

Kewara water— an infusion made from scented flowers used for aroma in desserts.

Karai— like a wok, used for stir-frying and deep-frying. It has a heavy bottom and can be made of stainless steel, or any other metal.

Kidney beans (Rajmah)— kidney shaped red legumes that are available dry, canned, or frozen.

Legumes— include dry beans, lentils and 'dal' or Indian lentils such as Mung, Urad, Chana, and Toor.

Makhane (lotus puffs)— whitish soft roasted nuggets derived from lotus plant that are used in some dishes to give a nutty taste.
Mango powder (Amchoor)— made from raw mangoes that are dried, it gives sour taste to dishes. It may be substituted by lemon juice.

Masala— a dry combination of spices, e.g. 'garam masala'; or a wet mixture of herbs and spices prepared by sauté, e.g. 'garlic and onion masala' (page 33).

Mouth fresheners— different types of nuts and seeds such as cardamom, betel nut, and fennel, with scented and sweet coating. They are widely used to chew after meals to aid in digestion.

Mustard (Rai)— blackish seeds that splutter and jump when put in hot oil to sauté a dish. There are also yellow mustard seeds that are sometimes used. Mustard powder is used in pickles.

Onion seeds (Kalonji)— black tiny seeds used in pickles and some dishes.

Paan (betel leaf)— a folded green leaf generally served after meals. The leaf is smeared with a slightly pungent paste, and piled with scented delicacies such as betel nut pieces, cardamom, and fennel seeds. It can be made sweet by adding ingredients such as grated coconut and rose petals paste. Some may add little tobacco. The leaf is folded and held together by a clove.

Paneer (fresh cheese)— made by curdling milk (see page 31). Also available in Indian grocery stores in the refrigerator or freezer section.

Papad or Pappadum (spicy wafers)— made from 'dal', rice, or other grains and spices, they are available in ethnic grocery stores. They are very thin; can be quickly deep–fried or roasted in the oven (or microwave) to use as snacks.

Poha (Flat parboiled rice)— ragged-edged translucent rice flakes used in some dishes.

Pomegranate (Anardana)— seeds (or powder) used for tartness.

Poppy seeds (Khuskhus)— whitish seeds used to thicken gravy.

41

Raita— made from plain yogurt by adding vegetables such as cucumber, onion, tomato, and spices.

Rasam powder— a ready-made mixture of spices used to make 'Rasam'.

Raw peanuts— unroasted peanuts with inner reddish skin. They are roasted, with skin, in oven or little oil before use.

Rice flour— used to add crispness to some snacks. It can generally be interchanged with ground rice (made by grinding soaked rice).

Sacred basil (Tulsi)— considered holy by the Hindus who use its leaves in worship. It is known to have medicinal value, especially, for cure and prevention of colds, allergy, and even malaria.

Saffron (Kesar)— orange-red threads that are stigma of a crocus family flower; it is soaked in warm water or milk to extract the brilliant yellow color and aroma.

Sabodana (Tapioca)— tiny whitish nuggets used in place of flour, especially during a fast when grains are not eaten.

Sesame (Til)— tiny whitish seeds used for nutty flavor, generally in desserts.

Suji (Semolina)— coarsely ground wheat flour used in many Indian dishes. It can be substituted by cream of wheat or farina.

Tamarind (Imli)— a bean pod from the tamarind tree, it is available as a block with pulp, seeds and roughage, or a block with pulp only or as paste or as powder. The block is soaked or boiled and then strained to get pulp. It gives tartness.

Tawa— like a griddle, it is used for making flat breads and crepes. Generally it is made of cast iron.

Thali— a medium to large size plate, generally made of stainless steel. It is traditionally used to serve meals and therefore the term 'thali', often used for the serving of a complete meal with different delicacies.

Turmeric (Haldi)— yellow powder used for color and also for its disinfectant quality.

Varak (silver layer)— a very fine layer of edible silver attached to a fine tissue paper which is patted gently onto sweet delicacies, as a garnish.

Vermicelli (Sevia)— very thin pasta like sticks that are generally cooked in milk to make a dessert. They come as roasted or un–roasted.

Wadi (dried lentil drops)— made from ground lentils and spices, they are used for flavor and texture in some dishes. These can be stored for a long time.

Sample Menus

Use the menus on the following pages as guidelines to plan tasty and satisfying meals, formal or informal. These represent some popular dishes and are designed to provide servings from different Food Groups as described on page 10. Menus are based on 2000 calorie diet; adjust the number of servings according to your chemistry profile and metabolism. It is recommended to take plenty of water and use butter, oils, and sugars as sparingly as possible in cooking.

MENU 1	Grain	Vege-table	Fruit	Leg-ume/Meat	Dairy	Fat	Sugar
Breakfast 1 whole–wheat toast, 2 tablespoons Bean Dip, ¾ cup Dalia with 1 cup 1% milk, Tea w/o sugar, 1 fruit	1 1.5		1	.16	1		
Lunch ¾ cup Garlic Dal, ½ cup Stuffed Eggplant, ½ cup Rice Real, 1 Chapati, ½ cup Raita with onion, 1 cup Tossed Veg Tofu Salad, 1 cup Mango Milkshake, 1 fruit	1 1	.16 1 .16 1	.5 1	1 .12	.5 1	.16 .25	.5
Snack 1 cup Fruit Chaat, 3 tablespoons Spiced Nuts, 1 Veg Poore	.5	.2	1	1 .2		.16 .3	
Dinner ½ cup Saag, ¾ cup Cream of Carrot soup, ½ cup Mashed Potatoes, 1 Tandoori Roti	.12 .12 1 1	1 1			.12 .12	.12 .12 .12	
TOTAL	7.24	4.52	3.5	2.48	2.74	1.23	.5

MENU 2	Grain	Vege–table	Fruit	Leg–ume/Meat	Dairy	Fat	Sugar
Breakfast 1½ cups Upma, ½ cup Yogurt onion sauce, 1 cup 1% milk, Tea w/o sugar, 1 fruit	2	.5 .75	1	.5	.25 1	.4 .16	
Lunch ¾ cup Besan Kadhi w/o pakori, 1/3 cup Bhartha, 1 cup Pulao, ¾ cup Curly Carrot Salad, 1 cup Creamy Fruit Shake	2	1 .5 1	1	.5 .25	.12 .75	.12 .25 .12 .25	.25
Snack ¾ cup Sprouted Mung, ½ cup Tomato Salsa		1		1		.12	
Dinner ¾ cup Spinach Dal*, ½ cup Tandoori Spicy Veg, 2 Roti 2000, ¾ cup Kheer, 1 fruit	.25 2 .5	.5 1	1	1 .16	1	.12 .12	1
TOTAL	6.75	6.25 (6.75)	3	3.41	3.12	1.66 (1.91)	1.25

* You may substitute ½ cup Fish–do–Piazza for Spinach Dal. Legume/Meat intake remains the same but Vegetable intake increases by .50 and Fat intake increases by .25, as indicated in parenthesis.

MENU 3	Grain	Vege–table	Fruit	Leg–ume/ Meat	Dairy	Fat	Sugar
Breakfast ¾ cup Poha, ½ cup Mango Spicy Salsa, Coffee w/sugar & milk, 1 fruit	.75	.5	1 1		 .25	.12	.5
Lunch ¾ cup Cheesy Peas Curry, 2 pieces Stuffed Mushrooms, 1 cup Veg Finger Salad, 1 cup Bulgur Pulao, 2 pieces Banana Burfi	.12 2	.75 1 .75 .6 1			1 .25 .25	.12 .12 .25	 1
Snack ¾ cup Potato Chaat, ½ cup Spiced Beans, Chutney	1	.25 .25		1			
Dinner ¾ cup Dal Makhni, ¼ cup Quick Greens, 2 cups Lassi (salty), 2 Chapati, 1 fruit	2	.25 1	 1	1	 1	.3 .12	
TOTAL	5.87	5.35	4	2	2.75	1.03	1.5

Snacks and Appetizers

Snacks are very popular, served at tea–time or as appetizers before the meals. They generally bring back memories of great times together munching and meeting friends. Some of the easy and delicious hors d'oeuvres include 'Handva', Mushroom Patties, and Bread Vegetable Patties.

You can tailor the type and amount of seasonings to your taste and needs. Use hot or mild green chili, black pepper, or red chili powder as you may choose. Also modify quantity of onions, garlic, and ginger to your taste. For details of how to sauté, knead dough, and other techniques, see the chapter *Preparation Techniques.*

To help plan nutritious meals, each recipe gives nutritive value (calories, protein, carbohydrate (carb), fiber, fat, and cholesterol (chol)) and Food Group Exchange for a helping of the dish. Estimate is rounded off for ease of understanding. Garnishes, topping and small amounts of seasoning are not counted. (See page 13 for basis of estimating Food Group Exchange and nutritive value.)

Abbreviations:

carb: carbohydrate,	chol: cholesterol,	F: Fahrenheit,
g: gram,	lb: pound,	med: medium,
mg: milligram,	oz: ounce.	

ADAI DOSA (Rice and Lentil Crepes)

This is a special type of 'Dosa' (a South Indian dish), high in protein. These are best made fresh and served hot. If cold, reheat in a stack of four, properly wrapped, in the microwave oven (1–2 minutes) or in the conventional oven (10 minutes at 375°F). The batter can be easily made in advance, refrigerated or frozen.

1 cup rice
½ cup Toor split dal
¼ cup Chana split dal
¼ cup Mung split peeled dal
¼ cup Urad split peeled dal
Oil to pan-fry

Seasonings:
1 teaspoon chopped green chili
1 teaspoon grated ginger
1½ teaspoons salt

1. Check, rinse and soak the rice and different 'dal' in water for 3– 5 hours. Drain; grind them to a make a thick consistency batter, using minimum possible water. Mix in the seasonings.
2. Heat a griddle (or heavy skillet or tawa) on medium heat. Grease with ½ teaspoon of oil the first time only. Pour 2 tablespoons of the batter and spread evenly as thin as possible, with the back of a serving spoon, into a round shape. Add ½ teaspoon of oil around the edges. Cook for 1–2 minutes until the top appears dry and the bottom has just begun to brown. Turn over with a flat spatula; brown the other side very lightly.
3. Make all the 'dosa' the same way. Stack and serve hot with 'Coconut Chutney'

Healthy Alternative: Make on a heavy non–stick skillet, using minimum or no oil.

Makes about 18 servings, one piece each. Per serving –
Nutritive Value: 106 calories, 4 g protein, 15 g carb, 1 g fiber, 3 g fat, 0 mg chol.
Food Group Exchange: 1/3 Grain, 1/3 Legumes/Meat, 1/3 Fat.

ALU TIKKI (Potato Patty)

One of the traditional snacks of India, you find them being sold by venders on street corners. These can be prepared in advance, refrigerated, and pan-fried when ready to serve. If already cooked, reheat them in the oven, spread on a cookie sheet, at 375°F for 5–10 minutes until warm.

5 medium size potatoes
2 bread slices
2 teaspoons oil + oil for pan–frying

Seasonings:

1 teaspoon coriander powder	½ teaspoon red chili powder
1 teaspoon garam masala	½ teaspoon black pepper
½ teaspoon mango powder	1 teaspoon salt

Filling:

½ cup green peas	½ teaspoon chopped green chilies
1 teaspoon grated ginger	

1. Boil and peel the potatoes. Mash them while still little warm, along with bread slices and all the seasonings.
2. To make the filling, sauté the green peas, ginger and chilies in 2 teaspoons oil; cook until tender and dry.
3. Divide the potato mash into golf size balls. Flatten each ball between your palms, fill with about 2 teaspoons of the filling, fold from all sides, and make a flat round patty, about ½" thick.
4. Heat a flat skillet (or tawa) on medium heat. Grease with 1 teaspoon of oil the first time only. Put 5–6 patties that can fit on the skillet without touching. Add drops of oil around the edges of each patty. They should cook very slowly; lower heat as needed. As the bottom starts to brown, flip each patty with a flat spatula; brown the other side too, adding drops of oil on edges.
5. Repeat with the remaining patties. Serve hot with any chutney.

Variation: Use a different filling such as crumbled fresh cheese (paneer) mixed with grated ginger, chopped green chilies and chopped cashews.

Healthy Alternative: Instead of pan-frying (step 3), bake in the oven spread on a greased cookie sheet, at 400°F for 20 minutes until golden brown. Brush oil on top also. Flip and bake for another 20 minutes, until golden brown on the other side too.

Makes about 15 servings, two pieces each. Per serving –
Nutritive Value: 200 calories, 3 g protein, 21 g carb, 2 g fiber, 12 g fat, 0 mg chol.
Food Group Exchange: 1 Grain, 1/8 Vegetable, ½ Fat.

BATATA VADA (Potato Rounds)

Also called 'Alu Bonda', these are easy to make and are specially liked by children. Use all–purpose or boiling potatoes. Make them few days in advance, if necessary, and refrigerate or freeze. Reheat in the oven at 375°F, spread out on a cookie sheet, for 5–10 minutes until warm and crisp.

6 medium size potatoes boiled
1 cup gram flour (besan)
1 tablespoon oil + oil for deep-frying

Seasonings:

1 teaspoon mustard seeds	½ teaspoon mango powder
1 teaspoon cumin seeds	1 teaspoon garam masala
1 teaspoon crushed green chili	1 teaspoon red chili powder
1 teaspoon coriander powder	1 teaspoon salt

1. Sift the gram flour and mix with about one cup water to make a thin paste. Keep separately. Peel and break the boiled potatoes in small chunks.
2. Heat 1 tablespoon of oil in a skillet on medium-high heat. Sauté the mustard seeds and cumin seeds. After a few seconds, when the seeds splutter, add the potatoes and remaining seasonings; cook for about 5 minutes.
3. When the mixture is cold, make golf size balls. Heat the oil for frying in a deep skillet or wok on medium-high heat. Dip each potato ball in the gram flour mixture and put in the hot oil. Put as many that can fit in the skillet in single layer.
4. Deep fry, turning often so that all sides are cooked, until golden brown. (Regulate the heat as needed.)
5. Repeat with the remaining 'Batata Vada'. Serve hot with any chutney.

Makes about 25 servings, two pieces each. Per serving –
Nutritive Value: 249 calories, 3 g protein, 14 g carb, 2 g fiber, 20 g fat, 0 mg chol.
Food Group Exchange: ½ Grain, ¼ Legumes/Meat, 1 Fat.

BESAN POORE (Gram Flour Crepes)

These are best made fresh and served hot. The batter can be made in advance and refrigerated. However, if they are made ahead of time, then reheat in a stack of four, properly wrapped, in the microwave oven (1–2 minutes) or the conventional oven (10 minutes at 375°F).

1½ cup gram flour (besan), sifted
½ cup buttermilk
Oil to pan-fry

Seasonings:

1 finely chopped onion
1 teaspoon chopped green chili
½ teaspoon grated ginger

½ teaspoon black pepper
1 teaspoon salt

1. Mix everything together (except oil) with a whisk or your hand. Add more buttermilk if needed, to make a thick consistency batter, as for pancakes.
2. Heat a griddle (or skillet or tawa) on medium heat. Grease with 1 teaspoon of oil the first time only.
3. Pour 2 tablespoons of batter and spread evenly and thinly with the back of a serving spoon into a round shape. Add ½ teaspoon of oil around the edges. Cook for 1–2 minutes until the top appears dry and the bottom has just begun to brown. Turn over with a flat spatula; brown the other side very lightly, adding ½ teaspoon of oil around the edges.
4. Make all the crepes the same way. Serve hot with any chutney.

Variation: Use Bisquick baking mix or a pancake mix instead of gram flour.

Healthy Alternative: Make on a heavy non-stick skillet, using oil spray or very little oil. Use them as wraps and fill with sautéed vegetables or beans.

Makes about 10 servings, one piece each. Per serving –
Nutritive Value: 124 calories, 5 g protein, 14 g carb, 3 g fiber, 6 g fat, 0.4 mg chol.
Food Group Exchange: ½ Legumes/Meat, 1/8 Vegetable, ½ Fat.

BHEL (Spicy Mixture with Chutney)

This delicious and popular snack is made from some ready-made spicy mixes available from Indian grocery stores and chutney described in the chapter *Pickles and Chutney*. It makes a good salad bar item that everybody can enjoy. The mixture and chutneys can easily be made several days in advance. You may prepare potatoes and onions one day in advance, close in an airtight bag, and refrigerate.

4 10" flour tortillas (Burritos)
4 cup Indian rice krispies (Murmura), lightly roasted
1 cup "Hot Mix"
3 potatoes, boiled and chopped
1 chopped onion
1 cup Mint-Coriander Chutney
1 cup Tamarind Chutney
Oil to deep–fry (for tortillas)

<u>Garnish:</u> ½ cup 'Bikaner Mix' (optional)

1. Cut the flour tortillas in ½"x¾" strips. Deep–fry the strips (few at a time) on medium heat until light golden. Drain and put them in a brown paper bag or paper towels that absorb extra oil.
2. When ready to eat, mix everything together. Mix in additional salt and red chili powder if necessary. Serve sprinkled with 'Bikaner mix'.

Note: *For a large gathering, it is better to put everything on table and let everybody mix their own; or mix small batches at a time to prevent it from getting soggy.*

Variation: Use a 16 oz. bag of 'Bhel Mix' in place of tortillas, rice krispies, and 'Hot Mix'. May also add a cup of 'Sprouted Mung Beans'.

Healthy Alternative: Use whole–wheat tortillas (or pita bread). Bake them instead of deep-frying. Lightly moisten each tortilla or brush with little oil, and cut into strips or small wedges. Place them on a baking sheet in single layer, and bake in the pre–heated oven at 400°F for 5–10 minutes until lightly browned and crisp. Let them cool before using.

Makes about 16 servings, one cup each. Per serving –
Nutritive Value: 208 calories, 3 g protein, 27 g carb, 2 g fiber, 10 g fat, 0 mg chol.
Food Group Exchange: 1 Grain, 1 Fat, ½ Sugar, ¼ Vegetable.

BIRD'S NEST (Potato Roll)

These are very delicious and decorative, great for children. These can be made in advance and refrigerated. Reheat in the oven, spread on a cookie sheet, at 400°F for 5–10 minutes until warm.

4 medium size potatoes, boiled
½ cup green peas
1 chopped onion
¾ cup bread crumbs
2 teaspoons lemon juice
1 cup un–roasted vermicelli (sevia), broken
Oil for deep-frying

Seasonings:

½ teaspoon black pepper   1 teaspoon salt (to taste)
½ teaspoon red chili powder

1. Peel and mash the boiled potatoes. Mix all the ingredients (except vermicelli and oil) and the seasonings; it should be like semi-hard dough.
2. Divide the potato mixture in about 12 parts. Shape each part with your hands into an oval shape, like an egg (about 1"x2"). Coat each 'egg' with the vermicelli pieces to look like a nest.
3. Deep–fry the rolls, few at a time, at high heat until golden brown on all sides.
4. Remove and drain extra oil on paper towels or brown paper bag. Serve hot with 'Mint–Coriander Chutney' or ketchup.

Makes about 12 servings, one piece each. Per serving –
Nutritive Value: 197 calories, 4 g protein, 22 g carb, 1 g fiber, 11 g fat, 0 mg chol.
Food Group Exchange: ½ Grain, ¼ Vegetable, 1 Fat.

BREAD–VEGETABLE PATTIES

Bread patties are especially popular because they are not fried and are delicious. You can prepare them in advance and refrigerate; bake them when ready to serve. They can be reheated in the oven, spread on a cookie sheet, at 400°F for 5–10 minutes until warm.

6 medium potatoes
10 oz. green peas or vegetables
1 large (24 oz.) potato bread thin sliced (or any other)
1 tablespoon oil + oil for coating

Seasonings:

1 teaspoon cumin seeds	½ teaspoon mango powder
2 teaspoons coriander powder	½ teaspoon red chili powder
½ teaspoon turmeric powder	½ teaspoon black pepper
1/8 teaspoon asafetida powder	1 teaspoon salt
1 teaspoon garam masala	

To Make Filling:

1. Boil the potatoes (in the microwave or on the stove). Peel and mash into small pieces.
2. Heat 1 tablespoon of oil in a skillet on medium heat. Sauté the cumin seeds. Immediately add the green peas (or vegetables), potatoes, and remaining seasonings. Cook, stirring as needed, for 5 minutes. Let it cool.

To Make Patties:

3. Put about 2 tablespoons water in a plate; dip a slice of bread, turn and flatten, pressing with your hand. Hold the flattened bread in your palm, fill with 1+ tablespoon of filling, fold from all sides, bringing the ends together, and press gently to make a flat round patty. (It does not matter if the top is slightly open.) Use a paper towel to absorb extra moisture, if any.
4. Make all the patties and put them on a greased baking sheet. Spread little oil on the top of the patties too.
5. Bake in the oven at 450°F for 20 minutes until golden brown. Turn; bake for another 20 minutes, until golden brown on the other side too. (Instead of baking, you may pan-fry in batches in a large skillet.)
6. Serve hot with any chutney.

Makes about 15 servings, one piece each. Per serving –
Nutritive Value: 252 calories, 5 g protein, 36 g carb, 3 g fiber, 8 g fat, 0 mg chol.
Food Group Exchange: 1.5 Grain, ¼ Vegetable, 1/3 Fat.

CABBAGE ROLLS

Serve them as a snack or as an appetizer before parties. You may refrigerate or freeze them. Reheat in the microwave oven, covered.

1 head cabbage, grated (5–6 cups)
1–2 cup gram flour (besan), sifted

Seasonings:

1 chopped onion
1 teaspoon crushed garlic
1 teaspoon chopped green chili
2 teaspoons grated ginger

¼ teaspoon turmeric powder
1 tablespoon chopped green coriander
1 teaspoon salt

To Sauté:

2 teaspoons oil
1 teaspoon mustard seed
½ teaspoon sesame seed

Pinch of asafetida powder
4 whole green chilies, halved

Garnish: 1 tablespoon chopped green coriander

1. Squeeze the grated cabbage to remove excess liquid. Mix the cabbage with the gram flour and seasonings to make like semi–hard dough that can be shaped into rolls. Make rolls, about 3" long and ¾" in diameter. Make sure the ends are flat.
2. Use a metal colander that can fit in a large wide pot and covered. Put 2–3" deep water in the pot. Place a stand in water on which the colander can be positioned without touching water. Cover the pot and let the water boil.
3. Place the rolls in single layer in the colander and steam on high heat for 10–15 minutes, covered, until the rolls are done (a fork comes out clean when pricked). Remove the rolls with a spatula. Continue with the remaining rolls, adding more water before every batch.
4. When cool, cut the rolls into ¾" pieces, like little squares. Smooth the edges as needed. You may refrigerate or freeze the pieces for later use.
5. Heat the oil and sauté the spices. Mix in the rolls. Garnish and serve warm.

Variation: Deep–fry the steamed pieces on medium–high heat for a crispy taste and then sauté.

Makes about 10 servings, four pieces each. Per serving –
Nutritive Value: 109 calories, 6 g protein, 19 g carb, 5 g fiber, 2 g fat, 0 mg chol.
Food Group Exchange: ½ Legumes/Meat, ¾ Vegetable, 1/8 Fat.

CHAAT PAPRI (Crackers in Spicy Mixture)

This delicious and popular snack is made using tortillas. Generally it is put together for each person or served in a salad bar where people serve themselves. You may make tortilla and chutney several days in advance. Prepare the potatoes the same day or one day in advance, close in an airtight bag, and refrigerate.

4 10" flour tortillas (Burritos)
3 potatoes, boiled and chopped
1 cup plain yogurt, whipped
½ cup Tamarind Chutney
Oil to deep–fry, about 2" deep in a wok

Seasonings:

1 tablespoon chopped green chili	3 teaspoons chaat masala
1 teaspoon red chili powder	1 teaspoon salt

1. Cut the flour tortillas in ½"x¾" strips. Deep–fry the strips (few at a time) on medium heat until light golden. Drain and put them in a brown paper bag or couple of paper towels that absorb extra oil.
2. For each person, put a handful of fried tortilla pieces in a plate. Top with some boiled potato pieces. Spread 1 tablespoon of yogurt and 2 teaspoons Tamarind chutney over the potatoes and tortilla.
3. Sprinkle the seasonings to taste and serve.

Healthy Alternative: Add 1 tablespoon of 'Sprouted Mung Beans' or boiled chickpeas along with potatoes.

Variation: Use small thin 'Mathri' (Salted Crackers) instead of tortilla.

Makes about 8 servings, one cup each. Per serving –
Nutritive Value: 316 calories, 5 g protein, 40 g carb, 1 g fiber, 15 g fat, 1 mg chol.
Food Group Exchange: 1 Grain, 1 Fat, ¼ Sugar, 1/6 Dairy.

CHAKLI (Flour Pretzels)

These can be stored for a long time and served anytime. You need the 'chakli machine' to make the special shape.

3 cup whole–wheat flour
¼ cup oil + oil for deep-frying

Seasonings:

1 teaspoon turmeric powder	2 teaspoons lemon juice
1 teaspoon sesame seeds	1 teaspoon red chili powder
1 teaspoon caraway (ajwain) seeds	2 teaspoons salt

1. Tie the flour in a cloth. Put the tied flour in a small bowl that can fit in a pressure cooker. Add 2–3 cups water in the pressure cooker. Place the cooker on high heat with the bowl inside it and cover. As soon as the steam starts coming, place the pressure regulator on top. Lower heat and let it steam for about 10 minutes. (May steam in a large pot instead of pressure cooker; will take about 20 minutes to steam.)
2. When the pressure cooker has cooled down, remove the pressure regulator and take out the flour. Mix it with ¼ cup oil and all the seasonings. Knead the dough, adding water as needed, until it becomes smooth and supple.
3. Fill a chakli machine (available from Indian stores) with the dough. Turn the machine, dropping strings of dough in round pretzel shape on wax paper.
4. Heat the oil in a deep skillet or wok on medium-high heat. Deep fry 'chakli' in hot oil, few at a time, turning so that all sides are cooked, until light brown. (Do not make too dark.) Regulate the heat as needed.
5. Fry all the same way. Serve or store when cold.

Variation: Instead of whole-wheat flour, make the dough out of 1 cup gram flour (besan) and 3 cups rice flour mixed with ½ cup oil, seasonings, and water. Add yogurt also if desired. There is no need to steam this mixture.

Makes about 25 servings, two pieces each. Per serving –
Nutritive Value: 199 calories, 2 g protein, 11 g carb, 2 g fiber, 16 g fat, 0 mg chol.
Food Group Exchange: ½ Grain, 1 Fat.

CHICKPEA-POTATO CASSEROLE

This delicious low–fat side dish is made from potatoes, 'Chhole' (Curried Chickpeas page 136), and chutneys described in the chapter *Pickles and Chutney.*

8 medium size potatoes
5 cup 'Chhole' (Curried Chickpeas) of semi–thick
consistency, partially mashed
1 cup Mint-Coriander Chutney
1 cup Tamarind Chutney
1 tablespoon oil

1. Wash and boil the potatoes in their skin; peel and mash.
2. In a 9x13" baking dish, spread a thin layer (about 1/3") of the mashed potatoes, then 'Chhole', and then very thin layer of 'Tamarind Chutney'. Top with another layer of potatoes, 'Chhole' and then 'Mint–Coriander Chutney'. End with the potato layer. Brush the oil on top.
3. Bake at 350°F until the top crust is brown (about 20 minutes). Cut into squares and serve.

Makes about 20 servings, two pieces each. Per serving –
Nutritive Value: 126 calories, 3 g protein, 24 g carb, 1.4 g fiber, 2 g fat, 0 mg chol.
Food Group Exchange: ½ Grain, ½ Legumes/Meat, ½ Vegetable, 1/8 Fat.

Foods that are bitter, sour, salty,
Very hot, pungent, rough or burning
Are dear to the person of Rajas (passion).
They bring pain, misery and sickness.

The Bhagavad Gita, chapter 17, verse 9

CHIVDA (Cereal Mixture)

This is easy to make mixture that can be served any time. Use your imagination to mix any cereals and nuts. Make in advance and store in airtight containers.

**8 cup of mixed cereals such as Special K,
Rice Krispies, Chex, Total
1 cup peanuts, preferably shelled raw
1 cup whole or halved almonds
1 cup fried Chinese noodles
½ cup raisins (optional)
1 tablespoon oil**

Seasonings:

1 teaspoon mustard seeds	1 teaspoon mango powder
¼ teaspoon asafetida powder	1 teaspoon red chili powder
1 teaspoon cumin powder	1 teaspoon garam masala
1 teaspoon fennel seed powder	1 teaspoon salt

1. Heat the oil in a large pot on medium heat; sauté mustard seeds. Roast the peanuts (if raw) and almonds slightly.
2. Add the asafetida powder; add different cereals and noodles; keep stirring. Mix at low heat for 10–15 minutes.
3. Add the remaining seasonings and raisins. Stir for another 5 minutes. Store when cold.

Baking Method: Reduce the oil if desired. After the sauté and roasting of nuts, mix everything and spread evenly on a large baking pan. Bake in the oven at 325°F for 25-30 minutes, until golden brown. Stir occasionally for even toasting.

Variation: Add different types of spicy mixes available from the Indian grocery stores.

Makes about 20 servings, one cup each. Per serving –
Nutritive Value: 166 calories, 5 g protein, 24 g carb, 4 g fiber, 7 g fat, 0 mg chol.
Food Group Exchange: 1 Grain, 1/3 Legumes/Meat, 1/8 Fat.

CHUTNEY COVERED PEANUTS

Peanuts, rich in protein, are delightful anytime. Raw peanuts, with reddish skin, are available from specialty stores. You can roast the peanuts well in advance and keep in a covered bottle. Mix with chutney when ready to serve.

**1 cup shelled raw peanuts, with skin
2 teaspoons Mint–Coriander Chutney**

1. Bake the peanuts in the oven at 350°F for 10–15 minutes, checking often, until lightly brown. (You can also roast in a skillet with little oil.)
2. Remove some of the skin that easily falls off when rubbed between your hands. Serve mixed with chutney or serve chutney on the side.

Variation: Use roasted peeled peanuts if desired. Also mix in chopped red onions and green coriander.

*Makes about 4 servings, ¼ cup each. Per serving –
Nutritive Value: 212 calories, 10 g protein, 7 g carb, 4 g fiber, 18 g fat, 0 mg chol.
Food Group Exchange: 1 Legumes/Meat.*

**It has been discovered that
baking soda destroys the vitamin C content of vegetables.**

CORN VADA (Flour Patties)

Make these snacks for high tea or before dinner. The batter has to be started a day in advance. You may refrigerate or freeze the 'vada'. To serve, reheat in the microwave, properly wrapped, or in the oven at 375°F spread on a baking sheet. Makes about 20 medium size 'vada'.

1 cup plain yogurt, divided
1 cup corn flour
½ cup whole–wheat flour
¼ cup oil + for deep–frying (about 2" deep in a wok)

Seasonings:

1 teaspoon fenugreek seeds or powder	½ teaspoon turmeric powder
2 teaspoons crushed ginger	½ teaspoon red chili powder
2 teaspoons chopped green chili	1 teaspoon salt

1. Soak the fenugreek seeds in ¼ cup yogurt for 2–3 hours. Grind the seeds with yogurt. (If using the fenugreek powder, mix it with the flour.) Mix in the remaining yogurt, ¼ cup oil, and corn and wheat flour. Add water as needed to make like soft dough. Leave it covered 4–5 hours or overnight to condition the dough.
2. Mix the remaining seasonings into the dough. Make golf size balls; flatten to make patties and press in the middle with your thumb to make a tiny hole.
3. Heat the oil for frying in a deep skillet or wok on medium-high heat. Deep fry 'vada' in the hot oil, few at a time, turning so that all sides are cooked, until golden brown. Regulate the heat as needed. Fry all the same way.
4. Drain; serve hot with any chutney.

Makes about 10 servings, two pieces each. Per serving –
Nutritive Value: 361 calories, 3 g protein, 15 g carb, 2 g fiber, 32 g fat, 1 mg chol.
Food Group Exchange: 2/3 Grain, 2 Fat, 1/8 Dairy.

DAL VADA (Lentil Patties)

These are delicious, high in protein snacks made out of dry dal (lentils) and rice. They can be refrigerated or frozen. Reheat in the oven or microwave before serving. Makes about 50 medium size 'vada'.

**1 cup brown lentils
1 cup Chana dal
1 cup Urad peeled split dal
½ cup rice
Oil for deep–frying (about 2" deep in a wok)**

Seasonings:

2 cloves garlic	½ teaspoon mango powder
1" piece ginger	1 teaspoon red chili powder
2 teaspoons chopped green chili	2 teaspoons chopped green coriander
1 teaspoon coarsely ground coriander seeds	1 teaspoon salt

1. Check, rinse, and soak the lentils, Chana dal, Urad dal, and rice for 4–5 hours. Drain; grind using minimum possible water in a food blender or grinder to make like soft dough. Also grind garlic and ginger and remaining seasonings into the dough. Mix it well and make golf size balls; flatten to make small patties.
2. Heat the oil in a deep skillet or wok on medium-high heat. Deep–fry the 'vada' in hot oil, few at a time, turning so that all sides are cooked, until golden brown. Regulate the heat as needed. Fry all the same way.
3. Drain; serve hot with any chutney.

Variation: Put a filling of mashed potatoes, grated carrots and cauliflower, or green peas, mixed with spices, in each 'vada'. May make 'vada' from only 'Chana dal' or 'Urad dal'.

*Makes about 25 servings, two pieces each. Per serving –
Nutritive Value: 217 calories, 6 g protein, 17 g carb, 3 g fiber, 14 g fat, 0 mg chol.
Food Group Exchange: ¾ Legumes/Meat, 1/8 Grain, 1 Fat.*

DALIA (Multi–Grain Porridge)

You can custom blend any grains in this healthy morning treat and true winter comfort food. Serve it as a sweet or spicy dish. When refrigerated or frozen, it becomes stiffer and requires additional liquid.

**2 cups grains such as cracked wheat, rolled oats,
oat bran, wheat bran
½ cup wheat germ**

Seasonings:
    Milk, sugar or honey, or salt and pepper (to taste)

1. Heat 9 cups water in a pot.
2. Meantime put all the grains in a 3–4 quart pot on low–medium heat. Stir for a few minutes until lightly roasted.
3. Add the hot water to the grains slowly, taking care not to splash. Increase the heat to medium–high for a few minutes to let everything boil.
4. Reduce the heat; cook half–covered until the grains are soft (about 20 minutes). It should be like a pudding. Add more hot water if needed.
5. Serve hot with milk and the desired seasonings.

*Makes about 15 servings, ½ cup each. Per serving (without seasonings) –
Nutritive Value: 63 calories, 3 g protein, 12 g carb, 3 g fiber, 1 g fat, 0 mg chol.
Food Group Exchange: 1 Grain.*

DHOKLA (Lentil Cakes)

This is the traditional way to make 'dhokla', a popular dish from Gujarat, west of India. As for *'Rava Dhokla'* on page 87, you need a large pot and metal plate (thali) to make it. You may steam them in advance and refrigerate or freeze. Sauté and heat in a wide pot before serving. Makes about 80 pieces.

1 cup Urad peeled split dal (or 1¼ cups Urad dal flour)
2 cups cream of rice
1 cup plain yogurt (preferably sour)
1 tablespoon oil
1 teaspoon Eno powder (or ½ teaspoon baking soda)

Seasonings:

1 teaspoon chopped green chili	1 teaspoon salt
¼ teaspoon turmeric powder	

To Sauté:

2 teaspoons oil	Pinch of asafetida powder
1 teaspoon mustard seeds	4 whole green chilies, halved
½ teaspoon sesame seeds	

Garnish: 1 tablespoon chopped green coriander

1. If using 'dal', check it, rinse, and soak in enough water for about 6 hours. Drain and grind it in the food blender finely with little water. (Skip this step if using 'Urad dal flour'.)
2. Mix the ground 'Urad dal' (or flour) with cream of rice, yogurt, and 1 tablespoon oil, adding water as needed, and make a semi-thick consistency batter. Leave it covered for 3–4 hours until it rises.
3. When ready to cook, mix the seasonings and Eno powder in the batter. Whip it well.
4. Spread the batter thinly in a greased flat dish that can fit in a large wide pot and covered. Put 2–3" deep water in the pot. Place a stand in water on which the flat dish can be positioned without touching the water. Tie a cloth around the lid of the pot so that moisture does not drop into the flat dish.
5. Steam on high heat, covered, for 15–20 minutes until 'dhokla' is done (a fork comes out clean when pricked). Remove the dish and let it cool before cutting the pieces into 1-2" squares. Repeat with the remaining batter.
6. To sauté, heat the oil in a small pot. Add the mustard seeds. As soon as they splutter, add the remaining spices and mix into the 'dhokla'. Garnish and serve.

Makes about 20 servings, four pieces each. Per serving –
Nutritive Value: 118 calories, 4 g protein, 21 g carb, 1 g fiber, 2 g fat, 0.5 mg chol.
Food Group Exchange: ½ Grain, 1/3 Legumes/Meat, 1/8 Fat.

FRUIT CHAAT

The word 'chaat' denotes something spicy, aromatic and delicious. There are times when you have too many fruits on your hands, or fruits that are not too sweet. Make a 'chaat' and everybody will love it. Be creative and use what you like, e.g., grapes, peaches, and papaya in a 'chaat'.

2 apples, cored and peeled
2 pears, cored
1 banana, peeled
2 tablespoons chopped nuts (optional)
1 tablespoon raisins (optional)

Seasonings:

1 tablespoon lemon juice
½ teaspoon black pepper

1 teaspoon chaat masala
1 teaspoon salt

1. Cut the fruits in ¾" cubes or rounds. Mix in the lemon juice and refrigerate for 1–2 hours.
2. Just before serving, toss with the remaining seasonings to taste.

Makes about 6 servings, one cup each. Per serving –
Nutritive Value: 78 calories, 0.5 g protein, 20 g carb, 3 g fiber, 0.5 g fat, 0 mg chol.
Food Group Exchange: 1 Fruit.

Man is what he eats.

– Ludwig Feuerbach

HANDVA (Baked Hot Cakes)

This is a delicious easy to make dish from Gujarat, west of India. Serve it any time with chutney. The pieces can be frozen. Reheat in the microwave or conventional oven. Makes 24 pieces.

1 cup semolina (suji)
1 cup cream of rice
1 cup cornmeal
2 cups plain yogurt
10-oz chopped spinach (or any other green)

Seasonings:

2 teaspoons salt	½ teaspoon sugar
1 teaspoon lemon juice	1 teaspoon crushed green chili
½ teaspoon baking soda	2 teaspoons grated ginger

To Sauté:

¼ cup oil	1 teaspoon sesame seeds
2 teaspoons mustard seeds	¼ teaspoon asafetida powder

1. Mix the semolina, cream of rice, cornmeal, yogurt, salt, and about ½ cup water into a thick batter. Leave covered overnight in a warm place.
2. Mix the chopped spinach and the remaining seasonings into the mixture.
3. To prepare the sauté, heat the oil in a small pan on medium–high heat. Put the mustard seeds and cover. As soon as they splutter, reduce the heat and add the remaining spices. Mix half of the sautéed oil and spices into the mixture.
4. Spread the mixture in a 9x13" baking dish. Pour the remaining sautéed oil and spices on top. Bake at 350°F for 45 minutes. It is done when a fork comes out clean when pricked.
5. Broil for about 5 minutes to get baked crust. Cut into squares. Serve hot.

Healthy Alternative: Reduce the amount of oil to half; for moisture, add another ½ cup pureed squash to the mixture before baking.

Makes about 12 servings, two pieces each. Per serving –
Nutritive Value: 209 calories, 6 g protein, 33 g carb, 2 g fiber, 5.5 g fat, 2 mg chol.
Food Group Exchange: 1 Grain, ¼ Vegetable, 1/6 Dairy, 1/3 Fat.

IDLI (Steamed Rice & Lentil Rounds)

These healthy round patties are delicious served with hot 'Sambhar' and 'Coconut Chutney'. You may make them in advance and freeze. Warm them, covered, in the microwave. You will need the 'Idli maker' to steam 'Idli'. Makes 40–45.

1 cup peeled split Urad dal
2 cups rice (or cream of rice)
½ cup flat parboiled rice (Poha)
Oil to grease

Seasonings:
2 teaspoons salt

1. Check, rinse, and soak the 'dal', rice (not cream of rice), and flat parboiled rice separately for about 4 hours. Drain; grind each, using minimum water, to a fine texture. (Urad dal should be like fluffy paste.) Blend in the salt, and make a thick consistency batter. (If using cream of rice in place of rice, mix it with the ground 'dal', adding little water as needed.)
2. Leave the batter, covered, in a warm place, overnight. Whip the batter before using.
3. Put the batter in greased 'Idli' molds (part of 'Idli Maker'). Stack the molds and stand them in a large pot with 1–2" deep boiling water at bottom. Keep on high heat. Cover tightly and let the 'Idli' steam for about 8 minutes. (You may use a pressure cooker to steam 'Idli'. Close the lid but do not put the pressure regulator.)
4. Remove 'Idli' from the molds. To help remove from the molds, sprinkle cold water on top or use buttered knife. (For easy clean-up, line the idli molds with coffee filters cut to fit.) Optionally, pat little butter on 'Idli' for moistness before serving.

Variation: Use 'Idli mix' available from Indian grocery store and follow directions.

Makes about 20 servings, two pieces each. Per serving –
Nutritive Value: 62 calories, 3 g protein, 11 g carb, 1 g fiber, 1 g fat, 0 mg chol.
Food Group Exchange: ¾ Grain, 1/3 Legumes/Meat.

KABOB

This snack can be made from any ground meat and does not use any oil. You may make them in advance and freeze.

1 lb. ground turkey (or chicken or beef)
2 teaspoons tandoori paste (from Indian grocery store)
1 egg, beaten

Seasonings:

1 teaspoon crushed garlic	2 teaspoons lemon juice
1 teaspoon crushed green chili	1 teaspoon salt

1. Mix all the ingredients and seasonings; make round patties.
2. Bake on a greased sheet at 450°F for about 15 minutes. Serve with any chutney and onion salad.

Variation: Can also make with ground lamb. Bake them at 350°F for 25–30 minutes.

Makes about 10 servings, two pieces each. Per serving –
Nutritive Value: 74 calories, 8 g protein, 0 g carb, 0 g fiber, 4 g fat, 54 mg chol.
Food Group Exchange: 2/3 Legumes/Meat.

Food must be treated respectfully.
                                          -Talmud

KELE Ki TIKKI (Plantain Patty)

This is similar to 'Alu Tikki' earlier in this chapter but is low in carbohydrates because it is made from plantains (kacche kele). These can be prepared in advance, refrigerated, and pan-fried when ready to serve. If already cooked, reheat in the oven, spread on a cookie sheet, at 375°F for 5–10 minutes until warm. Makes about 20.

4 plantains
2 medium size potatoes
½ cup gram flour (besan) (as needed)
Oil for pan frying

Seasonings:
1 tablespoon chopped cilantro
1 teaspoon coriander powder
1 teaspoon garam masala
½ teaspoon mango powder

½ teaspoon red chili powder
½ teaspoon black pepper
1 teaspoon salt

1. Boil the plantains and potatoes. Peel and mash them; mix thoroughly with the gram flour to make a stiff mixture. Add more gram flour if needed.
2. When ready to pan-fry, mix in the seasonings. Divide the mash into golf size balls (about 20). Form each ball into ½" thick round patty.
3. Heat a flat skillet (or tawa) on medium heat. Grease with 1 teaspoon of oil the first time only. Put 5–6 patties that may fit on the skillet without touching. Add drops of oil around the edges of each patty. Cook them slowly; lower heat as needed. As the bottom starts to brown, flip each patty with a flat spatula; brown the other side too, adding drops of oil on edges.
4. Make all the patties the same way. Serve hot with any chutney.

Variation: Add crushed peanuts or cashews to the mash.

Makes about 10 servings, two pieces each. Per serving –
Nutritive Value: 164 calories, 2.5 g protein, 30 g carb, 2 g fiber, 5 g fat, 0 mg chol.
Food Group Exchange: ½ Fruit, 1/3 Grain, ¼ Legumes/Meat, ½ Fat.

KHASTA KACHORI (Crispy Patties)

This popular snack is traditionally served at weddings and parties. Can be easily made in advance and stored at room temperature for several days. May also be refrigerated or frozen. Serve warmed in the oven or at room temperature.

To make Filling:

½ cup peeled split Urad dal
1 tablespoon oil

Seasonings:

1/8 teaspoon asafetida powder	½ teaspoon crushed fennel seeds
½ teaspoon garam masala	½ teaspoon salt (to taste)
1 teaspoon red chili powder	

1. Check, rinse, and soak the 'dal' for about 5 hours (or overnight). Drain; grind coarsely using minimum water.
2. Heat the oil in a skillet on medium heat. Stir–fry the ground 'dal' until dry (about 15 minutes). Mix the seasonings. **Note:** You may grind dry 'dal' without soaking. Grind it coarsely, mix with the seasonings, oil and water to make a dry consistency mixture. Let it rest for 4 hours. No need to stir-fry.

To make Dough and Patty:

2 cups all-purpose flour
¼ teaspoon salt
½ cup oil + oil for deep–frying

3. Mix the flour and ½ cup oil. Add salt. Knead the dough, adding water as needed, until it becomes semi–hard and supple. Take small pieces of the dough (golf ball size), make a round and flatten into 3" disc with a rolling pin.
4. Fill each disc with 1–2 teaspoons of the filling, bring all ends together and join them moisten the ends if needed, bring them together and close the opening completely, and shape into a patty. Pat or roll gently.
5. Heat the oil for deep–frying in a wok or deep skillet on low-medium heat. Put the patties, with joined side up, in single layer.
6. Deep–fry the patties at low-medium heat until golden brown on all sides (about 20 minutes for each batch). Remove and drain extra oil on paper towels or brown paper bag. Serve with any chutney or 'Alu Bhaji'.

Healthy Alternative: Replace part of all–purpose flour by whole-wheat.
Makes about 20 servings, one piece each. Per serving –
Nutritive Value: 203 calories, 3 g protein, 11 g carb, 2 g fiber, 16 g fat, 0 mg chol.
Food Group Exchange: ¾ Grain, 1/8 Legumes/Meat, 1 Fat.

MASALA DOSA (Potato–Lentil Wraps)

There is hardly anybody who does not drool at the mention of 'Masala Dosa'. These are best made fresh and served hot. If cold, reheat, properly wrapped, in the microwave oven (1–2 minutes). The batter can be easily made in advance, refrigerated or frozen. The filling can be refrigerated too.

1 cup peeled split Urad dal
2½ cups rice (or 3½ cups rice flour)
½ cup flat parboiled rice (Poha)
Oil to pan-fry

Seasonings:
    1 teaspoon fenugreek seeds
    1 teaspoon salt

1. Check, rinse, and soak the 'dal' and rice (not rice flour) separately for 4 hours or more. Soak the flat parboiled rice and fenugreek seeds for about ½ hour. Drain; grind each very fine using just enough water. (If using rice flour, mix with ground 'dal'; add warm water as needed.)
2. Whip everything together and salt to make a semi-thick consistency batter, as for pancakes. Leave the batter, covered, in a warm place, overnight.
3. Heat a griddle (or heavy skillet or tawa) on medium heat. (Lubricate with 1 teaspoon of oil to start with.) For every 'dosa', sprinkle a drop of water; wipe gently; spread about 2 tablespoons of batter (very thin layer) into a round shape with the back of a ladle or serving spoon. Add 1 teaspoon of oil around the edges.
4. Cook, covered, for 2–3 minutes until the top appears dry and the bottom has just begun to brown. Lower heat as needed.
5. Spread about 2 tablespoons stuffing (as described below) in middle and fold both ends. Serve hot with 'Coconut Chutney'.

STUFFING:

6 medium size potatoes, boiled, peeled
2 chopped onions
½ cup green peas
1 tablespoon oil

Seasonings:
1 teaspoon mustard seeds
2 teaspoons split peeled Urad dal
½ teaspoon turmeric powder
1 teaspoon chopped curry leaves

1 tablespoon chopped green chili
1 tablespoon chopped green coriander
1 teaspoon salt

6. Sauté the mustard seeds in a skillet on medium heat. As soon as they splutter, stir in the 'Urad dal'. Add the onions and cook until translucent. Add the remaining seasonings.
7. Add the green peas if desired. Add the potatoes that have been broken in small pieces. Stir for a couple of minutes.

Variation: Before folding the 'dosa' in step 5, spread about ½ teaspoon 'Coconut Chutney' along with the stuffing. Instead of grinding the batter yourself, you may use the 'Dosa mix' available from Indian grocery store and follow instructions.

Healthy Alternative: Make on a heavy non–stick skillet, using minimum or no oil.

Makes about 20 servings, one piece each. Per serving –
Nutritive Value: 205 calories, 5 g protein, 33 g carb, 4 g fiber, 6 g fat, 0 mg chol.
Food Group Exchange: 1 Grain, ¼ Legumes/Meat, 1/8 Vegetable, ½ Fat.

MATAR KACHORI (Pea Patties)

Similar to 'Khasta Kachori' on page 71, make them in advance and store at room temperature for a couple of days. May be refrigerated or frozen. You can also make a large amount of the filling and freeze it for use as needed. Serve warmed in the oven.

For Filling:

¾ cup dry green peas
1 tablespoon oil

Seasonings:

1 teaspoon cumin powder
½ teaspoon garam masala
1 teaspoon red chili powder

½ teaspoon mango powder
½ teaspoon salt

1. Check, rinse and soak the peas for about 5 hours (or overnight). Drain; grind coarsely using minimum water.
2. Heat the oil in a non–stick skillet on medium heat. Stir–fry the ground peas until dry (10–15 minutes). Reduce the heat to avoid sticking at bottom. Mix in the seasonings.

For Dough:

2 cups all-purpose or whole-wheat flour (or a mix)
¼ teaspoon salt
¼ cup oil + oil for deep-frying

3. Mix the flour and ¼ cup oil. Add salt. Knead the dough, adding water as needed, until it becomes semi–hard and supple. Take small pieces of the dough (golf ball size), and make small balls and flatten them.
4. Roll each disc on flat surface in a thin round. Fill each round with 1–2 teaspoons of filling, moisten the ends if needed, bring them together and close the opening completely, and shape into a patty.
5. Heat the oil for deep–frying in a wok or deep skillet on low-medium heat. Put the patties, with joined side up, in single layer. Deep fry until golden brown on all sides, turning as needed. Remove and drain extra oil on paper towels. Fry all the patties the same way. Serve warm with any chutney.

Variation: Use whole Mung dal instead of dry peas for filling.

Healthy Alternative: Use milk instead of water to make the dough. Add 1 tablespoon baking powder and desired spices. Make the patties as above and bake them in the preheated oven at 400°F for 5–10 minutes; turn and bake for another 5 minutes until light brown on all sides.

Makes about 10 servings, two pieces each. Per serving –
Nutritive Value: 334 calories, 3 g protein, 19 g carb, 1 g fiber, 28 g fat, 0 mg chol.
Food Group Exchange: 2/3 Grain, ¼ Legumes/Meat, 1 Fat.

> No scholar should live in a town where vegetables are unobtainable.
> -Talmud

MATHRI (Salted Crackers)

Also called 'Tikhi Puri', these can be made mild or spicy, as desired. You may store them, in an airtight bag, for a month or so.

½ cup semolina (suji)
½ cup whole–wheat flour
2 cups all-purpose unbleached flour
½ cup oil + oil for deep–frying

Seasonings:

1 teaspoon salt

2 teaspoons coarsely crushed black pepper

¼ teaspoon caraway seeds (ajwain)

1. Mix the semolina in just enough water to make it completely wet and let it soak for about 20 minutes. Mix the other flours, ½ cup oil, salt and caraway seeds together. Add the soaked semolina and knead the dough, adding about ¼ cup water as needed, until the dough becomes semi–hard and supple.
2. Make little balls (walnut size) and shape them into patties. On a flat surface, roll each patty, sprinkled with a pinch of black pepper, into a small round, about ¼" thick. Prick the rounds with fork for air vents.
3. Heat the oil in a deep frying pan or wok on medium heat. Fry the 'mathri', few at a time, turning as needed, until golden brown on all sides. Drain them on paper towels or brown paper bag. Repeat for the remaining 'mathri'. Serve when completely cold.

Variation: May add 1 cup fresh fenugreek leaves (½ cup dry leaves), black pepper and red chili powder, when making the dough. To get bite size snacks called 'namak pare', instead of step 2 above, make 2 large balls of dough and roll them into large rounds (like pizza), then cut into ½"x¾" strips or small diamond shapes. Continue with the remaining steps to deep–fry.

Healthy Alternative: Use milk instead of water to make the dough. Add 1 tablespoon baking powder and the desired spices. Take small pieces of dough and shape like bread sticks. Bake in the preheated oven at 425°F for 5 minutes; turn and bake for another 5 minutes until light brown.

Makes about 24 servings, one piece each. Per serving –
Nutritive Value:162 calories, 2 g protein, 11 g carb, .5 g fiber, 12 g fat, 0 mg chol.
Food Group Exchange: ½ Grain, 1Fat.

MUNG DAL PAKORI (Lentil Fritters)

This crispy snack can be served with tea or as appetizer before dinner. You may make them in advance and refrigerate or freeze them. Warm in the oven before serving.

2 cups Mung split peeled dal
1 cup chopped onions
1 tablespoon oil + oil to deep-fry

Seasonings:

1 teaspoon chopped green chili
1 teaspoon grated ginger
½ teaspoon red chili powder
½ teaspoon black pepper

1 teaspoon cumin powder
1 teaspoon fennel seeds
1 tablespoon chopped green coriander
1 teaspoon salt

1. Check and rinse the dal. Soak it in about 5 cups water for 4–5 hours. Drain extra water. Grind coarsely in food blender using minimum water.
2. Mix in the chopped onions, 1 tablespoon oil, and all the seasonings. Whip and make into smooth fluffy batter.
3. Heat the oil in a deep skillet or wok on medium-high heat. Take the mix in small balls (about ¾" round) and drop in hot oil. Fry, turning to make sure all sides are cooked, until golden brown.
4. Drain on paper towels. Serve hot with any chutney.

Healthy Alternative: Use Mung split dal (green and yellow with peel) and grind the soaked dal along with peel.

Makes about 15 servings, two pieces each. Per serving –
Nutritive Value: 161 calories, 5 g protein, 13 g carb, 3 g fiber, 10 g fat, 0 mg chol.
Food Group Exchange: ½ Legumes/Meat, 1 Fat.

MUNG DAL POORE (Lentil Crepes)

These are similar to 'Besan Poore'. If necessary, reheat in a stack of four, properly wrapped, in the microwave oven (1-2 minutes), or in the conventional oven (10 minutes at 375°F). The batter can be easily made in advance and refrigerated.

2 cups Mung split dal (green & yellow with peel)
Oil to pan-fry

Seasonings:
1 teaspoon chopped green chili   ½ teaspoon black pepper
½ teaspoon grated ginger   1 teaspoon salt
½ teaspoon red chili powder

1. Check and rinse the 'dal'. Soak it in about 5 cups water for 4–5 hours. (The outside shell of 'dal' may appear separated; use it all.) Drain extra water. Grind along with all the seasonings in a food blender, using some of the water. Whip and make into pancake batter consistency.
2. Heat a griddle (or heavy skillet or tawa) on medium heat. Grease with ½ teaspoon oil the first time only. Pour about 2 tablespoons batter and spread evenly and thinly with the back of a serving spoon into a round shape.
3. Add ¼ teaspoon of oil around the edges. Cook for 1–2 minutes until the top appears dry and the bottom has just begun to brown. Turn over with a flat spatula; brown the other side very lightly adding ¼ teaspoon oil.
4. Make all the crepes the same way. Stack and serve hot with any chutney.

Healthy Alternative: Make on a non-stick skillet, using minimum oil. Use them as wraps and fill with sautéed vegetables such as mushrooms and onions.

Makes about 20 servings, one piece each. Per serving –
Nutritive Value: 74 calories, 4 g protein, 9 g carb, 2 g fiber, 3 g fat, 0 mg chol.
Food Group Exchange: ½ Legumes/Meat, ½ Fat.

MUSHROOM TURNOVERS

Mushrooms are a favorite with many. Make several of these turnovers because they go fast. Make them in advance and refrigerate or freeze; bake when ready to serve.

1½ cup all-purpose unbleached or whole-wheat flour
9 oz cream cheese
½ cup (4 oz.) butter

<u>For the Filling</u>:

1 chopped onion
10 oz. chopped mushrooms
6 boiled, peeled, and chopped potatoes
2 tablespoons flour
½ cup sour cream
1 tablespoon oil

<u>Seasonings:</u>

1 teaspoon coriander powder   1 teaspoon black pepper
½ teaspoon garam masala   1 teaspoon salt

1. Mix the cream cheese and butter. Add the flour and work until smooth. Chill in the refrigerator (about 2 hours) until the dough can be handled.
2. To make the filling, heat the oil in a skillet on medium–high heat. Sauté the chopped onions until golden brown. Add all the ingredients and seasonings for filling (except flour and sour cream); cook together for 5 minutes. Sprinkle the flour, stir in sour cream, and cook until thick and dry (about 5 minutes).
3. Divide the dough into 20 small patties. Roll each patty into 1/8" thick round (3–4" round). Place about 1 tablespoon of filling on each round and fold in half. Press edges together (may use handle of a fork). Prick top for steam vents. (At this point you may freeze the turnovers if you want to bake them later.)
4. Preheat the oven to 400°F. Place the turnovers on cookie sheet. Bake for about 15 minutes or until golden brown. (Frozen turnovers take a little longer to cook.) Serve hot.

Healthy Alternative: Omit the sour cream in the filling. Use tomatoes or yogurt cheese.

Makes about 20 servings, one piece each. Per serving –
Nutritive Value: 176 calories, 3 g protein, 16.3 g carb, 1 g fiber, 11.4 g fat, 16 mg chol.
Food Group Exchange: ¾ Grain, 1/3 Vegetable, ½ Dairy, ½ Fat.

MUTHIA (Flour–Vegetable Scramble)

This dish from Gujarat can be served as a snack or a side dish. Steam the batter for 'Muthia' in advance, and freeze or refrigerate it. Sauté and use when needed. Use any greens such as tops of daikon (white radish or 'mooli') and beets.

2 cups whole–wheat flour
2 cups gram flour (besan)
½ cup semolina (suji)
1 cup cream of rice
1 cup plain yogurt
2 lb. finely chopped greens (spinach, cabbage,..)
2 tablespoons oil

Seasonings:

1 tablespoon lemon juice	¼ teaspoon turmeric powder
2 teaspoons chopped green chili	1 teaspoon baking soda
2 teaspoons grated ginger	2 teaspoons salt

To Sauté:

2 tablespoons oil	1 teaspoon sesame seeds
2 teaspoons mustard seeds	Pinch of asafetida powder (hing)

Garnish: 2 tablespoons chopped green coriander

1. Mix all the ingredients and seasonings to make thick consistency batter, adding little water as needed. Mix well to make the batter smooth and light.
2. To steam, spread the batter, about ¾" thick layer, in a greased metal dish that can fit in a large wide pot and covered. Put 1–2" deep water in the pot. Place a stand in water on which the dish can be positioned without touching water. Steam on high heat, covered, for 30–45 minutes until 'Muthia' is done (a fork comes out clean when pricked). Steam the batter in batches as needed.
3. Remove the dish and let it cool before cutting the steamed mixture into small pieces, about ½" squares.
4. To sauté, heat the oil in a wide skillet on medium–high heat. Add the mustard seeds. As soon as they splutter, add the steamed mixture and other spices. Brown everything together for a few minutes. Adjust the seasonings, garnish, and serve warm.

Makes about 20 servings, ½ cup each. Per serving –
Nutritive Value: 168 calories, 7 g protein, 26 g carb, 6 g fiber, 4 g fat, 0.5 mg chol.
Food Group Exchange: ¾ Grain, ½ Legumes/Meat, ½ Vegetable, 1/8 Fat.

NUTTY GRANOLA

You can custom blend the ingredients in this healthy snack; skip any of the nuts and fruits that you cannot find or do not like. Use it as a cereal with milk or as a topping on a dessert like ice cream. Makes about 12 cups.

2 cups rolled oats
½ cup wheat germ
¼ cup wheat flakes
1 cup cereal such as grape nuts
½ cup maple syrup
1 cup brown sugar
½ cup water, as needed
3 tablespoons oil

NUTS & FRUITS:

1 cup sesame seeds
1 cup sunflower seeds
½ cup almond halves
½ cup cashews

1 cup raisins
1 cup chopped dried apples
1 cup chopped dried apricots

1. Mix everything in a shallow baking pan. (You may line it with foil paper to make cleaning easier.) Layer should not be more than 1 inch deep.
2. Preheat the oven to 325°F. Bake the nuts mix for about 30 minutes, stirring occasionally. Add more water if needed. Take care that cereal does not burn.
3. Store in a covered container in the refrigerator when completely cool.

Makes about 24 servings, ½ cup each. Per serving –
Nutritive Value: 231 calories, 6 g protein, 36 g carb, 4 g fiber, 9 g fat, 0 mg chol.
Food Group Exchange: ¾ Grain, ½ Fruit, ½ Legumes/Meat, 1 Sugar, 1/8 Fat.

PAO BHAJI (Vegetables on Rolls)

This makes a good picnic food. May use pita bread instead of rolls. The vegetable mix can easily be made in advance and refrigerated. The special spice 'pao bhaji masala' adds a unique taste.

4 potatoes
½ head cauliflower
2 carrots
1 cup green peas
¼ cup Chana dal
2 onions, chopped
4 tomatoes, sliced
12 bread rolls (or buns)
2 tablespoons oil + oil to pan-fry the rolls

Seasonings:
1 teaspoon salt
1 teaspoon mustard seeds
2 whole red chilies
½ teaspoon red chili powder
2 teaspoons pao bhaji masala (available at Indian grocery stores)

1. Wash, peel, and cut the potatoes. Wash, trim, and chop (or grate) the cauliflower and carrots in small pieces.
2. Rinse and drain 'dal' and put in a 2-quart pot to boil in 2 cups water. When little cooked (after 10 minutes), add the potatoes and salt. Cook until the potatoes are done; mash them along with 'dal'.
3. Add the chopped (or grated) cauliflower, carrots, and green peas to the 'dal' mix. Cook for another 15 minutes until the carrots are tender. Add water, as needed.
4. Heat 2 tablespoons oil on medium heat in a skillet. Sauté the mustard seeds in hot oil. Add the whole red chilies (can be removed before serving). Add the onions; stir until translucent. Add the cooked mixture. Cook for about 5 minutes; it should be like a wet mixture. Stir in red chili powder and 'pao bhaji masala', to taste.
5. Separate the rolls. Toast them in a hot skillet, using little bit of oil for each roll. Put the prepared filling and a slice of tomato between two halves. Serve hot.

Makes 12 servings, one roll each. Per serving –
Nutritive Value: 258 calories, 8 g protein, 39 g carb, 5 g fiber, 9 g fat, 0 mg chol.
Food Group Exchange: 1 Vegetable, 1.3 Grain, 1/8 Legumes/Meat, ½ Fat.

PATULI (Gram Flour Rolls)

Also known as 'Khandvi', it is a quick snack or side dish to make anytime. You may refrigerate them for about a week. Sauté before serving. You may freeze them but they can easily break when thawed. Serve warm or at room temperature with chutney or salsa. Makes about 20 pieces.

**1 cup plain yogurt
3 cups water
1 cup gram flour (besan)**

Seasonings:

1 teaspoon minced green chili
1 teaspoon grated ginger
Pinch of asafetida powder (hing)

½ teaspoon turmeric powder
2 teaspoons salt

To Sauté:

1 tablespoon oil
2 teaspoons mustard seed

1 teaspoon chopped curry leaves

Garnish: 1 tablespoon chopped green coriander

1. In a heavy pot, whisk the yogurt and water. Blend with the flour and the seasonings, making sure there are no lumps.
2. Cook over medium heat, stirring all the time, until the mixture thickens (appears like layers), about 20 minutes. Reduce the heat so that it does not stick to bottom of the pot.
3. Pour the mixture in a 9x13" greased tray. Spread it quickly as even and thin as possible. When it solidifies, cut into 2x4" strips. Roll each strip.
4. To sauté, heat the oil in a small pan. Add the mustard seeds. As soon as they splutter, add the curry leaves. Spread the sauté over the rolls. Garnish and serve.

Variation: Also add some grated un–sweetened coconut or sliced onion to the sauté, and sprinkle on the rolls.

Makes about 10 servings, two pieces each. Per serving –
Nutritive Value: 61 calories, 3.3 g protein, 7 g carb, 1 g fiber, 2.3 g fat, 1.4 mg chol.
Food Group Exchange: ½ Legumes/Meat, 1/8 Dairy, 1/8 Fat.

POHA (Pressed Rice with Vegetables)

This is a quick side dish or snack that can be served any time and is liked by all.

2 cups poha or pressed parboiled rice
2 onions chopped
1 cup mixed vegetables or green peas
2 potatoes, boiled, peeled and cut
1 tablespoon oil
1 teaspoon lemon juice

Seasonings:

1 teaspoon mustard seeds	1½ teaspoons salt
1 teaspoon cumin seeds	1 teaspoon crushed green chili
pinch of asafetida powder	½ teaspoon red chili powder
½ teaspoon turmeric powder	

Garnish: 1 tablespoon chopped green coriander

1. Rinse and drain the 'poha' (pressed rice) and keep aside. Sprinkle some water before using.
2. Heat the oil in a skillet on medium heat. Add the mustard seeds. As soon as they splutter, add the cumin seeds; then chopped onions and the remaining seasonings. Stir until the onions are translucent. Add the mixed vegetables and potatoes. When cooked, stir in the 'poha' gently and cook for a couple of minutes.
3. Sprinkle the lemon juice. Garnish with green coriander and serve.

Healthy Alternative: For increased fiber, do not peel the potatoes; scrub with a vegetable brush and remove any blemishes. Cook in the microwave oven so that no nutrition is lost.

Makes about 8 servings, ¾ cup each. Per serving –
Nutritive Value: 109 calories, 2.4 g protein, 21 g carb, 1.4 g fiber, 2.2 g fat, 0 mg chol.
Food Group Exchange: ¾ Grain, ½ Vegetable, 1/8 Fat.

POTATO CHAAT

The word 'chaat' makes your mouth water; it denotes something spicy, aromatic and delicious. In India, it is a common thing sold by venders on street corners. Be creative and use what you like, e.g., cucumbers, black or red beans, or sweet potatoes. Make it colorful and adjust the spices accordingly.

8 red or yellow potatoes, boiled, peeled, and cooled
1 cup cooked green peas (or chickpeas)
½ cup chopped tomatoes
¼ cup chopped onions
2 tablespoons lemon juice

Seasonings:

2 teaspoons roasted cumin powder
½ teaspoon black pepper
1 teaspoon chaat masala

1 tablespoon chopped green coriander leaves
1 teaspoon salt (to taste)

Garnish: 2 tablespoons tamarind chutney

1. Cut the cooled potatoes in ½" cubes. Mix everything together to taste.
2. Garnish with the chutney and serve. Can be eaten with a fork or toothpick.

Variation: Make 'Sweet Potato Chaat' by mixing boiled and peeled sweet potatoes, potatoes, and the seasonings. Choose sweet potatoes with the most intense orange color for a greater jolt of beta–carotene.

Makes about 8 servings, ¾ cup each. Per serving –
Nutritive Value: 120 calories, 4 g protein, 26 g carb, 3 g fiber, 0.2 g fat, 0 mg chol.
Food Group Exchange: 1 Grain, ¼ Vegetable.

POTATO-PEAS CASSEROLE

This is an easy to make snack that uses very little oil. It can also be served as a side dish. Make it in advance and refrigerate; re-warm in the oven before serving. Makes about 45 pieces.

3 lb. potatoes (preferably Idaho potatoes), boiled
4 bread slices
1½ cup dry green peas
1 cup Mint-Coriander chutney
1 cup Tamarind Chutney
2 tablespoons oil

Seasonings:

3 teaspoons salt, divided
2 teaspoons coriander powder
1+2 teaspoons cumin powder

2 teaspoons crushed ginger
1 teaspoon mango powder
½ teaspoon red chili powder

1. Rinse and soak the dry green peas in about 3 cups water for 4–6 hours. Add more water if needed. Add half of the salt. Cook on top of the stove (45 minutes), or in a pressure cooker (15 minutes) or a slow cooker (3 hours) until the peas are tender. Drain any extra liquid and mash the peas a little, adding coriander powder and 1 teaspoon cumin powder.
2. Mash the boiled, peeled potatoes along with the bread slices. (It is better to mash potatoes while they are still hot.) Mix in rest of the salt, 2 teaspoons cumin powder, ginger, mango powder, and red chili powder.
3. In a greased 9x13" baking dish, spread a thin layer of the potato mash, then 'Tamarind chutney', then cooked peas, then 'Mint-Coriander chutney', topped by another layer of the potatoes. Brush with the oil.
4. Bake at 350°F until brown (about 45 minutes). Broil for a couple of minutes for crusty top. Serve hot with chutney.

Makes about 22 servings, two pieces each. Per serving –
Nutritive Value: 89 calories, 2.5 g protein, 17 g carb, 2 g fiber, 1.6 g fat, 0 mg chol.
Food Group Exchange: 1 Grain, 1/3 Legumes/Meat, ¼ Vegetable, 1/8 Fat.

RAVA DHOKLA (Semolina Cakes)

Dhokla is a popular dish from Gujarat, west of India. It is often served as an appetizer before parties. There are several ways to make it and the proportions of the flours can be changed. (See *'Dhokla'* on page 65.) You need the special pot and metal plate (thali) to make it. You may refrigerate or freeze them; reheat in the microwave oven, covered. Makes about 30 pieces.

1 cup semolina (suji)
2 tablespoons gram flour (besan)
1 cup plain yogurt
1 tablespoon oil, heated
1 teaspoon Eno powder (or ½ teaspoon baking soda)

Seasonings:

½ tsp. lemon crystals or citric acid
1 teaspoon chopped green chili
1 teaspoon grated ginger

¼ teaspoon turmeric powder
1 teaspoon salt

To Sauté:

2 teaspoons oil
1 teaspoon mustard seed
½ teaspoon sesame seed

Pinch of asafetida powder
4 whole green chilies, halved

Garnish: 1 tablespoon chopped green coriander

1. Mix the ingredients and seasonings (except oil and Eno powder) to make a thick consistency batter. Add about ½ cup water as needed. When ready to cook, add the heated oil, Eno powder (or baking soda), and mix well to make the batter smooth and light.
2. Spread the batter, about 1/3" thick layer, in a flat greased metal dish and steam for 15–20 minutes as on page 65. Cut the pieces into 1–2" squares.
3. To sauté, heat the oil in a small pot. Add mustard seeds. As soon as they splutter, add the remaining spices. Mix the sauté into the 'dhokla'. Garnish and serve warm.

Makes about 8 servings, four pieces each. Per serving –
Nutritive Value: 142 calories, 5 g protein, 21 g carb, 1 g fiber, 4 g fat, 2 mg chol.
Food Group Exchange: ½ Grain, 1/8 Dairy, 1/8 Fat.

RAVA DOSA (Semolina Crepes)

'Dosa' is a South Indian dish and is very popular everywhere as a savory meal. This is a quick way to make 'Dosa'. You may refrigerate or freeze them; reheat in the microwave oven, covered.

1 cup semolina (suji)
2 tablespoons rice flour
2 cups buttermilk
Oil to pan-fry

Seasonings:

1 teaspoon chopped green chili	1 teaspoon cumin seeds
1 teaspoon grated ginger	1½ teaspoons salt
1 tablespoon chopped curry leaves or green coriander	

1. Mix everything (except oil) to make a semi-thin consistency batter like that for pancakes. Add some water if needed. Let the mixture stand for at least 1 hour.
2. Heat a griddle (or heavy skillet or tawa) on medium heat. Grease with ½ teaspoon of oil the first time only.
3. For every 'Dosa', sprinkle a drop of water to ensure that the griddle is hot enough. Pour 2 tablespoons of batter; it should spread by itself as you tilt the griddle a little. Add ½ teaspoon of oil around the edges. Cook for 1–2 minutes until the top appears dry and the bottom has just begun to brown. Turn over with a flat spatula and brown the other side very lightly.
4. Serve them hot and crisp with 'Coconut chutney'.

Variation: Serve them as wraps filled with spiced potatoes as at 'Masala Dosa' on page 72.

Makes about 10 servings, one piece each. Per serving –
Nutritive Value: 104 calories, 3.7 g protein, 14 g carb, 0.7 g fiber, 3.3 g fat, 0 mg chol.
Food Group Exchange: ½ Grain, 1/5 Dairy, 1/3 Fat.

RAVA IDLI (Semolina Rounds)

Though similar to 'Idli' made from rice and dal, these are quicker to make. You will need the 'Idli maker' to steam 'idli'. Serve them with hot 'Sambhar' and 'Coconut chutney'. Makes about 12.

1 cup lightly roasted semolina (suji)
2½ cups yogurt

Seasonings:

1 teaspoon grated ginger	½ teaspoon chopped green chilies
1 tablespoon chopped curry leaves or green coriander	1 teaspoon salt

To Sauté:

2 teaspoons oil	1 teaspoon Urad split peeled dal
½ teaspoon mustard seeds	10 halved cashews
1 teaspoon Chana dal	

1. Whip the yogurt. Mix with the semolina. Leave the batter, covered, in a warm place, for 30 minutes.
2. Blend in all the seasonings and whip to make a thick consistency batter.
3. To sauté, heat the oil in a small pan. Add mustard seeds; as they splutter, add 'dal' and cashews. Turn off the heat. 'Dal' and nuts should be golden brown. Mix the sauté into the batter.
4. Put the batter in the greased 'Idli' molds (part of 'Idli Maker') and steam as on page 68. Remove 'Idli' from containers. To help remove from 'Idli containers', sprinkle cold water on top or use buttered knife. (For easy clean-up, line the 'Idli containers' with coffee filters cut to fit.)
5. Optionally, pat little butter on 'Idli' for moistness, before serving.

Variation: Use 'Rava Idli mix' available from any Indian grocery store and follow directions.

Makes about 6 servings, two pieces each. Per serving –
Nutritive Value: 214 calories, 9.4 g protein, 29 g carb, 1 g fiber, 6.4 g fat, 4.2 mg chol.
Food Group Exchange: ½ Grain, 1/3 Dairy, 1/8 Fat.

SAGO-POTATO VADA (Tapioca Rounds)

Sago or sabodana is made from tapioca and is widely used during the fasting days when no cereal is eaten. It replaces rice and flour in many dishes. Serve these patties hot. If cold, reheat in the oven at 375°F, spread out on a cookie sheet, for 5–10 minutes until warm and crisp.

¾ cup tapioca (sabodana)
4 medium size potatoes boiled
¼ cup crushed peanuts
Oil for deep–frying (about 2" deep in a wok)

Seasonings:

1 teaspoon crushed green chili
1 teaspoon coriander powder
½ teaspoon mango powder

½ teaspoon red chili powder
1 teaspoon salt

1. Rinse and soak the sabodana in 1–cup water for about ½ hour until soft. Drain excess liquid.
2. Peel and mash the boiled potatoes. Mix with the soaked sabodana, peanuts and all the seasonings. Make small round disks (vadas).
3. Heat the oil in a deep skillet or wok on medium–high heat. Put as many 'vada' that can fit in the skillet in single layer. Deep–fry, turning often so that all sides are cooked, until golden brown. (Regulate the heat as needed while the 'vada' are being fried.) Repeat with the remaining 'vada'.
4. Drain; serve hot with any chutney.

Healthy Alternative: Make ½" thick patties. Pan–fry them on a skillet instead of deep–frying.

Makes about 12 servings, two pieces each. Per serving –
Nutritive Value: 209 calories, 2 g protein, 16.3 g carb, 1 g fiber, 15.4 g fat, 0 mg chol.
Food Group Exchange: 1 Grain, 1/8 Legumes/Meat, 1 Fat.

SAMOSA (Stuffed Triangular Patties)

This is a very popular snack with everybody, served anytime. They can be made in advance and frozen before or after frying. Reheat in the oven at 350°F before serving.

PASTRY:

2¼ cups all-purpose unbleached flour
1 teaspoon salt
½ cup water (or milk)
3 tablespoons oil + oil to deep–fry, 2" deep in wok

1. Mix the dry ingredients; mix in 3 tablespoons oil; add water (or milk) and knead the dough until it becomes smooth and supple but a little stiff. Add more water if needed. Brush lightly with oil, cover and let stand for 15 minutes. (It can be made in advance and left at room temperature for 4–5 hours.)

For Filling:

1½ lb. potatoes, boiled
½ cup green peas
1 tablespoon oil

Seasonings:

2 teaspoons cumin seeds
1 teaspoon coriander powder
1 teaspoon chopped green chili
1 teaspoon crushed ginger
1 tablespoon chopped green coriander

½ teaspoon garam masala
½ teaspoon mango powder
½ teaspoon red chili powder
½ teaspoon salt

2. Peel the boiled potatoes and cut or mash in small pieces. Heat the oil in a skillet on medium heat. Sauté cumin seeds in hot oil. Add boiled potatoes, green peas and remaining seasonings for filling; stir for a couple of minutes until completely mixed. Let the filling cool a little before using.
3. Break the pastry dough in about 12 pieces. Make golf size balls; let them stand for 15 minutes, covered by a damp towel or plastic wrap.
4. On a floured surface, flatten each ball and roll into a very thin slightly oval shape. Cut each oval into half to make 2 semi-circles; each semi-circle makes a 'samosa'.

5. Moisten the bottom edge (base) of the semi-circle with your finger dipped in water; carefully join two sides of the base, overlapping by ¼", to make a cone.

6. Hold the cone in your hand, put a rounded tablespoon of the filling in center, push it down, leaving ¼" on top to close. Seal by moistening the inside of the top edge and pressing it tightly. Make all the 'samosas' and keep them covered by a damp towel or plastic wrap.

7. Bake the 'samosas' at 350°F for 15 minutes, turning once or twice, until light golden. (If the shell cracks and the filling is uncovered, cover with a thin layer of dough.) (At this point you may freeze the 'samosas', in single layer for couple of hours, and then put in a bag. Thaw and separate before frying.)

8. Heat the oil in a deep skillet or wok on medium heat (375°F). Test to make sure the oil is ready. Deep-fry few 'samosas' at a time, turning with a slotted flat spatula, until golden brown on all sides. (Regulate the heat as needed.)

9. Remove and drain on paper towels. Serve hot with any chutney.

Makes about 20 servings, one piece each. Per serving –
Nutritive Value: 189 calories, 2 g protein, 14.4 g carb, 1 g fiber, 13.7 g fat, 0 mg chol.
Food Group Exchange: ½ Grain, 1 Fat.

SPICED BEANS

You can use canned, frozen, or dry beans for this dish. If using dry beans, boil them in advance and refrigerate or freeze them. Spice them to your taste and serve as a super snack. Be creative and add what you like, e.g., chopped cucumbers, minced garlic or scallions.

**4 cups boiled chickpeas, black-eyed peas, or red kidney beans or a mixture
2 chopped tomatoes
2 tablespoons lemon juice**

Seasonings:

2 teaspoons roasted cumin powder
½ teaspoon black pepper
1 teaspoon chaat masala

1 teaspoon crushed green chili
1 tablespoon chopped green coriander
1 teaspoon salt

1. If using canned beans, drain them and rinse. Cook them for a couple of minutes to take away any metallic taste. (For frozen beans, cook them to ensure they are the right softness. See page 30 for how to cook dry beans.)
2. Mix everything together to taste. Add more lemon juice if needed. Serve at room temperature with any chutney.

Makes about 10 servings, ½ cup each. Per serving –
Nutritive Value: 104 calories, 6 g protein, 18.7 g carb, 4 g fiber, 1.3 g fat, 0 mg chol.
Food Group Exchange: 1 Legumes/Meat, ¼ Vegetable.

SPICED NUTS

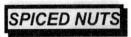

Be sure to make a lot of these as they will disappear fast. Serve them with drinks. Mix any nuts that you like. If you have unshelled nuts, gently press on the middle of the shell with a nutcracker and try to get the nutmeat intact. Generally one pound of unshelled almonds equals a cup of shelled whole almonds. Serve them at room temperature.

4 cups shelled whole almonds (or cashews or peanuts)
2 tablespoons butter (or clarified butter)

Seasonings:

1 teaspoon garam masala	½ teaspoon red chili powder
1 teaspoon mango powder	2 teaspoons salt
1 teaspoon chaat masala	2 tablespoons brown sugar

1. Spread the nuts evenly in a baking pan. Roast in the oven at 350°F for about 10 minutes, checking in between, until the nuts are brownish. (Cashews take less time than other nuts do.)
2. Heat the butter in a wide skillet on medium heat. Add the seasonings and nuts; stir for a couple of minutes until the nuts are coated with the spices. (Add more spices to your taste.) When cool, store in a covered container.

Makes about 16 servings, 3 tablespoons each. Per serving –
Nutritive Value: 231 calories, 6.4 g protein, 9.5 g carb, 0 g fiber, 20 g fat, 4 mg chol.
Food Group Exchange: 1 Legumes/Meat, 1/8 Fat.

Who eats food that is disagreeable violates
three prohibitions:
he hurts his health, wastes food,
and offers a prayer in vain.
-Midrash

SPINACH PAKORAS (Fritters)

These are considered the most readily available snack any time of the day. It is a treat especially in cold rainy weather when the aroma of fried dough and vegetables is very comforting. These can be made in advance and frozen. Warm in a 350°F oven before serving. Makes 40-45 pieces.

3 cups gram flour (besan)
½ cup rice flour
10 oz chopped spinach
2 chopped onions
2 chopped or grated potatoes
Oil for frying (about 2" deep in a wok)

Seasonings:

1 teaspoon crushed green chili
1½ teaspoon coriander powder
1 teaspoon garam masala
1 teaspoon mango powder

1 tsp. crushed pomegranate seeds (optional)
1 teaspoon red chili powder
1+ teaspoon salt

1. Sift the gram flour. Mix all the ingredients (except oil), to make a smooth and thick dough-like batter. Cover and let it stand for ½ hour. Sprinkle little water if needed. (If using frozen spinach, thaw before using.)
2. Blend in all the seasonings (except salt) and mix well. (You may chill the batter in the refrigerator for about 2 hours or more until it can be handled.) Mix in salt when ready to cook.
3. Heat the oil in a deep skillet or wok on medium–high heat. For each 'pakora', scoop a heaped teaspoon of the batter, and with a second spoon, scrape the mixture into the hot oil. Put the 'pakoras' in a single layer in the skillet. Fry, turning them with a slotted flat spatula, until all sides become golden brown. (Regulate the heat as needed while the 'pakoras' are being fried.)
4. Remove and drain on paper towels or brown paper bag lined with plastic.
5. Fry all the 'pakoras' this way. Serve hot with any chutney.

Variation: Add 1 cup corn kernels to the mixture for extra crispness. May also add ½ teaspoon baking soda to ensure softness.

Makes about 14 servings, three pieces each. Per serving –
Nutritive Value: 237 calories, 6 g protein, 20 g carb, 5 g fiber, 15 g fat, 0 mg chol.
Food Group Exchange: 1 Legumes/Meat, 1/3 Grain, 1/3 Vegetable, 1 Fat.

SPROUTED MUNG BEANS

Sprouts satisfy your protein needs without surplus calories usually associated with most protein–rich foods. The sprouting process also reduces the flatulence potential of beans. This dish needs to be started at least 2 days in advance. Serve them as an appetizer, a filling for sandwiches, or a side dish.

1 cup dry whole Mung dal
2 teaspoons oil

Seasonings:

¼ teaspoon cumin seeds
1/8 teaspoon asafetida powder
¼ teaspoon red chili powder

1 teaspoon crushed green chili
1 teaspoon crushed ginger
½ teaspoon salt

Garnish:

1 tablespoon chopped green coriander
½ chopped tomato

1 teaspoon lemon juice

1. Check, rinse and soak the 'dal' in water overnight or minimum 6 hours. Drain, wrap in a cloth, and keep in a warm dark place (e.g., oven) until it sprouts, about 36 hours. Check in between and sprinkle some water if needed. Rinse before using. (See *sprouting* on page 34.)
2. Heat the oil in a skillet on medium heat. Add cumin seeds and asafetida powder and stir. Immediately add the sprouted 'dal' and other seasonings. Let it cook covered for 10–15 minutes on low heat until the water dries out and the 'dal' is soft.
3. Serve warm, garnished with green coriander, tomato, and lemon juice.

Variation: Steam the sprouts in the microwave for a few minutes until tender; use them in salads.

Makes about 6 servings, ¾ cup each. Per serving –
Nutritive Value: 40 calories, 2.6 g protein, 5 g carb, 1.6 g fiber, 2 g fat, 0 mg chol.
Food Group Exchange: 1 Legumes/Meat, 1/8 Fat.

TOFU BURGERS

Serve these protein-rich burgers with pita bread or buns. If someone does not like tofu, this is a good way to hide it. You may prepare the patties in advance and refrigerate without cooking. Pan-fry them when ready to eat. They can be reheated in the microwave oven (1–2 minutes) or in the conventional oven (10 minutes at 400°F) or in a skillet.

1 pound soft tofu
2–3 potatoes, boiled, peeled and mashed
1 small onion, finely chopped
½ bunch scallions, finely chopped
2 slices of bread
Oil to pan–fry

Seasonings:

½ teaspoon chopped green chili	½ teaspoon black pepper
½ teaspoon grated ginger	2 tbls. chopped green coriander
1 teaspoon coriander powder	1½ teaspoons salt
¾ teaspoon mango powder	

1. Drain the tofu, pressing it to remove all excess liquid. Cut it in cubes and mash with a fork. Mix everything together (except oil) into stiff dough like mixture. Mix in more bread slices if the mixture does not hold. Use a food processor to mix if desired.
2. Using your hands, shape the mixture into 2–3" round patties, about ½" thick (makes about 20).
3. Heat a skillet on medium heat. Grease with ½ teaspoon of oil. Place the patties that can fit on the skillet, and cook until golden brown at bottom (about 5 minutes). Flip over with a spatula; brown the other side lightly too, adding ½ teaspoon of oil all around the edges. Repeat with all the patties.
4. Serve hot with any chutney and bread.

Variation: Instead of making in a skillet, spread the patties in a greased baking sheet. Brush little oil on top also. Bake at 400°F oven for about 25 minutes until the patties turn golden brown at bottom. Turn to brown the other side also.

Healthy Alternative: Instead of bread slices, add 1 cup mashed cooked beans like chickpeas.

Makes about 10 servings, two pieces each. Per serving –
Nutritive Value: 113 calories, 4.4 g protein, 11 g carb, 1 g fiber, 6 g fat, 0 mg chol.
Food Group Exchange: ½ Grain, ½ Legumes/Meat, 1/3 Fat.

UPMA (Semolina Salty Pudding)

This is generally served for breakfast with plain yogurt or 'Raita'. You may keep roasted semolina ready and also prepare the sauté in advance. Put together the dish when ready to eat. It can be reheated in the microwave oven (1–2 minutes).

2 cups semolina (suji)
½ cup raw peanuts or cashews
1 chopped onion
1 cup green peas
2 tablespoons oil, divided

Seasonings:
1 teaspoon mustard seeds
1 teaspoon peeled split Urad dal
1 tablespoon crushed green chili
½ teaspoon crushed ginger

1 teaspoon chopped curry leaves
½ teaspoon red chili powder
1 teaspoon salt
1 teaspoon lemon juice

Garnish:
1 tablespoon chopped green coriander

2 tablespoons grated un-sweetened coconut (optional)

1. Roast the semolina in a skillet (or in the microwave) until it changes color slightly; keep aside.
2. Heat 1 tablespoon oil on medium heat in a large pan. Lightly roast the peanuts (or cashews) on low heat. Remove from pan; reserve for garnish.
3. In the same pan, add the remaining oil, sauté mustard seeds and 'Urad dal'. When they brown or splutter, add the onions and the remaining seasonings except lemon juice. Stir until the onions are translucent. Stir in the peas.
4. Add 5–6 cups water. When it boils, gradually stir in the roasted semolina making sure there are no lumps. Lower the heat; stirring often, simmer until all the water is absorbed.
5. Mix in the lemon juice. Cover and keep for 5 minutes for semolina to absorb the liquid. Stir and take out in a serving dish, garnish with green coriander, roasted nuts and coconut.

Makes about 10 servings, ¾ cup each. Per serving –
Nutritive Value: 205 calories, 7 g protein, 29 g carb, 3 g fiber, 6.7 g fat, 0 mg chol.
Food Group Exchange: 1 Grain, ¼ Vegetable, ¼ Legumes/Meat, 1/5 Fat.

VEGETABLE CUTLETS

These delicious hors d'oeuvres can be served anytime. You may prepare the patties in advance and refrigerate without cooking. Fry them when ready to eat. They can be reheated in the microwave oven (1–2 minutes) or in the conventional oven (10 minutes at 400°F) or in a skillet.

5 large potatoes, boiled
2–3 bread slices
1 cup green peas
¾ cup grated carrots
¾ cup grated cabbage
2 tablespoons gram flour (or all–purpose flour)
½ cup bread crumbs
1 tablespoon oil + oil for deep–frying as needed

Seasonings:

1 teaspoon crushed green mild chili	½ teaspoon red chili powder
½ teaspoon garam masala	1 tablespoon chopped green coriander
½ teaspoon mango powder	1½ teaspoons salt

1. Mash the potatoes along with the bread slices. (It is better to mash potatoes while they are still hot.) Add all the seasonings.
2. Sauté the green peas, carrots, and cabbage in 1 tablespoon oil; cook until tender and dry; mix with the potato mash and make like a hard dough.
3. Make a thin mixture of gram flour (or all-purpose flour) by adding about ½ cup water.
4. Take small balls of the potato vegetable mixture on palm of your hand and make into oval or round patties. Wet the patties in the flour solution, roll in the bread crumbs, and deep–fry at high heat (cutlets tend to break on low heat) until golden brown on all sides.
5. Drain the cutlets on paper towels. Serve hot with 'Mint–Coriander Chutney' or ketchup.

Healthy Alternative: Instead of deep–frying, brown the cutlets in a wide skillet on low–medium heat, using a teaspoon of oil on both sides. Or arrange the patties on a well–greased cookie sheet; bake in the pre–heated oven at 400°F for 20 minutes. Turn, adding more oil as needed. Bake for another 15 minutes.

Makes about 20 servings, one piece each. Per serving –
Nutritive Value: 178 calories, 3 g protein, 16 g carb, 2 g fiber, 12 g fat, 0 mg chol.
Food Group Exchange: ¾ Grain, ¼ Vegetable, 1 Fat.

VEGETABLE OMELET

This is an easy to fix, healthy dish for breakfast or lunch. An omelet folded with your favorite vegetables and a piece of whole–wheat bread, is a complete meal. Top it with salsa or tomato sauce.

3 eggs
1 tablespoon milk
1½ tablespoons oil

Filling:

1 cup finely chopped onions, spinach, mushrooms or any other vegetable
1 tablespoon chopped green coriander

2 tablespoons grated Mozzarella or Cheddar cheese

Seasonings:

1 teaspoon black pepper
¼ teaspoon red chili powder

½ teaspoon salt

1. In a small bowl, whisk together the eggs, milk, and about 1 tablespoon water.
2. To sauté the vegetables for the filling, heat half of the oil in a non–stick skillet on high heat. Add the onions and stir for 1–2 minutes until tender. Add other vegetables and stir in the seasonings; sauté for a few minutes. Take the sautéed vegetables out in a plate.
3. In the same skillet, add the remaining oil. As the oil sizzles, pour in the egg mixture, covering the whole pan. Reduce the heat to medium. (If there is egg liquid on top, tilt the pan as you lift edges of the omelet to let the liquid go underneath where it will cook.)
4. When the eggs start to solidify, spread the sautéed vegetables, cheese and green coriander on one half, and carefully lift the other half over the filled part. Cover and cook for another minute.
5. Cut into desired portions and serve hot.

Healthy Alternative: Use only egg whites mixed with ½ teaspoon turmeric powder or egg substitute if you want to cut down on cholesterol. May also increase the amount of vegetables.

Makes about 3 servings, one egg each. Per serving –
Nutritive Value:162 calories, 8 g protein, 5 g carb, 1 g fiber, 12 g fat, 190 mg chol.
Food Group Exchange: 1 Legumes/Meat, 1/3 Vegetable, 1/3 Dairy, ½ Fat.

VEGETABLE PAKORAS (Fritters)

Any vegetable can be used to make 'pakoras'—also called 'bhajia'—a favorite for many. You generally cut vegetables in thin rounds or long slices. Cut green chilies in half (or keep whole), and use un-peeled eggplant. The 'pakoras' can be made in advance and frozen. Warm in a 350°F oven before serving.

3 cups gram flour (besan)
½ cup rice flour (optional)
4 potatoes (or 4 onions, or ½ head cauliflower,
or 20 green chilies, or 1 eggplant, or a mixture)
Oil for frying, 2–3" deep in a wok

Seasonings:

1 teaspoon coriander powder

1 teaspoon garam masala
1 teaspoon mango powder

1 tsp. crushed pomegranate seeds (optional)
1 teaspoon red chili powder
2 teaspoons salt

1. Sift the gram flour. Mix with the rice flour and about 2 cups water to make smooth thick consistency batter (thicker than that for pancakes. Use more water if needed). Whisk it well. Cover and let stand for ½ hour. Blend in all the seasonings.
2. Wash and scrub or peel the potatoes. Cut them in thin rounds.
3. Heat the oil in a deep skillet or wok on medium-high heat. Dip the cut vegetables in the batter, one at a time; and drop in the hot oil in a single layer. (You may do so with your hand or use a metal tong.) Turn 'pakoras' with a slotted flat spatula, and fry until golden brown on all sides. (Regulate the heat as needed while the 'pakoras' are being fried.)
4. Remove from the oil and drain on paper towels. Make all the 'pakoras' this way. Serve hot with any chutney.

Variation: You may double–fry the fritters for greater crispness. The first time, remove them from the wok when half done. Fry again when ready to serve.

Makes about 13 servings, three pieces each. Per serving –
Nutritive Value: 243 calories, 6 g protein, 24 g carb, 3 g fiber, 14 g fat, 0 mg chol.
Food Group Exchange: 1 Legumes/Meat, ¼ Grain, 1 Fat.

VEGETABLE POORE (Crepes)

These crepes make a complete meal followed by some fruit or something sweet, such as 'Kheer' (rice pudding) for dessert. Serve them with chutney or soup. If prepared in advance, reheat them in a stack of four, properly wrapped, in the microwave oven (1–2 minutes) or in the conventional oven (10 minutes at 375°F). The batter can be easily made in advance and refrigerated.

2 cups whole–wheat flour
¾ cup gram flour (besan)
½ cup rice flour
1 cup plain yogurt
2 cups finely chopped (or pureed) vegetables such as spinach, onions, green fenugreek leaves (methi), or grated zucchini or bottle gourd (ghiya/dhudi)
Oil to pan–fry

Seasonings:

1 teaspoon chopped green chili	½ teaspoon black pepper
½ teaspoon grated ginger	1 teaspoon salt

1. Mix the different flours, yogurt, and vegetables with a whisk to make a thick consistency batter, making sure there are no lumps. Add 1–2 cups water as needed. Leave it covered for minimum 2 hours.
2. Mix the seasonings into the batter and whip again to make it into pancake batter consistency.
3. Heat a griddle (or non–stick skillet or 'tawa') on medium heat. Grease with 1 teaspoon of oil the first time. Pour about ½ cup of batter and spread evenly and thinly with the back of a serving spoon into a round shape. Add ½ teaspoon of oil around the edges. Cook for 1–2 minutes until the top appears dry and the bottom has just begun to brown. Turn over with a spatula; brown the other side very lightly, adding ¼ teaspoon of oil.
4. Make all the crepes the same way. Stack and serve hot with any chutney or yogurt.

Healthy Alternative: Make on a non-stick griddle, using minimum or no oil.

Makes about 15 servings, one piece each. Per serving –
Nutritive Value: 128 calories, 4 g protein, 18 g carb, 3 g fiber, 4.7 g fat, 0 mg chol.
Food Group Exchange: ½ Grain, 1/5 Legumes/Meat, 1/5 Vegetable, 1/3 Fat.

VEGETABLE TRIANGLES

Served anytime, they make an excellent finger food and can be quickly prepared from flour or corn tortillas. Generally the flour tortillas are better because they are more pliable. You may use any vegetable like shredded cabbage or cauliflower for filling. The filling can be made in advance. Warm them in the microwave for 1–2 minutes or in the conventional oven at 350°F for about 10 minutes.

8 flour (or whole–wheat) tortillas (10" size)
1 zucchini
2 bell peppers
2 red onions
1 cup chopped scallions
1 tomato
½ cup sour cream (or yogurt cheese)
¼ cup oil

Seasonings:

1 teaspoon mustard seeds	1 teaspoon crushed green chili
1 teaspoon cumin seeds	½ teaspoon crushed ginger
1 teaspoon peeled split Urad dal	½ teaspoon red chili powder
1 teaspoon crushed garlic	1 teaspoon salt

Garnish: 1 cup salsa

1. Prepare and chop the vegetables in thin strips.
2. Heat 2 teaspoons oil on medium heat in a skillet. Sauté the mustard seeds, cumin seeds, and 'Urad dal'. When they splutter or brown, add garlic; stir for a minute. Stir in the vegetables and remaining seasonings; cook until soft. Slowly add sour cream until the mixture is creamy. May use yogurt cheese instead. Use the mixture as filling.
3. Heat another skillet on medium heat. Spread ½ teaspoon oil. Place one tortilla in the skillet. When light brown at bottom (about 30 seconds), spread 2–3 tablespoons vegetable mixture on half of the tortilla. Fold the other half of the tortilla over the mixture.
4. Remove and arrange in a serving platter. Cut each tortilla into 3 wedges. Keep them warm in the oven at 300°F.
5. Repeat with all the tortillas. Serve with salsa.

Variation: Use a filling of cheese and any vegetable such as onions, mashed potatoes, and tomatoes. Can also use beans like red kidney beans and chickpeas.

Makes about 16 servings, ½ tortilla each. Per serving –
Nutritive Value: 135 calories, 3 g protein, 17 g carb, 1 g fiber, 7 g fat, 5 mg chol.
Food Group Exchange: ½ Grain, ½ Vegetable, ½ Fat.

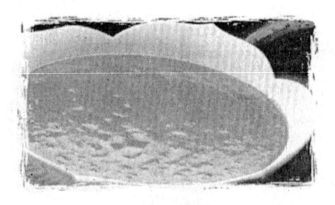

Good to the Last Drop

Soups and Beverages

The most popular beverage in India is 'Chai' (hot tea) or coffee. In hot summer months, it is fresh lemon drink (shikanjavi) or 'Lassi' (yogurt drink). Soups, however, have become very popular these days because of the flexibility of combining different vegetables and presenting them with artistic garnishes. They are a healthy combination of vegetables, beans, and pasta. Adding vegetable stock further enriches a soup. There are some soups and shakes in the chapter *Cooking by Children* also.

To help plan nutritious meals, each recipe gives nutritive value (calories, protein, carbohydrate (carb), fiber, fat, and cholesterol (chol)), and Food Group Exchange for a helping of the dish. Estimate is rounded off for ease of understanding. Garnishes, topping and small amounts of seasoning are not accounted for. (See page 13 for basis of estimating Food Group Exchange and nutritive value.)

Abbreviations:
carb: carbohydrate,	chol: cholesterol,	F: Fahrenheit,
g: gram,	lb: pound,	med: medium,
mg: milligram,	oz: ounce.	

CABBAGE SOUP

Little tartness in this soup makes it very tasty. It can be made in advance and refrigerated or frozen. Serve hot with crackers.

½ head (about 1½ lb.) cabbage
3 carrots
1 tart apple or mango

Seasonings:
1 teaspoon salt
½" ginger piece

1 green chili
½ teaspoon red chili powder

Garnish: Thin slices of apple or mango

1. Cut the vegetables and apple (or mango) in ½–1" pieces. Boil them with the seasonings in 3–4 cups water as needed. Cover and cook until the cabbage is tender (about 10 minutes).
2. When little cold, puree the soup in a blender. Heat and serve, garnished with apple or mango slices.

Variation: Swirl in some yogurt or sour cream before serving. May sauté the seasonings and some cumin seeds before adding to the soup.

Makes about 6 servings, ¾ cup each. Per serving –
Nutritive Value: 46 calories, 1.5 g protein, 11 g carb, 3.3 g fiber, 0.4 g fat, 0 mg chol.
Food Group Exchange: 1 Vegetable.

CREAM OF BROCCOLI SOUP

Broccoli is considered one of the super foods in terms of nutrition as well as taste. This creamy soup is made with milk, not cream. Make it in advance and refrigerate or freeze. Serve with bread and desired topping such as yogurt cheese or sour cream.

1 head (about 1½ lb.) broccoli
1 medium bell pepper
1 carrot
1 large onion chopped
1 cup milk
1 tablespoon oil

Seasonings:

3 garlic pods (peeled and lightly mashed)	1 green chili
½" ginger piece (peeled and lightly mashed)	½ teaspoon red chili powder
½ teaspoon cumin powder	1 teaspoon salt
½ teaspoon paprika	1 teaspoon garam masala

1. Cut the vegetables in ½–1" pieces.
2. Heat the oil in a pot on medium heat. Add garlic and onion pieces. Stir until the onions are translucent. Stir in the remaining seasonings (except garam masala) and vegetables. After a couple of minutes, add 2–3 cups water as needed. Cover and cook until the broccoli is tender (about 10 minutes). Add garam masala.
3. When little cold, puree the soup in a blender, in batches if necessary. Heat with milk before serving.

Variation: Whisk in ½ cup yogurt, evaporated skim milk, or sour cream instead of milk.

Healthy Alternative: Reduce or cut out oil; stir onions with little salt on dry heat. You may grill or microwave the vegetables. Stir in low-fat milk or yogurt cheese when serving. Or add any chutney, salsa or 'Tomato–Yogurt Curry'.

Makes about 6 servings, ¾ cup each. Per serving –
Nutritive Value: 81 calories, 5 g protein, 11 g carb, 4 g fiber, 3.2 g fat, 1.7 mg chol.
Food Group Exchange: 1 Vegetable, 1/8 Dairy, 1/8 Fat.

CREAM OF CARROT SOUP

This soup gives your menu a special beta–carotene boost. If desired, make the soup in advance and refrigerate. Omit potatoes if you want to freeze it. Serve hot with crackers, carrots and celery sticks.

1 onion
2 potatoes
6 carrots
1 medium bell pepper
1 stalk of celery
1 cup evaporated milk
1 tablespoon oil

Seasonings:

½ teaspoon fenugreek seeds
½ teaspoon caraway seeds
1 teaspoon salt (to taste)
½" ginger piece

1 teaspoon fennel powder
1 green chili (to taste)
½ teaspoon red chili powder

1. Cut the onion and other vegetables in ½–1" pieces so that they can be cooked and pureed.
2. Heat the oil in a pot on medium heat. Add fenugreek seeds; as soon as they start turning color, immediately add caraway seeds. After couple of seconds, add the onion pieces and salt; stir until the onions are translucent.
3. Add the potatoes. After about 5 minutes when potatoes are little cooked, add the remaining seasonings and other vegetables; stir. Add 2–3 cups water as needed. Cover and cook until the potatoes are tender (about 15 minutes). **Note:** To reduce time, you may cook the potatoes in the microwave before adding to the soup.
4. When little cold, puree the soup in a blender. Before serving, whisk in the evaporated milk and heat the soup.

Variation: Use leeks (white part only) instead of onions.

Healthy Alternative: Cook onions and other seasonings with minimum or no oil in a non-stick pan. Or grill or microwave the vegetables and then puree them. Garnish with green coriander or parsley, or swirl in some chutney when serving.

Makes about 8 servings, ¾ cup each. Per serving –
Nutritive Value: 111 calories, 4 g protein, 15 g carb, 2.5 g fiber, 4.5 g fat, 9 mg chol.
Food Group Exchange: 1 Vegetable, 1/8 Grain, 1/8 Dairy, 1/8 Fat.

DAL SOUP

It is a very healthy appetizer and very appealing. 'Dal' almost triples in quantity when cooked.

**1 cup dal (lentils, peeled Mung split,
Toor split, or a mixture)
1 onion chopped
1 bell pepper diced
1 carrot chopped
1 tablespoon oil**

Seasonings:

1 teaspoon salt
½ teaspoon turmeric powder
½ teaspoon cumin powder
½ teaspoon paprika

1 teaspoon chopped green chili
½ teaspoon red chili powder
1 teaspoon crushed ginger
1 teaspoon garam masala

Garnish:

1 tablespoon chopped green coriander
1 tomato cut into cubes

1. Remove any grit or discolored pieces from 'dal', and rinse. Cook the 'dal' in 5 cups water, salt, and turmeric powder. Let it simmer for 30–40 minutes until the 'dal' is soft and blended.
2. Heat the oil in a small pot on medium heat. Add onions; stir until the onions are translucent. Stir in the remaining seasonings (except garam masala). Add chopped vegetables.
3. When the vegetables are little tender (about 5 minutes), add everything to the cooked dal. Add more water, as desired. Cover and cook until everything is mixed (about 10 minutes). Add garam masala.
4. Serve hot garnished with chopped green coriander and tomato pieces.

Makes about 6 servings, ¾ cup each. Per serving –
Nutritive Value: 120 calories, 6 g protein, 19 g carb, 5 g fiber, 3 g fat, 0 mg chol.
Food Group Exchange: ¾ Legumes/Meat, ¼ Vegetable, 1/8 Fat.

HERBAL CHAI (Tea)

A healthy drink, without caffeine, it is known to relieve cramps, coughs, and poor digestion. Combine any or all of the following herbs, as desired. To save time, grind larger quantities of different herbs and spices for use as needed.

3½ cups cold water
2 teaspoons fennel seeds
2 green cardamom pods
½" cinnamon stick
2 peppercorns
2 cloves
½" ginger piece
1 tablespoon fresh mint leaves (or 1 teaspoon dried leaves)
6–8 sacred basil (Tulsi) leaves

<u>Seasonings</u>: Honey (or sugar) and milk (to taste)

1. Crush all the herbs and spices coarsely. Boil the water with the herbs. (Put ¾ teaspoon herbs for 1 cup water.) Simmer for 15–20 minutes, covered.
2. Strain; serve hot with milk and honey (or sugar) to taste.

Variation: Let the tea cool down. Add honey (or sugar) to taste and serve cold on ice, garnished with thin lemon slices.

Makes about 3 servings, 1 cup each. Per serving (without seasonings) –
Nutritive Value: 10 calories, 0.3 g protein, 2 g carb, 0.8 g fiber, 0 g fat, 0 mg chol.
Food Group Exchange: 1/8 Vegetable.

HOT CIDER

Apple cider, widely available in many countries, makes an excellent drink before dinner, especially in wintertime.

1 gal apple cider
½ gal cranberry juice

Seasonings:

¼ cup sugar

2 cinnamon sticks

4–6 cloves

4 black peppercorns (optional)

1. Combine everything in a large pot. Simmer on low heat, covered, for about an hour.
2. Remove the seasonings and serve medium hot. (Keep warm or reheat to serve.)

Makes about 24 servings, 1 cup each. Per serving –
Nutritive Value: 129 calories, 1 g protein, 31 g carb, 0 g fiber, 1 g fat, 0 mg chol.
Food Group Exchange: 1 Fruit, ½ Sugar.

> **Men of Tamas (ignorance) love the food**
> **That is stale and tasteless,**
> **Rotten, impure, left over**
> **And unfit for serving.**
>
> The Bhagavad Gita, chapter 17, verse 10

JAL JEERA (Tamarind Drink)

This delicious drink is very popular, served by itself or with snacks especially 'golgappa' (round puffed crackers) available from any Indian store. Poke the 'golgappa' with a fork and fill with boiled chopped potatoes and boiled chickpeas. Dip in 'Jal Jeera' and serve.

1 lb. tamarind
1 bunch mint leaves
1 bunch green coriander
2–4 green chilies (to taste)
1 gallon water

Seasonings:

2 teaspoons red chili powder
½ cup sugar
3 tablespoons dark roasted cumin seeds, powdered
2 tablespoons roasted coriander seeds, powdered

1 teaspoon black pepper
3 teaspoons salt
1 teaspoon black salt

1. Rinse the tamarind; soak for 1–2 hours in 4 cups warm water. Mash well to separate the pulp; strain through a colander to remove seeds and roughage.
2. Wash the mint leaves and coriander; discard any hard stems. Grind in a food blender, along with green chilies, adding water as needed.
3. Mix everything together in a large jug. Add water and seasonings to taste. Refrigerate and serve cold with 'golgappa' or in glasses with ice and thin lemon slices.

Makes about 20 servings, 1 cup each. Per serving –
Nutritive Value: 78 calories, 1 g protein, 20 g carb, 1.5 g fiber, 0 g fat, 0 mg chol.
Food Group Exchange: ½ Vegetable, 1 Sugar.

KANJI *(Carrot Drink)*

This drink is specially served in winter in India when carrots are available in plenty and people bask in bright sun. Serve along with few carrot sticks to munch on.

2 lb. carrots
1 beet (for color)
1 gallon warm water

Seasonings:

3 teaspoons ground mustard seeds (rye)   3 teaspoons salt

1. Scrub the carrots; cut into long sticks. Peel and chop the beet in small pieces. Combine everything in a glass or plastic (not aluminum) container. Keep in sun, covered, to marinate for 2–3 days. 'Kanji' will be little tart.
2. Refrigerate when ready. Serve cold.

Makes about 20 servings, 1 cup each. Per serving –
Nutritive Value: 21 calories, 0.5 g protein, 5 g carb, 1.5 g fiber, 0 g fat, 0 mg chol.
Food Group Exchange: ½ Vegetable.

Identify and manage
the powerful "I" within you that controls your life including your eating pattern.

LASSI (Yogurt-Shake)

A very hearty drink, it is generally taken for breakfast or lunch. Modify the proportions of yogurt, fruit and water as you like.

3 cups plain yogurt
2 cups water
2 cups crushed ice

Seasonings:

6 teaspoons sugar   1 teaspoon cardamom powder

Garnish: 2 teaspoons crushed almonds and pistachio

1. Combine the ingredients and seasonings in a blender. Blend at high speed for few seconds until smooth and frothy.
2. Pour in glasses, garnish and serve immediately.

Variation: Add 2 cups chopped (fresh or frozen) fruit like mango, strawberries, or banana to yogurt before blending.

Healthy Alternative: Use salt and black pepper instead of sugar. Add 1 cup of chopped cucumber or carrots and little mint, if desired. Garnish with dark roasted cumin powder.

Makes about 8 servings, 1 cup each. Per serving –
Nutritive Value: 68 calories, 4.5 g protein, 9 g carb, 0 g fiber, 1 g fat, 5 mg chol.
Food Group Exchange: ½ Dairy, 1 Sugar.

LEMONY REFRESHER

Lemons are used in Indian diet in several different ways. Some people squeeze ½ lemon in a glass of warm water and drink every morning for better digestion. This lemon drink, called 'shikanjavi' in Hindi, is popular in summer.

1 fresh lemon
Ice

<u>Seasonings:</u> 4 teaspoons sugar (to taste)

1. Put two glasses of water (less ½ cup to allow for ice) in a jug. Stir in sugar. Squeeze lemon juice to taste.
2. Put the ice in glasses, pour the lemon drink and serve.

Variation: Use salt and pepper instead of sugar.

Makes about 2 servings, 1 glass each. Per serving –
Nutritive Value: 40 calories, 0 g protein, 11 g carb, 0.8 g fiber, 0 g fat, 0 mg chol.
Food Group Exchange: 2 Sugar, ½ Fruit.

MANGO MILKSHAKE

Milkshake is a hearty beverage any time of the year. There are many varieties of mangoes and they come in green, yellow and red color. Choose ripe mangoes. You may take out mango pulp in advance and refrigerate or freeze it.

2 ripe mangoes (or 1½ cups mango pulp)
4 cups milk
1 cup crushed ice
3 scoops vanilla ice cream or frozen yogurt

<u>Seasonings:</u> 1 teaspoon sugar (to taste)

1. If using a fresh mango, soften it between your palms; make a wide slit at top and squeeze out the pulp. (You may peel the mango and cut into small pieces.)
2. Combine everything in a blender. Blend at high speed for few seconds until smooth and frothy, being careful not to over-process. Serve immediately.

Variation: Instead of mangos, you may use other fruits such as bananas, strawberries, or canned pineapple.

Healthy Alternative: Omit ice cream; just add some flavor (1 teaspoon crushed cardamom, ½ teaspoon saffron, and sugar to taste).

Makes about 10 servings, 1 cup each. Per serving –
Nutritive Value: 113 calories, 4 g protein, 16 g carb, 1 g fiber, 3 g fat, 11 mg chol.
Food Group Exchange: 1 Dairy, ½ Fruit, ½ Sugar.

MANGO PUNCH

You can make this punch from mango pulp available in cans. Optionally, take pulp from fresh ripe mangoes and whip it before using. Mix juices of your choice.

32 oz. can mango pulp (or pulp from 3 mangoes)
1 quart each of apple juice, white grape juice and
orange juice
2 liter ginger–ale

1. Combine the mango pulp, desired juices, and ice cubes in a punch bowl.
2. Add ginger ale when ready to serve.

Variation: Float some chopped fruit pieces, such as grapes and strawberries on top.

Makes about 20 servings, 1 cup each. Per serving (without ginger–ale) –
Nutritive Value:98 calories, 0.4 g protein, 24 g carb, 0.6 g fiber, 0 g fat, 0 mg chol.
Food Group Exchange: 1 Fruit.

MILK with ALMONDS

A delicious healthy drink, you'll like it in winter months.

8 almonds chopped lengthwise
½ teaspoon butter
2 cups milk

Seasonings:

2 threads of saffron   1 teaspoon sugar or honey (to taste)

1. Put the butter and almonds in a cup. Microwave for about 1 minute till the butter sizzles and almonds change color. Stir with a spoon.
2. Add milk and saffron. Microwave so that milk is nice and hot (2–3 minutes). Add sugar or honey, if desired. Serve hot with a spoon to eat almonds.

Makes about 2 servings, 1 cup each. Per serving –
Nutritive Value: 193 calories, 9.5 g protein, 12.5 g carb, 0 g fiber, 10.5 g fat, 12.6 mg chol.
Food Group Exchange: 1 Dairy, ½ Legumes/Meat, 1/8 Fat, ½ Sugar.

POTATO SOUP

This chunky soup goes with any meal. You may make it in advance and refrigerate; don't freeze. Heat before serving.

1 chopped onion
4 potatoes, peeled and chopped in ¼" cubes
2 tomatoes chopped
1 tablespoon oil

Seasonings:

1 teaspoon cumin seeds
1/8 teaspoon asafetida powder
½ teaspoon grated ginger
½ teaspoon turmeric powder

1 chopped green chili
½ teaspoon red chili powder
1 teaspoon salt

Garnish: 1 tablespoon chopped green coriander

1. Heat the oil in a pot on medium heat. Add cumin seeds; as soon as they splutter, add the chopped onions and asafetida powder; stir until the onions are translucent.
2. Add potatoes and the remaining seasonings. After 10–15 minutes when the potatoes are cooked, add tomatoes and stir for a couple of minutes. Add 2–3 cups water. Cover and cook until the soup is of desired consistency (about 20 minutes).
   Note: To reduce time, you may cook potatoes in the microwave before adding to the soup
3. Mash the potatoes a little to thicken the gravy. Serve hot garnished with green coriander.

Variation: Add 1 cup washed and chopped leeks (white part only) along with potatoes.

Healthy Alternative: Reduce or cut out oil. Instead of peeling, scrape and clean the potatoes. Use vegetable stock instead of water.

Makes about 8 servings, ¾ cup each. Per serving –
Nutritive Value: 75 calories, 2 g protein, 13 g carb, 1.6 g fiber, 19 g fat, 0 mg chol.
Food Group Exchange: ¾ Grain, ½ Vegetable, 1/8 Fat.

SPICED CHAI (Masala Tea)

Tea, or popularly known as 'chai', is India's national drink, served any time when people get together. Darjeeling tea from India is known for its aroma. The seasonings can be used in any combination. It is still customary to grind fresh seasonings using mortar and pestle when making tea.

2¾ cups cold water
3 tea bags or 3 teaspoons loose tea
½ cup whole or 2% milk

Seasonings:

¼ teaspoon semi-crushed cardamom seeds

½ teaspoon crushed ginger

2 cloves semi-crushed

2 teaspoons sugar or honey (to taste)

1. Boil the water with the desired seasonings (except honey or sugar). When boiling, add tea bags or loose tea; simmer for a couple of minutes, covered.
2. Add milk and, if desired, sugar. Bring to a boil. Turn off the heat and let it rest for a couple of minutes. Remove tea bags, strain, and serve hot.

Variation: After boiling, let the tea and seasonings steep for 5–10 minutes. Strain; serve hot tea separately with warm milk and any sweetener.

Makes about 3 servings, 1 cup each. Per serving –
Nutritive Value: 32 calories, 1.3 g protein, 5 g carb, 0 g fiber, 0.8 g fat, 3 mg chol.
Food Group Exchange: ½ Sugar, 1/8 Dairy.

THANDAI (Cooling Almond Drink)

This is a popular drink at festival time, especially 'Holi', the festival of color. Some may mix an intoxicant to it. Grind the almonds and seasonings in advance; mix when ready to serve. Makes about 1 gallon (16 cups).

3¼ cup almonds (about 500 grams)
½ gallon water
½ gallon milk, 2% or whole
1 cup sugar (to taste)

Seasonings:

½ cup cardamom seeds
1/3 cup whole black or white pepper

1/3 cup poppy seeds
½ cup fennel seeds

1. Blanch the almonds and grind them in a blender with little water as needed. Strain using thin muslin cloth. Squeeze it to extract as much liquid as possible, adding water as needed. Grind the solids one more time with some water and squeeze out the liquid.
2. Grind the seasonings also with some water and strain using thin muslin cloth. Squeeze out as much liquid as possible, adding water as needed. It is better to grind the seasonings with water once again and squeeze out the essence.
3. Mix the two extracts which should be about ½ gallon. Mix equal amount of milk. Add sugar to taste. Serve cold with ice.

Makes about 16 servings, 1 cup each. Per serving –
Nutritive Value: 335 calories, 12 g protein, 31 g carb, 7 g fiber, 20 g fat, 10 mg chol.
Food Group Exchange: ¾ Legumes/Meat, ½ Dairy, ¾ Sugar.

TOMATO SOUP

This is an easy to make appetizer from fresh tomatoes. You may refrigerate or freeze this soup; re–warm on top of stove.

1 onion, chopped
2 carrot, chopped
2 lb. ripe tomatoes, cut in large pieces
1 tablespoon oil

Seasonings:

2 cloves garlic, peeled and cut	1 teaspoon black pepper
1 small piece of ginger	2 teaspoons salt
2 green chilies	

Garnish: ½ cup grated Mozzarella (or Cheddar) cheese

1. Heat the oil in a large pot on medium heat. Add garlic and onions; stir until the onions are translucent.
2. Stir in ginger. Stir in the carrots and remaining seasonings. After about 5 minutes, add the tomatoes and about 1 cup water. Cover and cook for 8–10 minutes until the carrots are soft. Turn off the heat.
3. When slightly cold, puree in a blender until everything is mixed. Add water as needed. Just before serving, heat the soup and garnish with cheese.

Healthy Alternative: Reduce or cut out oil. Use vegetable stock instead of water.

Makes about 10 servings, ¾ cup each. Per serving –
Nutritive Value: 41 calories, 1 g protein, 6.4 g carb, 1.6 g fiber, 2 g fat, 0 mg chol.
Food Group Exchange: 1 Vegetable, 1/8 Fat.

VEGETABLE COMBO SOUP

A wonderful mix of vegetables, make this soup from fresh or frozen vegetables.

2 onions
1 carrot
3 cups chopped vegetables, such as celery, cabbage, and green beans
2 tomatoes
1 cup cooked kidney beans
1 tablespoon oil

Seasonings:

2 teaspoons crushed garlic
1 teaspoon crushed ginger
1 teaspoon crushed green chili

1 teaspoon black pepper
2 teaspoons salt

Garnish:

½ cup grated Mozzarella (or Cheddar) cheese
1 cup tofu cubes

¼ cup chopped parsley or green coriander

1. Prepare and chop the onions, carrots and other vegetables in small cubes. Heat the oil in a large pot on medium heat. Add garlic and onions; stir until the onions are translucent. Stir in the carrots, celery, cabbage and green beans. Add the seasonings; cook for few minutes.
2. Add about 2 cups water (or vegetable stock). Cover and cook for 15–20 minutes until the vegetables are soft. Add tomatoes and kidney beans; cook for 5–10 minutes, mashing the kidney beans and vegetables a little.
3. Add more water to get the desired consistency and bring to a boil. Just before serving, heat the soup and garnish with cheese, tofu cubes, and parsley or green coriander.

Variation: Try different vegetables such as red cabbage, corn, asparagus, green peas, and leeks (white part only).

Healthy Alternative: Reduce or cut out oil. Use vegetable stock instead of water. You may add ½ cup pearl barley or presoaked and cooked hulled barley to soup along with vegetables.

Makes about 12 servings, ¾ cup each. Per serving –
Nutritive Value: 48 calories, 2 g protein, 7.7 g carb, 2.6 g fiber, 1 g fat, 0 mg chol.
Food Group Exchange: 1 Vegetable, 1/8 Legumes/Meat, 1/8 Fat.

Vegetables and Beans

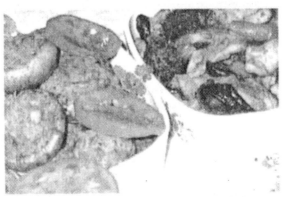

Vegetables and beans abound in the tropical climate of India. It is so refreshing to see vendors displaying different greens, squashes, cauliflower, eggplant, green peas and many other vegetables every morning. When you buy any vegetable, you get sprigs of green coriander (cilantro) and some green chilies free. You'll see some new vegetables like bitter melon and bottle gourd (long pale squash) when you visit an Indian grocery store. Prepare them using the recipes given in this chapter.

To help plan nutritious meals, each recipe gives nutritive value (calories, protein, carbohydrate (carb), fiber, fat, and cholesterol (chol)) and Food Group Exchange for a helping of the dish. Estimate is rounded off for ease of understanding. Garnishes, topping and small amounts of seasoning are not counted in the estimate. (See page 13 for basis of estimating Food Group Exchange and nutritive value.)

Abbreviations:

carb: carbohydrate,
g: gram, .
mg: milligram,

chol: cholesterol,
lb: pound,
oz: ounce.

F: Fahrenheit,
med: medium,

ALU BHAJI (Curried Potatoes)

Potatoes cooked any way are an important part of Indian meals. They can be cooked alone or mixed with any other vegetable. In this recipe, potatoes are cooked almost like a stew with all the spices.

6 medium size potatoes
½ cup crushed tomatoes
1 tablespoon oil

Seasonings:

1 teaspoon cumin seeds
2 teaspoons crushed garlic
1 chopped onion
1 teaspoon crushed ginger
½ teaspoon turmeric powder

2 teaspoons coriander powder
½ teaspoon paprika
½ teaspoon red chili powder
1 teaspoon salt (to taste)
1 teaspoon garam masala

Garnish: 1 tablespoon chopped green coriander

1. Wash and peel (or scrub) the potatoes. Cut them into about ½" pieces. Heat the oil in a medium-size pot on medium heat. Add cumin seeds, garlic, and onions; stir until the onions are translucent.
2. Add potatoes and the remaining seasonings (except garam masala); stir until the potatoes start to brown and soften (about 10 minutes). (You may sprinkle little water and cover the pot when you are not stirring.) **Note:** For faster cooking, microwave the cut potatoes until tender and then add to the sauté. Or boil them in their skin, peel and break into pieces before adding.
3. Add the tomatoes. Cook for a couple of minutes. Add about 1 cup of water and increase the heat to high. After the water starts to boil, reduce the heat back to medium. Cook until the gravy is thick (about 15 minutes). Add more water if needed.
4. Mix in garam masala. Garnish and serve hot.

Variation: Mix in 10 oz. green peas when the potatoes are little cooked, before adding tomatoes.

Makes about 10 servings, ¾ cup each. Per serving –
Nutritive Value: 78 calories, 2 g protein, 15 g carb, 1 g fiber, 1.5 g fat, 0 mg chol.
Food Group Exchange: ¾ Grain, ¼ Vegetable, 1/8 Fat.

ALU GOBHI (Potatoes & Cauliflower)

Cauliflower (gobhi) is a popular dish in Indian cuisine, served in many different ways, at formal and informal meals. When you cut the cauliflower, break it from the stem and keep the florets as intact as possible.

4 medium potatoes
1 head cauliflower cut into small florets
1 chopped red onion
1 tablespoon oil

Seasonings:

1 teaspoon mustard seeds
1 teaspoon cumin seeds
2 teaspoons crushed garlic
1 teaspoon crushed ginger
2 teaspoons coriander powder

½ teaspoon red chili powder
1 teaspoon salt (to taste)
1 teaspoon garam masala
1 teaspoon mango powder

Garnish: 1 tablespoon chopped green coriander

1. Wash and peel (or scrub) the potatoes. Cut into long ½" thick pieces. Microwave for 6–8 minutes, covered, for faster cooking.
2. Heat the oil in a wide skillet on high heat. Add mustard seeds and cover. As soon as the seeds start popping, reduce the heat and add cumin seeds. As they change color, add garlic.
3. Add the half–cooked potatoes, cauliflower pieces, and remaining seasonings (except garam masala and mango powder). Cook covered until ready (about 15 minutes). Stir and sprinkle water if needed; lower the heat to prevent burning.
4. Mix in garam masala, mango powder, and chopped red onion. Serve hot garnished with green coriander.

Note: Instead of cauliflower, use any vegetable such as green beans, bell pepper, onions, fenugreek (methi) or eggplant with potatoes.

Variation: Mix in 1 cup green peas and/or chopped carrots along with cauliflower. Use lemon juice instead of mango powder for a lemony taste. May also add a chopped tomato.

Makes about 10 servings, ½ cup each. Per serving –
Nutritive Value: 69 calories, 2 g protein, 13 g carb, 2 g fiber, 1.5 g fat, 0 mg chol.
Food Group Exchange: ½ Grain, ½ Vegetable, 1/8 Fat.

ALU WADI (Curried Potatoes with Lentil Drops)

'Wadi' or lentil drops can be added to any dish for a distinct flavor. Use 'urad dal wadi' for this dish. These are larger and spicier than 'mung dal wadi' (called 'mangori'). Break 'wadi' into small pieces.

6 medium size potatoes
½ cup wadi (dried lentil drops) pieces
½ cup crushed tomatoes
1 tablespoon oil

Seasonings:

1 teaspoon cumin seeds	½ teaspoon paprika
1 teaspoon crushed ginger	½ teaspoon red chili powder
½ teaspoon turmeric powder	1 teaspoon salt
2 teaspoons coriander powder	

Garnish: 1 tablespoon chopped green coriander

1. Wash and peel (or scrub) the potatoes. Cut into ¾" pieces.
2. Heat the oil in a medium size pot on medium heat. Add 'wadi'; stir for about a minute until they change color. Stir in cumin seeds. Add potatoes; stir until the potatoes start to brown (about 10 minutes). (You may cover the pot when you are not stirring.) Add the remaining seasonings. *Note:* For faster cooking, microwave the cut potatoes until tender before adding.
3. Add the tomatoes. Cook for a couple of minutes; add 1 cup water. Increase the heat for water to boil and then reduce it. Cook until the gravy is thick (about 15 minutes). Add more water if needed.
4. Serve hot garnished with green coriander.

Variation: Add ½ cup soy nuggets, along with tomatoes in step 3.

Makes about 10 servings, ¾ cup each. Per serving –
Nutritive Value: 93 calories, 3 g protein, 17 g carb, 2 g fiber, 1.5 g fat, 0 mg chol.
Food Group Exchange: ¾ Grain, ¼ Vegetable, 1/8 Legumes/Meat, 1/8 Fat.

BESAN KADHI (Gram Flour Stew)

'Besan Kadhi' is a special treat and is often served at auspicious and festive occasions. 'Besan' or gram flour is high in protein. It makes a complete meal served with rice and some greens on the side.

**2 cups gram flour (besan) sifted
6 cups plain yogurt
1 tablespoon oil**

Seasonings:

½ teaspoon fenugreek seeds
2 dry red chilies
1 teaspoon cumin seeds
1 teaspoon coriander powder
1/8 teaspoon asafetida powder
½ teaspoon turmeric powder

2 teaspoons salt
½ teaspoon red chili powder
1 teaspoon garam masala
½ teaspoon black pepper
1 teaspoon mango powder
1 tablespoon fresh (or dry) fenugreek leaves

1. Whisk together gram flour and yogurt until smooth; stir in 2 cups of water; keep aside.
2. Heat the oil in a 4-quart pot on medium heat. Sauté fenugreek seeds. As soon as they splutter (couple of seconds), stir in red chilies, cumin seeds, asafetida powder and coriander powder.
3. Immediately add the gram flour mixture. As it cooks, keep stirring and adding water (6–8 cups). Keep stirring until the mixture starts to boil, taking care not to make any lumps. Add turmeric powder and salt. Add more water as needed.
4. Lower the heat; simmer partially covered for about an hour; stirring occasionally until 'Kadhi' becomes semi-thick consistency. Add about 30 'pakoris' (see below) and continue cooking for a few minutes until 'pakoris' absorb the liquid and become soft. Stir in the remaining seasonings.

To Make Pakori: (about 30)

**1 cup gram flour, sifted
½ cup chopped vegetables such as spinach, fenugreek leaves or chopped potatoes and onions**

Seasonings:

½ teaspoon salt
¼ teaspoon caraway seeds

1 teaspoon red chili powder

Recipes with a Spice

1. Mix everything together with vegetables and little water to make a very thick batter. Blend well and let it stand for about 20 minutes.
2. Drop small round balls (about ½" diameter) in hot oil; deep–fry until golden brown. Drain on paper towels before using.

Variation: Sauté chopped potatoes, onions, ginger (or any other vegetable) along with other spices in step 2; then continue with remaining steps. There is no need to add 'pakori'.

Makes about 16 servings, ¾ cup each. Per serving –
Nutritive Value: 165 calories, 9 g protein, 16 g carb, 2 g fiber, 7.5 g fat, 5 mg chol.
Food Group Exchange: ½ Legumes/Meat, 1/8 Dairy, 1 Fat.

**I feel a recipe is only a theme,
which an intelligent cook can play each time with a variation.**
Madame Benoit

BESAN MIRCH (Bell Peppers in Gram Flour)

This is a good side dish, a mix of vegetables and flour that brings out excellent taste and texture. Besides bell peppers (also known as capsicums), you can use other vegetables such as green beans and eggplant.

¾ cup gram flour (besan)
6 green bell peppers, seeded and cut in cubes or strips
3 tablespoons oil

Seasonings:

1 teaspoon cumin seeds
2 teaspoons coriander powder
½ teaspoon turmeric
½ teaspoon red chili powder

1½ teaspoons salt (to taste)
1 teaspoon mango powder
1 teaspoon garam masala

1. Roast the gram flour in the oven at 400°F for 10–15 minutes until golden brown. Stir once or twice as needed to make sure there are no lumps. (Can also roast in the microwave for 1–2 minutes.)
2. Heat the oil in a skillet on medium-high heat. Add cumin seeds. As soon as they splutter, add chopped bell peppers, coriander, turmeric, red chili powder and salt. Cook covered, while stirring, for 5–10 minutes until the peppers are done.
3. Add roasted gram flour, mango powder, and garam masala. Cook covered for a few more minutes.

Healthy Alternative: Reduce the oil; add 1–2 tablespoons of crushed tomatoes and ¼ cup water when adding gram flour.

Makes about 10 servings, 1/3 cup each. Per serving –
Nutritive Value: 81 calories, 2 g protein, 9 g carb, 2 g fiber, 5 g fat, 0 mg chol.
Food Group Exchange: 1 Vegetable, ¼ Legumes/Meat, ½ Fat.

BHARTHA (Barbecued Eggplant)

'Bhartha' is known for its barbecue flavor. You may prepare the whole dish in advance and freeze; or roast eggplants in bulk, especially outside on a hibachi on a nice summer day and freeze baked eggplant pulp in small containers to be used as needed. Use it as a main dish in any meal.

2 medium size eggplants
3 onions (chopped and divided in 2 parts)
2 large tomatoes (chopped)
10 oz. frozen green peas
3 tablespoons oil

Seasonings:

2 hot red whole chilies	1 teaspoon paprika
6 cloves garlic, crushed	1 teaspoon red chili powder
1 teaspoon cumin seeds	2 teaspoons crushed ginger
2 chopped green chilies	1 teaspoon garam masala
2 teaspoons coriander powder	2 teaspoons salt

Garnish: 2 tablespoons chopped green coriander.

1. Wash the eggplants; keep the stem on. Lightly brush them with oil and roast whole on grill or hibachi. The skin will be black. When little cool, peel the skin and mash the eggplants. Use all the juice that comes out. You may freeze the mashed eggplant pulp at this time. *Note:* There are several ways to roast eggplants, e.g., on top of gas stove or in oven at broil. You can also peel and chop the eggplants and cook in a microwave oven, covered, for about 8 minutes. Mash the pulp as usual.

2. Heat 2 tablespoons oil in a large skillet on medium heat. Add red chilies and garlic and let them brown. (May have to remove the pan from heat if the oil is too hot and the spices start to burn.) Add cumin seeds and half of the onions. When the onions are light brown, add the roasted and mashed eggplant pulp. Stir for about 15 minutes. It should be thick consistency.

3. Add green chilies, coriander powder, paprika, red chili powder and salt; stir for a few minutes. Stir in the tomatoes and cook for another 5–10 minutes. Set aside.

4. In a small pan, heat 1 tablespoon oil. Stir-fry the green peas and ginger. When tender, add garam masala and remaining half of the onions. Cook the onions for 1 minute only; they must remain crunchy.

5. Mix the peas and onion mixture with cooked hot eggplants at serving time. Garnish with green coriander.

Healthy Alternative: Reduce or omit oil (see *no–fat sauté* on page 26); add additional 2–3 tablespoons of crushed tomatoes for moistness.

Makes about 12 servings, 1/3 cup each. Per serving –
Nutritive Value: 90 calories, 2.5 g protein, 12 g carb, 4 g fiber, 4 g fat, 0 mg chol.
Food Group Exchange: 1 Vegetable, ¼ Fat.

Foods that promote a fuller life,
Virtue, strength, health, happiness and satisfaction,
And which are delicious, pleasant, nutritious and agreeable
Are dear to the person of Sattwa (purity).

The Bhagavad Gita, chapter 17, verse 8

BHINDI (Spiced Okra)

Okra, the so called 'slimy' vegetable, is very popular in Indian cuisine. Use it in any meal or in a sandwich or pita bread. You may prepare spiced okra in advance, and refrigerate or freeze it. Or you may freeze uncooked okra. Buy fresh tender okra, when available, and rinse, pat–dry, trim, and cut them before freezing.

1 lb. fresh okra (or cut frozen okra)
2 onions, cut lengthwise
1 small chopped tomato
2 tablespoons oil

Seasonings:

1 teaspoon cumin seeds
Pinch of asafetida powder
¼ teaspoon turmeric powder
¼ teaspoon red chili powder

1 teaspoon salt
1½ teaspoon coriander powder
½ teaspoon mango powder
½ teaspoon black pepper

1. Rinse fresh okra and pat dry. Trim the bottom tip and the top cone. Cut into small rounds or lengthwise into two halves. (If using frozen okra, thaw it in microwave.)
2. Heat the oil in a skillet on medium heat. Add cumin seeds; as soon as they change color (a couple of seconds), add the asafetida powder and onions. Stir for a minute.
3. Add the okra, turmeric powder, red chili powder and salt. Cook slowly on medium heat, half covered, until the okra is tender and lightly browned. In between keep stirring using a flat spatula. *Note:* Okra should fit the skillet almost in a single layer to get the browning effect.
4. Add coriander powder, mango powder, and black pepper. Stir gently for another 5 minutes. Mix in the chopped tomato before serving.

Variation: To make **STUFFED BHINDI**, use fresh okra.

1. Mix all the seasonings, substituting 1 teaspoon cumin powder for cumin seeds, and use for stuffing. Trim the ends of okra. With a paring knife, make a long slit in each okra, from one end to another (leaving two ends and bottom of the pod intact). Keep the slit open with your thumb and use a small spoon to fill the opening with stuffing. Stuff all the okra this way.
2. Cook the okra in a wide skillet using 2 tablespoons oil, almost in a single layer, on medium heat. Add the onions. Stir the okra gently so

that stuffing does not come out. Reduce the heat to medium low, cooking slowly, half covered, until the okra is lightly browned.

Makes about 10 servings, 1/3 cup each. Per serving –
Nutritive Value: 50 calories, 1 g protein, 6 g carb, 2 g fiber, 3 g fat, 0 mg chol.
Food Group Exchange: 1 Vegetable, ¼ Fat.

CHANA SAAG (Chickpeas & Spinach)

Chickpeas and Chana dal provide protein for vegetarians. This is a nice colorful way to combine protein and vegetables. It can be made in advance and frozen. You may also freeze cooked chickpeas, 'Chana dal', and spinach separately. Prepare them to desired taste when needed.

**32 oz. canned chickpeas (garbanzos), drained,
(or 4 cups frozen chickpeas or 2 cups dry chickpeas)
½ cup Chana dal
1 cup spinach, pureed or finely chopped
1 tablespoon tamarind pulp soaked in hot water
1 tablespoon oil**

Seasonings:

2 teaspoons minced garlic	1 teaspoon crushed green chilies
1 chopped onion	½ teaspoon red chili powder
1 teaspoon crushed ginger	½ teaspoon black pepper
½ teaspoon cumin powder	½ teaspoon mango powder
1 teaspoon coriander powder	1 teaspoon garam masala
½ teaspoon cinnamon powder	

1. If using canned or frozen chickpeas, keep them aside. Boil the Chana dal in 2 cups water and cook until tender. Add the frozen chickpeas to dal when it is half-cooked. If using dry chickpeas, cook them and 'Chana dal' together, until soft. (See *Dry Beans–Cooking* on page 30.)
2. Heat the oil in a 2–3 quart pot on medium heat. Add garlic and onions; stir until translucent. Add ginger, cumin powder, and coriander powder. Stir for a minute.
3. Stir in the pureed spinach and cook for 3–5 minutes. Add the boiled chickpeas, 'dal', and the remaining seasonings (except 'garam masala'). Add water as needed.
4. Boil and simmer for 15 minutes until it is of desired thickness. Strain the tamarind mixture to remove any roughage and add to 'Chana-Saag'. Continue to cook for another 5 minutes. Add garam masala and serve hot.

Makes about 12 servings, ¾ cup each. Per serving –
Nutritive Value: 116 calories, 5 g protein, 18 g carb, 1 g fiber, 3 g fat, 0 chol.
Food Group Exchange: 1 Legumes/Meat, 1/3 Vegetable, 1/8 Fat.

CHEESY PEAS CURRY

This is an easy delicious main dish made from Ricotta cheese, a substitute for fresh cheese (paneer), and green peas that contain an abundance of disease fighting vitamins.

16 oz. frozen (or fresh) green peas
1½ lb. Ricotta cheese
½ cup tomato puree (canned or fresh)
1½ tablespoons oil

Seasonings:

1 onion chopped
1 teaspoon chopped ginger
½ teaspoon cumin powder
1 teaspoon coriander powder
½ teaspoon turmeric powder
½ teaspoon paprika

½ teaspoon ground black pepper
½ teaspoon red chili powder
1 teaspoon crushed green chili
1 teaspoon salt
1 teaspoon garam masala

Garnish: 1 tablespoon chopped green coriander

1. Heat the oil in a pan on medium-high heat. Add chopped onions and stir until they are light brown. Add ginger, cumin powder, coriander powder and peas. Cook, while stirring, for a few minutes until the peas are little tender.
2. Add the tomatoes, Ricotta cheese and remaining seasonings (except garam masala). Stir; cook until it is of semi-thick consistency (about 15 minutes), adding ½–1 cup water as needed.
3. Mix in 'garam masala'. Serve garnished with green coriander.

Variation: Instead of Ricotta cheese, use crumbled fresh cheese (paneer) and add it towards the end, in step 2.

Makes about 12 servings, ¾ cup each. Per serving –
Nutritive Value: 145 calories, 9 g protein, 9 g carb, 2 g fiber, 8 g fat, 20 mg chol.
Food Group Exchange: 1 Dairy, ¾ Vegetable, 1/8 Fat.

CHHOLE (Curried Chickpeas)

This dish, generally of semi-liquid consistency, is almost a must in any party and is very popular with children. It can be made in advance and frozen. You may also freeze cooked chickpeas and prepare them to desired taste when needed.

**2 16-oz. cans of chickpeas (garbanzos), drained, or
4 cups frozen, or 2 cups dry chickpeas
1 tablespoon tamarind pulp soaked in hot water
1 tablespoon oil**

Seasonings:

1 chopped onion	½ teaspoon red chili powder
1½ teaspoons crushed ginger	1 teaspoon garam masala
½ teaspoon cumin powder	½ teaspoon black pepper
1 teaspoon coriander powder	½ teaspoon mango powder
½ teaspoon cinnamon powder	

Garnish: 1 tablespoon chopped green coriander

1. If using canned or frozen chickpeas, keep them aside. If using dry chickpeas, cook them as at page 30.
2. Heat the oil in a 2–3 quart pan on medium heat. Add the onions; stir until translucent. Add ginger, cumin powder, and coriander powder. Stir for a few seconds.
3. Add the chickpeas and remaining seasonings. Add ½–1 cup water as needed. Boil and simmer for 5–10 minutes until the gravy is of desired thickness. (Frozen chickpeas may take a little longer to cook.)
4. Strain the tamarind mixture to remove any roughage. Stir it into 'Chhole' and continue to cook for another 5 minutes. Garnish and serve hot.

Variation: Instead of using tamarind, add ¼ cup pureed tomatoes. If using dry chickpeas, mix some black chickpeas for color. Also add ¼ cup rinsed Chana dal when you cook soaked chickpeas. This gives a creamier texture. You may garnish with onion wedges that have been marinated in lemon juice and salt.

*Makes about 8 servings, ¾ cup each. Per serving –
Nutritive Value: 143 calories, 5 g protein, 22 g carb, 7 g fiber, 4 g fat, 0 mg chol.
Food Group Exchange: 1 Legumes/Meat, 1/8 Vegetable, 1/8 Fat.*

CRISPY RICE POTATOES

This is an alternative way to serve whole potatoes, which are always popular. Potatoes are well coated with crunchy masala.

1 lb. tiny potatoes (or small potatoes cut into halves)
½ cup rice, soaked 2 hours, ground coarsely
2 tablespoons plain yogurt
3 tablespoons oil

Seasonings:

½ teaspoon fenugreek seeds
1 teaspoon crushed garlic
1 chopped onion
½ teaspoon crushed ginger
1 teaspoon crushed green chili
1 teaspoon coriander powder

¼ teaspoon turmeric powder
½ teaspoon mango powder
1½ teaspoons salt
½ teaspoon red chili powder
1 tbls. chopped green coriander

1. Scrub and wash the potatoes; stir-fry in 2 tablespoons oil on medium heat until cooked and golden brown. Remove the potatoes.
2. In the same pan, add the remaining oil, sauté fenugreek seeds. As soon as they start to brown, stir in garlic and onions. When the onions are light brown, add remaining seasonings (except green coriander) and stir for a minute.
3. Add the crushed rice and ½ cup of water; cook about 15 minutes. If the mixture is too thick, add water as needed.
4. Add cooked potatoes and yogurt; stir for 5–10 minutes. Mix in green coriander and serve.

Makes about 7 servings, ¾ cup each. Per serving –
Nutritive Value: 157 calories, 2 g protein, 23 g carb, 1 g fiber, 6 g fat, 0 mg chol.
Food Group Exchange: 1 Grain, 1/8 Vegetable, ½ Fat.

DAM ALU (Spiced Steamed Potatoes)

Small whole potatoes are used for this delicious dish, traditionally served at parties. Freshly roasted spices give a wonderful aroma.

12 small potatoes
3 tablespoons plain yogurt
3 tablespoons oil

Seasonings:

½ teaspoon crushed ginger
1 tablespoon coriander seeds (lightly roasted and ground)
¼ teaspoon black peppercorn (lightly roasted and ground)
½ teaspoon turmeric powder

1½ teaspoon salt
½ teaspoon red chili powder
½ teaspoon sugar
1 teaspoon cumin seeds

Garnish:

¼ teaspoon clove powder
½ teaspoon cinnamon powder

½ teaspoon cardamom powder

1. Scrub or peel potatoes; boil until half cooked. (You may cook them in the microwave, covered, for about 5 minutes). Prick the potatoes with a fork.
2. Mix all the seasonings (except cumin seeds), yogurt, and 2 tablespoons of water. Cover the potatoes with the paste like mixture.
3. Sauté cumin seeds in hot oil in a skillet on medium heat. Add the potatoes coated with the mixture; stir for 5-10 minutes. Add about 1 cup water; simmer, covered, on low heat until the potatoes are tender and dry.
4. Garnish with clove, cinnamon, and cardamom powder; cover to let the potatoes absorb the aroma.

Variation: Use long thin potatoes. Make 2–3 parallel cuts in each potato, about ¾ way through but not cutting to the end of the potato. Fill them with spices. Stir–fry, adding water as needed.

Makes about 12 servings, 1 piece each. Per serving –
Nutritive Value: 105 calories, 2 g protein, 17 g carb, 1.5 g fiber, 4 g fat, 0 chol.
Food Group Exchange: 1 Grain, ¼ Fat.

KADAI PANEER (Wok-fried Cheese)

This rich delicious dish has special aroma of freshly ground spices. Make fresh cheese (paneer) at home or buy from any Indian store. Serve it as a side dish at formal dinners.

Paneer strips (fresh cheese) made from ½ gallon whole or 2% fat milk
2 green bell peppers
2 chopped tomatoes
3 tablespoons oil

Seasonings:

2 red whole chilies and
1½ tsp whole coriander seeds (roasted and ground)
1 teaspoon crushed garlic
1 teaspoon crushed ginger

½ teaspoon chopped green chili
¼ teaspoon fenugreek seeds
1 teaspoon salt (to taste)

Garnish: 1 tablespoon chopped green coriander

1. Make 'paneer' (see page 31). Instead of cutting into squares, cut the 'paneer' in 2"x½" strips and do not fry. Seed and cut the bell peppers in strips.
2. Heat 1 tablespoon oil in a skillet on medium–high heat. Add the bell pepper strips and stir for a few minutes until soft. Take them out.
3. Put the remaining oil in the skillet. Sauté garlic until light brown. Add red chili powder and coriander, ginger and green chili. Stir for a couple of seconds and enjoy the aroma of herbs.
4. Stir in tomatoes and the remaining seasonings. Cook at medium heat for about 5 minutes.
5. Stir in the bell peppers and 'paneer' strips. Cook for 2–3 minutes. Mix in green coriander and serve hot.

Healthy Alternative: Use drained firm tofu instead of 'paneer'.

Makes about 8 servings, ½ cup each. Per serving –
Nutritive Value: 146 calories, 7 g protein, 7 g carb, 1 g fiber, 9.6 g fat, 6 mg chol.
Food Group Exchange: 1 Dairy, ½ Vegetable, ½ Fat.

KARELA (Bitter Melon)

As the name suggests, 'karela' are bitter but are known to have therapeutic value, especially for those suffering from diabetes. When tomatoes and other vegetables are mixed with it, the bitterness is reduced. Traditionally people first scrape 'karela' and remove the hard skin. Then they rub salt in them and let them rest for about 1 hour. Then they squeeze out bitter water before using.

'Karela' can be used with any meal or in a sandwich or pita bread. You may prepare them in advance, and refrigerate or freeze them. Or you may freeze uncooked 'karela'. Buy them fresh, when in season, and rinse, trim, and cut them before freezing.

1 lb. bitter melon (karela)
2 potatoes, peeled, cut in long strips and
half cooked
2 chopped onions
2 chopped tomatoes
2 tablespoons oil

Seasonings:

1 teaspoon cumin seeds
¼ teaspoon turmeric powder
¼ teaspoon red chili powder
1½ teaspoon coriander powder

½ teaspoon mango powder
½ teaspoon black pepper
1 teaspoon salt

1. Rinse bitter melon. Trim on both ends as needed and scrape any blemishes or hard skin. Cut into small rounds.
2. Heat the oil in a skillet on medium-high heat. Add 'karela' almost in a single layer; stir and cook until brownish. Reduce the heat if they tend to burn.
3. Add the onions, potatoes and all the seasonings; stir until the potatoes are cooked.
4. Add the tomatoes. Cook slowly on medium low heat, half covered, stirring as needed, until everything is cooked.

Variation: To make **STUFFED KARELA:**

1. Mix all the seasonings for stuffing, substituting 1 teaspoon cumin powder for cumin seeds.
2. Using a paring knife, make a long slit in each 'karela', from one end to another (leaving two ends and bottom of the pod intact). Keep the slit open with your thumb and use a spoon to fill the opening with the stuffing. Stuff all the 'karela' this way.
3. Cook 'karela' in a wide skillet using 2 tablespoons oil, almost in a single layer, on medium heat. Stir gently so that stuffing does not come out. When half–cooked, add the onions. Reduce heat to medium low, cooking slowly, half covered or uncovered, until 'karela' are browned.

Makes about 8 servings, ½ cup each. Per serving –
Nutritive Value: 86 calories, 2 g protein, 12 g carb, 2 g fiber, 3.6 g fat, 0 mg chol.
Food Group Exchange: 1 Vegetable, ¼ Grain, ¼ Fat.

MALAI KOFTA (Cheese Balls)

This is a rich fancy main dish served at formal dinners. 'Malai' means cream though these are made from fresh cheese (paneer).

CHEESE BALLS:

Paneer (fresh cheese) made from ½ gallon whole
or 2% fat milk
1 grated carrot
4 medium size potatoes, boiled and mashed
1/3 cup green peas
¼ cup finely chopped almonds or cashews
2 tablespoons all-purpose flour
1 tablespoon cornstarch
Pinch of baking powder
Oil to fry (about 2" deep in a wok)

Seasonings:

½ teaspoon red chili powder	½ teaspoon black pepper
1½ teaspoons coriander powder	1 teaspoon salt
½ teaspoon mango powder	

Filling: 40 raisins and 2 tablespoons crushed green chili

1. Make fresh cheese (paneer; see page 31). Let it drain for a couple of hours. When dry, beat it with a fork until it is fluffy and light. (You may give it a few rounds in a food processor.) Dry the grated carrot in a skillet (or in the microwave) to remove extra moisture.
2. Mix all the ingredients (except oil) and seasonings to make a hard dough like mixture. Add more flour if needed. Break into walnut size pieces (about 40). Take each piece, flatten, put 1 raisin and touch of green chili in middle, and make into a smooth ball, round or oval.
3. Deep–fry in a deep skillet or wok on high heat, turning, until golden brown on all sides. (Test fry one ball first. If the ball breaks, dip the balls in a solution of 1 tablespoon of flour and 1/3 cup water before frying.) At this point, you may freeze these balls for later use.

GRAVY:

2 medium size onions finely chopped or crushed
½ cup crushed tomatoes
½ cup heavy cream
2 tablespoons oil

Seasonings:

1 teaspoon crushed garlic

½ teaspoon cumin seeds

1 teaspoon crushed ginger

½ teaspoon turmeric powder

1 teaspoon coriander powder

1 teaspoon crushed poppy seeds

½ teaspoon paprika

½ teaspoon red chili powder

1+ teaspoon salt

1 teaspoon garam masala

Garnish: 1 tablespoon chopped green coriander

4. Heat the oil in a pan on medium–high heat. Add garlic and cumin seeds. Stir for a couple of seconds; add onions; stir until they are light brown.
5. Stir in the tomatoes and remaining seasonings (except garam masala). Cook at medium heat for about 10 minutes.
6. Stir in the heavy cream slowly and enough water (about 4 cups) to make it liquidy (liquid is later absorbed by the cheese balls). Cook until the gravy is well mixed (about ½ hour). Blend in garam masala.
7. To serve, arrange the cheese balls in a serving dish. (If the cheese balls are frozen, thaw at room temperature, not in the microwave because they may break.) About ½ hour before serving, pour the hot gravy on top so that the cheese balls soak. Serve hot garnished with green coriander.

Healthy Alternative: Use yogurt or sour cream instead of heavy cream in gravy.

Makes about 15 servings, ¾ cup each. Per serving –
Nutritive Value:260 calories, 5 g protein, 12 g carb, 2 g fiber, 21 g fat, 14 mg chol.
Food Group Exchange: 2 Fat, 1/3 Grain, ½ Vegetable, ½ Dairy, 1/8 Legumes/Meat.

MASALA ALU (Spiced Potatoes)

This is a quick way to fix potatoes with a lot of spices. Use them in sandwiches or pita bread.

8 medium size potatoes
1 large tomato (chopped)
2 tablespoons oil

Seasonings:

1 teaspoon mustard seeds	1 teaspoon garam masala
1 teaspoon cumin seeds	½ teaspoon mango powder
1/8 teaspoon asafetida powder	½ teaspoon paprika
1 teaspoon crushed ginger	½ teaspoon red chili powder
½ teaspoon turmeric powder	1 teaspoon salt
1 teaspoon coriander powder	

Garnish:

1 tablespoon chopped green coriander   1 tablespoon roasted peanuts (optional)

1. Rinse and boil the potatoes in their skin. Peel and cut into small pieces. (You may peel and chop the potatoes, and cook them covered in the microwave for 8 minutes.)
2. Heat the oil in a skillet on medium-high heat. Add mustard seeds. Cover the pot. As soon as the seeds start to pop, add cumin seeds and asafetida powder. (May have to remove the pan from the heat if the spices start to burn.)
3. Add ginger and tomato. Stir for a minute, add the potatoes and remaining spices. Stir together with a fork or flat spatula; cook for 5–6 minutes.
4. Garnish with green coriander and roasted peanuts when serving.

Makes about 10 servings, ¾ cup each. Per serving –
Nutritive Value: 105 calories, 2 g protein, 18 g carb, 2 g fiber, 3 g fat, 0 mg chol.
Food Group Exchange: ¾ Grain, 1/8 Vegetable, 1/8 Fat.

MASALA (Spiced) MUSHROOMS

Mushrooms can be served with any meal or in a sandwich or any bread as a wrap. You may prepare them in advance, and refrigerate or freeze them.

½ lb. mushroom
2 onions, chopped
2 small chopped tomatoes
1 tablespoon oil

Seasonings:

1 tablespoon minced garlic
½ teaspoon cumin powder
½ teaspoon turmeric powder
½ teaspoon crushed green chili
¼ teaspoon red chili powder

1 teaspoon coriander powder
1 teaspoon salt
1 tablespoon dry fenugreek leaves
½ teaspoon garam masala

1. Rinse mushrooms, pat–dry, and dice.
2. Heat the oil in a skillet on medium-high heat. Add garlic and onions; stir until light brown. Add all the seasonings except fenugreek leaves and garam masala; stir for less than a minute. (May sprinkle a little water if the spices burn.)
3. Add tomatoes; cook for a couple of minutes. Add the mushrooms; cook for 5–7 minutes, increasing heat if the mushrooms leave too much water. Stir in garam masala and fenugreek leaves before serving.

Variation: Add some green peas and cubed tofu along with mushrooms.

Makes about 8 servings, ½ cup each. Per serving –
Nutritive Value: 39 calories, 1.4 g protein, 5 g carb, 1 g fiber, 2 g fat, 0 mg chol.
Food Group Exchange: 1 Vegetable, 1/8 Fat.

MASALA PHULGOBHI (Spiced Whole Cauliflower)

This decorative dish can be prepared in advance. Bake for a few minutes when ready to serve.

1 cauliflower (stem removed)
2 chopped onions
2 chopped tomatoes
½ cup plain yogurt
3 tablespoons oil

Seasonings:

4 cloves minced garlic
1 tablespoon crushed ginger
1 teaspoon crushed green chilies
½ teaspoon turmeric powder
1½ teaspoon coriander powder
½ teaspoon cumin powder

1½ teaspoons salt
½ teaspoon paprika
½ teaspoon red chili powder
1 tablespoon crushed poppy seeds
2 tablespoons crushed cashews

Garnish: 2 tablespoons chopped green coriander

1. Soak cauliflower in about 4 cups salted water for ½ hour. Drain and put several half cuts on the stem side of the cauliflower. Steam it until tender. (You may microwave at high, covered, for about 8 minutes.)
2. Heat the oil in a wide skillet on medium–high heat. Stir fry garlic and onions until translucent. Add crushed ginger, green chilies, coriander, cumin, turmeric, and salt. Stir until the onions are golden brown. Add the remaining spices (except poppy seeds and cashews). Keep on stirring. Add tomatoes and ¼ cup water to cook them.
3. Blend in the yogurt gradually and keep on stirring until the oil is separated. Add crushed cashews and poppy seeds and ¼ cup water. Now add the cauliflower, head down, and coat with masala to let everything cook together for 5–10 minutes.
4. Place the cauliflower, stump down, in a casserole dish. Coat with all the masala. (Put more cuts in the cauliflower to ensure that all sides are covered with the masala.)
5. Before serving, bake for 15 minutes at 350°F. Garnish with green coriander. You may also decorate with cooked green peas and pan–fried potato slices.

Makes about 10 servings, ½ cup each. Per serving –
Nutritive Value: 80 calories, 2.4 g protein, 7 g carb, 2 g fiber, 5 g fat, 0.5 mg chol.
Food Group Exchange: 1 Vegetable, ½ Dairy, ½ Fat.

MIXED BEANS and VEGGIES

Different beans and vegetables are cooked together to make this tasty side dish. You may cook almost any vegetable in this manner.

1 cup frozen baby Lima beans
½ cup frozen green peas
1 cup snow peas
½ cup wax beans
1 cup thin eggplants, chopped in small cubes
1 green pepper chopped
¼ cup scallions chopped
1½ tablespoons oil

Seasonings:

1 teaspoon mustard seeds
½ teaspoon red chili powder

1 teaspoon crushed ginger
2 teaspoons salt

Garnish: 1 tablespoon chopped green coriander leaves

1. Heat the oil in a skillet on medium-high heat. Add mustard seeds. Cover the pot. As soon as the seeds start to pop, add all the ingredients and seasonings except scallions. Reduce heat to medium; cover and cook, stirring frequently.
2. Add the scallions when the beans and vegetables are almost done (about 10 minutes). Cook for a few more minutes. Serve hot, garnished with green coriander leaves.

Makes about 8 servings, ½ cup each. Per serving –
Nutritive Value: 75 calories, 3 g protein, 10 g carb, 3 g fiber, 2.6 g fat, 0 mg chol.
Food Group Exchange: ½ Vegetable, ½ Legumes/Meat, 1/8 Fat.

MULTANI KADHI (Lentil Nuggets Stew)

This is a regional dish passed from mother to daughter. A special main dish, it is served with bread or rice. The nuggets can be made in advance and frozen.

Lentil Nuggets:

2 cups Mung split peeled yellow dal
Oil to fry (about 2" deep in a wok)

Seasonings:

½ teaspoon cumin powder   ½ teaspoon salt
¼ teaspoon red chili powder

1. Check, rinse and soak 'dal' in enough water for 3–4 hours. Drain; grind into fine paste using minimum water and whip. Mix the seasonings; it should be thick consistency batter.
2. Spread the batter thinly in a greased flat dish that can fit in a large wide pot and covered. Steam as for 'Dhokla' on page 65. Remove the dish. When little cold, cut into 40–50 small pieces.
3. Deep–fry the pieces in a deep skillet or wok on medium-high heat, turning, until golden brown on all sides. At this point, you may freeze these nuggets for later use.

GRAVY:

2 medium size onions finely chopped or crushed
½ cup crushed tomatoes
2 tablespoons oil

Seasonings:

1 teaspoon cumin seeds   ½ teaspoon paprika
1 teaspoon crushed garlic   ½ teaspoon red chili powder
1 teaspoon crushed ginger   1 teaspoon salt
¼ teaspoon turmeric powder   1 teaspoon garam masala
1 teaspoon coriander powder

Garnish: 1 tablespoon chopped green coriander

4. Heat the oil in a skillet on medium heat. Add cumin seeds. As they change color, add garlic and onions; stir until they are light brown.
5. Stir in tomatoes and remaining seasonings (except garam masala). Cook at low-medium heat for about 10 minutes. Add about 4 cups

water, enough to make it liquidy (liquid is later absorbed by the nuggets). Cook until the gravy is well mixed (about ½ hour).

6. Add the fried nuggets. Blend in garam masala. Cook for a couple of minutes. Garnish with green coriander. Leave covered for about ½ hour before serving.

Variation: Instead of steaming in a flat dish, tie the batter tightly in a thick cloth. (It looks like a ball of batter.) Put it in boiling water in a pot; cover and cook until the batter becomes hard (about 30 minutes).

Healthy Alternative: Instead of deep-frying, stir-fry the lentil nuggets in little oil. Add some yogurt to the gravy for creamy flavor.

Makes about 12 servings, ¾ cup each. Per serving –
Nutritive Value: 249 calories, 7 g protein, 17 g carb, 4 g fiber, 17 g fat, 0 mg chol.
Food Group Exchange: 1 Fat, ½ Legumes/Meat, ¼ Vegetable.

Cooking is like love.
It should be entered into with abandon
or not at all.

Harriet Van Horne

NAVRATNA (Nine Jewels) CURRY

This rich delicious main dish is like a gem in a formal dinner. It can be made in advance and refrigerated. Make fresh cheese (paneer) at home or buy from any Indian grocery store. Fry the cheese pieces and keep them in the freezer for use when needed.

20 oz. canned or frozen green peas
1 lb. chopped mushrooms
½ cup makhane (lotus puffs), rinsed
20 oz. can crushed tomatoes
1 lb. Ricotta cheese
½ cup chopped cashews
½ cup chopped blanched almonds
Paneer (fresh cheese pieces) made from ½ gallon whole or 2% fat milk
2 tablespoons oil

Seasonings:

3 tablespoons crushed ginger
1 teaspoon cumin seeds
1 teaspoon ground cinnamon
2 pods of large brown cardamoms
½ teaspoon ground black pepper
½ teaspoon turmeric powder

1 teaspoon coriander powder
¼ teaspoon asafetida powder
½ teaspoon red chili powder
2 teaspoons salt
2 teaspoons paprika

Garnish: 1 tablespoon chopped green coriander

1. Fry 'paneer' (fresh cheese pieces; see page 31), and keep them aside.
2. Heat the oil in a 4-quart pot on medium-high heat. Sauté ginger and cumin seeds (enjoy the delicate smell and aroma).
3. Add the remaining seasonings (except paprika). Cook for a few minutes; add peas, mushrooms, and 'makhane'.
4. When cooked (5–10 minutes), add the tomatoes and Ricotta cheese. Cook, stirring often, until the oil is separated and it is of semi-thick consistency (about 15 minutes). Add 1–2 cups water as needed.
5. Stir in the nuts. Add the fried cheese pieces. Cook for a couple of minutes. Mix in paprika. Serve garnished with green coriander. (Remove brown cardamoms before serving.)

Healthy Alternative: Use the cheese pieces without frying or use firm tofu.

Makes about 15 servings, ¾ cup each. Per serving –
Nutritive Value: 259 calories, 13 g protein, 15 g carb, 3 g fiber, 17 g fat, 14 mg chol.
Food Group Exchange: ¾ Vegetable, ¾ Dairy, ¼ Legumes/Meat, 1/8 Fat.

PALAK PANEER (Spinach & Cheese)

'Palak' or spinach is often combined and cooked with other ingredients. This popular main dish can be served in any formal setting and goes well with 'Nan'.

**20 oz. chopped (frozen or fresh) spinach
1 chopped onion
1 chopped tomato
4 oz. cream cheese (or sour cream)
Paneer (fresh cheese pieces) made from ½ gallon whole
or 2% fat milk
2 tablespoons oil**

Seasonings:

2 teaspoons crushed ginger
2 chopped green chilies
½ teaspoon turmeric powder
1 teaspoon salt
1 teaspoon crushed garlic

1 teaspoon cumin powder
1 teaspoon coriander powder
1 teaspoon red chili powder
1 teaspoon garam masala

1. Make 'paneer' (fresh cheese pieces; see page 31), and fry them. Keep them aside.
2. Cook spinach, onion, tomato, ginger, green chilies, turmeric powder and salt in one cup water for about 10 minutes, on medium heat. When little cold, blend everything together in the food processor or blender. Add more water as needed.
3. Heat the oil in a pan on medium heat. Add garlic; stir until light brown. Stir in cumin and coriander powder. Add cream cheese (or sour cream). Add the spinach mixture, red chili powder and garam masala; cook for 15 minutes.
4. Before serving, add the cheese pieces; serve hot.

Healthy Alternative: Use fresh cheese pieces without frying them. Or drain and cut firm tofu in small squares and add to the spinach.

Variation: Use creamed spinach instead of plain spinach; delete cream cheese or sour cream.

Makes about 12 servings, ½ cup each. Per serving –
Nutritive Value: 127 calories, 7 g protein, 4 g carb, 5 g fiber, 9 g fat, 5.5 mg chol.
Food Group Exchange: 1 Dairy, ½ Vegetable, ½ Fat.

RAJMAH (Curried Red Kidney Beans)

'Rajmah', an extremely popular dish, is like chili. It is generally served with rice. It can be frozen. Thaw in the refrigerator before using.

1 chopped onion
2 16-oz. cans of red kidney beans, drained
½ cup crushed tomatoes (fresh or canned)
1 tablespoon oil

Seasonings:

1 teaspoon chopped ginger	½ teaspoon red chili powder
1 teaspoon cumin powder	1 teaspoon garam masala
1 teaspoon coriander powder	½ teaspoon black pepper

Garnish: 2 tablespoons chopped green coriander

1. Heat the oil in a sauce–pan on medium–high heat. Add chopped onions and stir until they are translucent. Add ginger, cumin powder and coriander powder. Stir for a minute.
2. Add the tomatoes, kidney beans, and red chili powder. Add water as needed. Boil and let it simmer for 15 minutes until the gravy is thick. Add black pepper and garam masala to make it spicy.
3. Serve garnished with green coriander.

Variation: Substitute frozen or dry beans for canned beans. To cook dry beans, see *Dry Beans–Cooking* on page 30.

Makes about 8 servings, ¾ cup each. Per serving –
Nutritive Value: 121 calories, 6 g protein, 20 g carb, 8 g fiber, 2 g fat, 0 mg chol.
Food Group Exchange: 1 Legumes/Meat, ¼ Vegetable, 1/8 Fat.

ROASTED TOFU

In this dish you can also use 'paneer' (fresh cheese). Alter the seasonings to your taste.

**1 lb. firm tofu, drained and cut into 1"squares
about ½" thick
2 tablespoons plain yogurt**

Seasonings:

2 tablespoons chopped green coriander

3 tablespoons grated coconut

1 chopped green chili

½ teaspoon red chili powder

1 teaspoon salt

½ teaspoon black pepper

1 tablespoon lemon juice

1. Blend all the seasonings and yogurt together to make a paste.
2. Put the tofu pieces on aluminum foil in a baking dish. Spread the paste on the pieces. Wrap the foil around loosely and bake at 400°F for 15 minutes until cooked.
3. Open the foil and broil for 5–10 minutes for brownish look. Serve hot.

Variation: You can also roast the tofu in a wide skillet in 1 tablespoon of oil. Add the seasonings as desired. May use 'paneer' (fresh cheese) pieces instead of tofu.

Makes about 5 servings, ½ cup each. Per serving –
Nutritive Value: 68 calories, 7 g protein, 3 g carb, 1 g fiber, 4 g fat, 0 mg chol.
Food Group Exchange: 1 Legumes/Meat.

SAAG (Mixed Greens)

Leafy greens are perhaps the most nutrient–dense foods. This dish is very popular in North India. You can mix any greens, fresh or frozen, as you like. If buying fresh greens, discard limp and yellow leaves. Remember that greens usually cook down; 1 lb. may yield less than 2 cups cooked. It can easily be made in advance and refrigerated or frozen.

10 oz. chopped spinach (or collard greens)
10 oz. chopped broccoli rabe
20 oz. mustard greens
½ cup corn flour
½ cup green or dried fenugreek leaves (optional)
1 chopped tomato
1 tablespoon oil

Seasonings:

1 teaspoon salt	1 teaspoon coriander powder
1 tablespoon crushed garlic	½ teaspoon red chili powder
2 teaspoons chopped ginger	1 teaspoon garam masala
1 teaspoon cumin powder	½ teaspoon black pepper

1. If using fresh greens, trim and remove all fibrous material, and wash in a colander immersed in a large bowl filled with water; dirt will settle down. Remove the colander and throw away the water. Repeat until water is clear.
2. Chop or tear the leaves and boil them in about 3 cups of water and salt, on medium–high heat, for about 10 minutes until soft.
3. When little cool, give it a few rounds in the food processor or blender to make it smooth and creamy, adding corn flour, fenugreek leaves, and tomatoes. Add more water as needed.
4. Heat the oil in a 4–quart pot on medium–high heat. Add garlic. Add ginger, cumin powder and coriander powder. Stir for a minute. Stir in the cooked greens gradually (making sure there are no lumps). Add the remaining seasonings.
5. Cook, stirring occasionally, and let it simmer for 20 minutes until everything is mixed and 'Saag' is to your taste.

Variation: For creamier taste, mix 1 tbls. of butter or sour cream before serving.

Makes about 10 servings, ½ cup each. Per serving –
Nutritive Value: 65 calories, 4 g protein, 10 g carb, 3 g fiber, 2 g fat, 0 mg chol.
Food Group Exchange: 1 Vegetable, 1/8 Grain, 1/8 Fat.

SARSON kA SAAG (Mustard Greens)

This is a treat in cool winter months in North India. Traditionally, people sit in the sun, peel the mustard green stalks to remove fibrous material, chop it very fine, and then cook on low fire for long hours until creamy and smooth. You can use fresh or frozen mustard greens for this dish.

3 lb. mustard greens
1 cup Mung whole (green) or Moth whole (brown) dal
½ cup corn flour
1 tomato
2 cups buttermilk
2 tablespoons oil

Seasonings:

1 teaspoon salt	2 teaspoons cumin powder
1 teaspoon turmeric powder	2 teaspoons coriander powder
1 tablespoon crushed garlic	1 teaspoon red chili powder
2 chopped onions	2 teaspoons garam masala
3 teaspoons chopped ginger	1 teaspoon black pepper

1. If using fresh greens, trim and remove all fibrous material, wash until water runs clear, and chop. Check 'dal' for grit; and rinse.
2. Put the greens, 'dal', about 4 cups of water, salt, and turmeric in a large pot, and boil for about ½ hour on medium heat.
3. When little cool, give it a few rounds in the food processor or blender to make it smooth and creamy, adding corn flour and tomato. Add more water as needed.
4. Heat the oil in a 4-quart pot on medium–high heat. Sauté garlic and onions. Add ginger, cumin and coriander powder. Stir for a minute. Stir in the cooked mustard greens gradually (making sure there are no lumps) and cook for about 30 minutes. Add the remaining seasonings.
5. Mix in buttermilk slowly and let it cook on low-medium heat for about 15 minutes until everything is mixed and 'Saag' is to your taste.

Variation: For creamier taste, mix 1 tbls. of butter or sour cream before serving.

Makes about 15 servings, ½ cup each. Per serving –
Nutritive Value: 122 calories, 7 g protein, 19 g carb, 6 g fiber, 2.6 g fat, 1 mg chol.
Food Group Exchange: 1 Vegetable, ½ Legumes/Meat, 1/8 Grain, 1/8 Fat.

SINDHI BESAN KADHI (Gram Flour & Veggie Stew)

This is one of the regional dishes from India, served with rice. Traditionally drumsticks, a bean–like pod is used in this dish. You may substitute by long beans or artichokes.

½ cup gram flour (besan)
1 potato, chopped
1 small eggplant, chopped
1 cup green peas
3 chopped tomatoes
12 oz. can drumsticks
1 teaspoon tamarind paste
3 tablespoons oil

Seasonings:

½ teaspoon fenugreek seeds
½ teaspoon cumin seeds
1 teaspoon chopped ginger
1 teaspoon chopped green chili
1 teaspoon coriander powder
½ teaspoon turmeric powder

½ teaspoon red chili powder
1 teaspoon garam masala
½ teaspoon black pepper
1 tbls. fresh or dry fenugreek leaves
2 teaspoons salt

1. Heat the oil in a 4–quart pot on medium-high heat. Sauté fenugreek seeds. As soon as they brown (couple of seconds), stir in cumin seeds, ginger and green chilies.
2. Immediately add gram flour; stir on low-medium heat until gram flour is golden brown (10–15 minutes). (it is a wonderful smell of roasted gram flour.)
3. Lower the heat to low. Add about 4 cups water slowly, while stirring, taking care not to make any lumps. Increase the heat to medium. When the mixture starts boiling, add potatoes, eggplant, salt, coriander powder, turmeric powder, and red chili powder; simmer partially covered.
4. Add the remaining vegetables; simmer (for about ½ hour); stirring occasionally, until it becomes semi-thick consistency. Add water as needed.
5. Stir in tamarind and the remaining seasonings; cook another 10-15 minutes.

Healthy Alternative: To reduce oil, roast the gram flour in oven before using.

Makes about 10 servings, about ¾ cup each. Per serving –
Nutritive Value: 107 calories, 3.6 g protein, 14 g carb, 4 g fiber, 5 g fat, 0 mg chol.
Food Group Exchange: 1 Vegetable, ¼ Legumes/Meat, ¼ Fat.

STUFFED BELL PEPPERS

Look for shiny green peppers (also known as capsicums) of medium size for this dish. You may make the filling and stuff the peppers in advance. Bake them when ready to serve.

6 medium green bell–peppers
1 chopped onion
4 boiled potatoes, peeled & mashed
3 tablespoons oil

Seasonings:

1 teaspoon crushed ginger	1 teaspoon crushed green chilies
1 teaspoon cumin powder	½ teaspoon turmeric
1 teaspoon coriander powder	½ teaspoon red chili powder
1½ teaspoons salt	1 teaspoon mango powder
1 teaspoon tamarind paste mixed in 2 tablespoons water	1 tablespoon chopped green coriander

1. Remove the stem and rinse the bell peppers. Microwave them for 4 minutes to make them little soft. Cut them half lengthwise; remove seeds.
2. For stuffing, heat 1 tablespoon oil in a small pot on medium-high heat. Sauté the onions until translucent. Stir in ginger, cumin and coriander powder, and salt. Add tamarind paste mixed in water, mashed potatoes, and the remaining seasonings. Cook, while stirring for about 5 minutes. Let it cool.
3. Stuff each half of bell-pepper with 2–3 tablespoons of potato stuffing, making a neat, round mound. Brush the remaining oil all around the stuffed peppers and place them, stuffing side up, in a baking pan.
4. Bake at 375°F for 30–40 minutes, until the stuffing turns light brown and the peppers are cooked. Serve hot.

Makes about 12 servings, one piece each. Per serving –
Nutritive Value:83 calories, 1.5 g protein, 12 g carb, 2 g fiber, 3.6 g fat, 0 mg chol.
Food Group Exchange: ½ Grain, ½ Vegetable, ¼ Fat.

STUFFED EGGPLANTS

Eggplants are known by different names. In India, they are called brinjal or 'baingan', and in some countries they are called aubergine. There are several ways to cook them. Small eggplants are used in this dish.

2 lb. small eggplants, thin long or round
1 teaspoon tamarind paste mixed in 2 tablespoons
warm water
3 tablespoons oil

Seasonings:

1 teaspoon crushed garlic
1 medium chopped onion
1 teaspoon crushed ginger
1 teaspoon crushed green chilies
1 teaspoon coriander powder

2 teaspoons salt
½ teaspoon turmeric
½ teaspoon red chili powder
1 tablespoon chopped green coriander
1 teaspoon each of poppy seeds, sesame seeds and coconut flakes (slightly roasted and ground)

1. Remove the stem and rinse the eggplants. Make a slit lengthwise.
2. Heat a small pot on medium–high heat. Sauté garlic and onion in 1 tablespoon oil until translucent. Stir in ginger, green chilies, coriander powder and salt. Add tamarind paste mixed in water and the remaining seasonings; cook, while stirring for about 10 minutes until the filling is smooth and paste–like consistency. Add water as needed.
3. Fill the eggplants through the slit with the prepared mixture (masala).
4. Put the remaining oil in a large skillet on low-medium heat. Place the stuffed eggplants in a single layer and cook, turning them gently with a spatula to make sure all the sides are cooked (about 20 minutes). Add about one cup water, as needed.
5. Pour any leftover 'masala' over the eggplants. Mix gently; serve hot.

Variation: If you want to skip stuffing, cut eggplants in long thick pieces, stir fry for 5 minutes and then add the seasonings as described and cook.

Makes about 12 servings, 2 pieces each. Per serving –
Nutritive Value: 44 calories, 1 g protein, 3 g carb, 1 g fiber, 3.5 g fat, 0 mg chol.
Food Group Exchange: 1 Vegetable, ¼ Fat.

STUFFED GHIYA (Bottle Gourd)

The most popular Indian squash is 'ghiya' (or 'loki' or 'dhudi'). Also called Italian squash, it is pale green and long (2–4 ft), with nutty flavor, more like zucchini. This makes a festive dish. It can be made in advance and frozen.

1 long ghiya, about 3 lb.
2 tablespoons oil

Seasonings:

1 teaspoon crushed ginger	2 teaspoons salt
1 teaspoon crushed green chilies	½ teaspoon turmeric
1 teaspoon cumin powder	½ teaspoon red chili powder
2 teaspoons coriander powder	1 teaspoon garam masala
½ teaspoon mango powder	

1. Remove stem, rinse, and peel the 'ghiya'. Cut it in half lengthwise. Remove any seeds. Cut each half in ½" thick slices. Using a paring knife, make a slit on the flat end of each slice, leaving sides and bottom intact.
2. Mix all the seasonings to make the stuffing. Fill the slit with the stuffing using a spoon or with your fingers. Stuff all the pieces.
3. Heat a wide skillet on medium heat. Put oil. Place the pieces in the skillet almost in a single layer. (Cook in batches if necessary.) When lightly brown at bottom, flip gently so that stuffing does not come out. Brown the other side too. Sprinkle little water or tomato sauce if needed. Serve hot.

Makes about 12 servings, 2 pieces each. Per serving –
Nutritive Value: 44 calories, 1 g protein, 3 g carb, 1 g fiber, 3.5 g fat, 0 mg chol.
Food Group Exchange: 1 Vegetable, ¼ Fat.

STUFFED MUSHROOMS

Serve them as a snack or a side dish. Choose any other vegetable such as grated cabbage or carrots for stuffing. Baby–bella mushrooms work well in this recipe.

20 oz. medium–large fresh mushrooms
10 oz. creamed spinach
½ cup seasoned bread crumbs
½ cup grated Parmesan cheese
1 teaspoon oil

1. Rinse the mushrooms under cold running water and pat dry. Remove stems from the mushrooms as close to the caps as possible.
2. Chop the stems. Heat the oil in a small skillet; sauté chopped stems for about 5 minutes. Add creamed spinach and cook for another 5 minutes. Turn off the heat and mix in bread crumbs and cheese to the filling.
3. Hold each mushroom in your hand and fill with 1–2 tablespoons of stuffing, making a neat, round mound. Repeat with remaining mushrooms, placing them, stuffing side up, in a baking pan.
4. Bake at 350°F for 20–30 minutes or until the stuffing turns light brown and the mushrooms begin to give up their liquid.
5. Serve hot or at room temperature; can be reheated in the oven or microwave.

Healthy Alternative: For filling use any combination of vegetables or potatoes with some yogurt cheese or sour cream.

Makes about 10 servings, 2 pieces each. Per serving –
Nutritive Value: 84 calories, 5.6 g protein, 9 g carb, 1.5 g fiber, 3 g fat, 4 mg chol.
Food Group Exchange: 1 Vegetable, ¼ Dairy, 1/8 Grain, 1/8 Fat.

TANDOORI SPICY VEGETABLES

'Tandoori' means from the oven. This dish fits the busy lifestyle perfectly, especially when you have to make larger quantities. The baked look is very appealing too. Use frozen veggies as desired. You may make it in advance and refrigerate.

4 medium size potatoes
3 carrots
½ head of cauliflower
1 cup green beans
3 bell peppers
½ eggplant
1 chopped onion
2 tablespoons oil

Seasonings:

2 teaspoons cumin seeds	2 teaspoons coriander powder
1 teaspoon minced garlic	½ teaspoon paprika
2 teaspoons crushed ginger	½ teaspoon red chili powder
1 teaspoon crushed green chili	1 teaspoon salt
½ teaspoon turmeric powder	1 teaspoon garam masala

1. Wash and peel (or scrub) the potatoes. Cut into small pieces and microwave them, covered, for about 6 minutes until half–cooked. Prepare and cut all other vegetables into small pieces.
2. Heat the oil in a saucepan on medium heat. Sauté cumin seeds, garlic and onions; stir until onions are translucent.
3. Put the potatoes and vegetables in a large baking dish. Mix in the sautéed spices and the remaining seasonings (except garam masala). Bake covered at 400°F until the vegetables are tender (about ½ hour). (Stir the vegetables in between and sprinkle water if necessary.)
4. Bake uncovered at 450°F for another 10 minutes to get a roasted look. Stir in garam masala. Garnish as desired and serve.

Variation: Stir in 1 tablespoon of butter or clarified butter (ghee) for flavor before serving.

Microwave Method: Cook the vegetables in the microwave oven, covered, for 10–12 minutes. Then combine everything else and put in the oven as in step 4 for a roasted look.

Healthy Alternative: Add a chopped tomato towards the end.

Makes about 16 servings, ½ cup each. Per serving –
Nutritive Value: 71 calories, 2 g protein, 12 g carb, 3 g fiber, 2 g fat, 0 mg chol.
Food Group Exchange: 1 Vegetable, ¼ Grain, 1/8 Fat.

TOFU with VEGETABLES

Tofu, a protein-rich food, can be used in a variety of ways. Sliced and sautéed with vegetables; it adds to the texture of the dish. You may substitute or combine other vegetables such as broccoli and mushrooms. Use this as a side dish or in sandwiches.

**1 lb. firm tofu, drained and cut into ½" cubes
1 cup chopped onion
1 cup diced carrots
1 cup diced green and red bell–peppers
1 cup green peas
1 tablespoon oil**

Seasonings:

½ teaspoon crushed ginger	1 teaspoon salt
1 chopped green chili	½ teaspoon black pepper
½ teaspoon red chili powder	1 teaspoon lemon juice

1. Heat the oil in a skillet on medium heat. Sauté the onions until translucent.
2. Add the carrots; stir for a few minutes. Add peas, red and green bell peppers (or other vegetables) and the seasonings (except lemon juice); cook until the vegetables are tender (about 10 minutes), stirring occasionally.
3. Mix in the tofu cubes and cook for a couple of minutes to let tofu absorb the flavors. Sprinkle lemon juice. Serve hot.

Variation: Instead of lemon juice, use soy sauce that gives a different aroma and darker color. You may use frozen tofu, well drained.

*Makes about 8 servings, ½ cup each. Per serving –
Nutritive Value: 84 calories, 6 g protein, 8 g carb, 2.6 g fiber, 3.5 g fat, 0 mg chol.
Food Group Exchange: ½ Legumes/Meat, ¾ Vegetable, 1/8 Fat.*

TOMATO CUPS

This is a delicious decorative side dish suitable for any dinner. Make them in advance and bake before serving.

6 medium size firm tomatoes
½ onion, chopped
2–3 potatoes, boiled and mashed
½ cup green peas
1 cup shredded Mozzarella cheese
¼ cup bread crumbs
1 tablespoon oil + oil to coat tomatoes

Seasonings:

1 teaspoon crushed green chili
½ teaspoon cumin powder
½ teaspoon coriander powder

½ teaspoon red chili powder
½ teaspoon black pepper
1 teaspoon salt

1. Slice off tops of the tomatoes; scoop out some pulp, leaving the shell intact.
2. Heat the oil in a skillet on medium heat. Sauté onions until translucent. Add all the seasonings; stir for a minute. Stir in the tomato pulp, mashed potatoes and peas.
3. Cook until the vegetables are tender (about 5 minutes). Turn off the heat. Mix in bread crumbs and Mozzarella cheese.
4. Fill the tomato shells with the mixture and place in a greased baking sheet. Brush oil on top; bake at 400°F until the tomatoes are tender (about 15 minutes). Serve hot.

Healthy Alternative: Use yogurt cheese or sour cream instead of Mozzarella cheese.

Makes 6 servings, one piece each. Per serving –
Nutritive Value: 155 calories, 9 g protein, 20 g carb, 3 g fiber, 5 g fat, 1.7 mg chol.
Food Group Exchange: 1 Vegetable, ½ Grain, 1/3 Dairy, ¼ Fat.

VEGETABLE KOFTA (Balls)

This is a delicious, fancy main dish that goes very well with rice or some kind of bread. It almost looks like meatballs. Make the 'koftas' (balls) in advance and freeze them. Put them in the curry when needed.

Vegetable Balls:

1 small head cabbage or 2 lb. bottle gourd (ghiya), grated
2–3 carrots, grated
¼ cup finely chopped almonds or peanuts
2–3 cups gram flour (besan), sifted
Oil to fry (about 2" deep in a wok)

Seasonings:

½ bunch chopped green coriander   ½ teaspoon salt
½ teaspoon red chili powder or
chopped green chilies

1. Squeeze the vegetables to remove excess water. Mix all the ingredients and seasonings to make hard batter that can be shaped. Let it rest for about ½ hour. Mix again and refrigerate for easier handling. (Add more gram flour as needed.)
2. Break the dough–like batter into walnut size round balls (about 40).
3. Deep–fry in a deep skillet or wok on high heat, turning, until golden brown on all sides. (If the balls break, dip them in a solution of 1 tablespoon of gram flour and 1/3 cup water before frying.) At this point, you may freeze these balls for later use.

Gravy:

2 medium size onions finely chopped or crushed
½ cup crushed tomatoes
½ cup heavy cream
2 tablespoons oil

Seasonings:

1 teaspoon crushed garlic   1 teaspoon crushed poppy seeds
1 teaspoon crushed ginger   ½ teaspoon paprika
1 teaspoon cumin powder   ½ teaspoon red chili powder
½ teaspoon turmeric powder   1+ teaspoon salt
1 teaspoon coriander powder   1 teaspoon garam masala

Garnish: 1 tablespoon chopped green coriander

4. Heat the oil in a pot on medium-high heat. Add garlic and onions; stir until they are light brown. Stir in the remaining seasonings (except garam masala). Add tomatoes; Cook at low-medium heat for about 10 minutes.
5. Add 4 cups water to make it liquidy (liquid is later absorbed by the vegetable balls). Cook until the gravy is well mixed (20–30 minutes), adding more water as needed. Blend in heavy cream and garam masala.
6. To serve, arrange the vegetable balls in a serving dish. (If frozen, thaw at room temperature, not in the microwave because they may break.) About 10 minutes before serving, pour very hot gravy on top so that the vegetable balls soak. Keep the dish warm in the oven. Garnish with green coriander. *Note:* If the vegetable balls appear hard, boil them in the gravy for a few minutes.

Healthy Alternative: Use yogurt or sour cream instead of heavy cream.

Variation: Also add some grated cauliflower. May use corn flour instead of gram flour.

Makes about 20 servings, ¾ cup each. Per serving –
Nutritive Value: 226 calories, 4 g protein, 11 g carb, 3 g fiber, 19 g fat, 8 mg chol.
Food Group Exchange: 1.5 Fat, ½ Legumes/Meat, ½ Vegetable.

VEGETABLE MEDLEY

Grated vegetables are used in this tasty side dish. You may use just one vegetable or a mix. It can be served as a snack too with crackers.

1 head cauliflower
2 carrots
1 tablespoon oil

Seasonings:

1 teaspoon mustard seeds
2 teaspoons Urad split
peeled dal
½ teaspoon red chili powder

1 teaspoon crushed ginger
2 teaspoons salt
2 teaspoons lemon juice

Garnish: 1 tablespoon chopped green coriander leaves

1. Trim and grate the cauliflower and carrots. Heat the oil in a skillet on medium-high heat. Add mustard seeds. Cover the pot. As soon as the seeds start to pop, add the Urad dal. Add the remaining seasonings except lemon juice. Stir for a few seconds until 'dal' is golden brown.
2. Stir in the grated vegetables. Cook until they are tender but crisp, 5–10 minutes. Mix in lemon juice. Serve hot, garnished with green coriander leaves.

Variation: Use other vegetables such as cabbage and turnips. May use a few 'wadi' (dried lentil drops) pieces in the sauté.

Makes about 10 servings, ½ cup each. Per serving –
Nutritive Value: 43 calories, 1.5 g protein, 7 g carb, 2.6 g fiber, 1.6 g fat, 0 mg chol.
Food Group Exchange: 1 Vegetable, 1/8 Fat.

VEGETARIAN CHILI

This main dish combines a number of vegetables and beans. Mix them to your liking.

2 cups diced peeled eggplant
1 cup diced zucchini
1 cup diced carrots
1 cup diced green and red bell peppers
1 cup diced trimmed green beans
2 cups chopped tomatoes
3 cups cooked chickpeas or red kidney beans
½ cup plain yogurt
2 tablespoons oil

Seasonings:

1 teaspoon crushed garlic
1 cup chopped onion
1 teaspoon red chili powder
1 teaspoon cumin powder

1 teaspoon salt
½ teaspoon black pepper
2 chopped green chilies

Garnish: 1 tablespoon chopped green coriander

1. Heat the oil in a large saucepan on medium heat. Add garlic and onions. Cook until the onions are translucent.
2. Add the red chili powder and cumin powder; stir for a minute. Reduce the heat to low, add all the vegetables (except tomatoes), salt and pepper, and cook for 10 minutes, stirring occasionally.
3. Increase the heat to medium; add the tomatoes, green chilies, yogurt, beans and about one cup water. Boil and let them simmer for 30–40 minutes until the gravy is thick. Add more water if needed.
4. Serve hot garnished with green coriander.

Makes about 12 servings, ¾ cup each. Per serving –
Nutritive Value: 109 calories, 4 g protein, 16 g carb, 5 g fiber, 9 g fat, 0 mg chol.
Food Group Exchange: ½ Legumes/Meat, 1 Vegetable, 1/8 Fat.

Fish, Poultry, Meat and Eggs

Vegetarianism is a way of life in Indian culture but by no means are all Indians vegetarian. Fish (macchali in Hindi) with rice is common food in the coastal areas of India. Chicken (murga in Hindi) and lamb (bakra in Hindi) are more popular in the northern states. Spices add an aroma of their own to the meat preparations. Some popular non-vegetarian dishes include Curried Chicken and Biryani. (Also see "Kabob" under Snacks.) You can adapt the recipes, especially the seasonings, to your taste and convenience. For information on the seasonings, refer to the chapter *Ingredients and Terms*.

To help plan nutritious meals, each recipe gives nutritive value (calories, protein, carbohydrate (carb), fiber, fat, and cholesterol (chol)), and Food Group Exchange for a helping of the dish. Estimate is rounded off for ease of understanding. Garnishes, topping and small amounts of seasoning are not accounted for. (See page 13 for basis of estimating Food Group Exchange and nutritive value.)

Abbreviations:

carb: carbohydrate,	chol: cholesterol,	F: Fahrenheit,
g: gram,	lb: pound,	med: medium,
mg: milligram,	oz: ounce.	

BAKED FISH

This spicy delicious fish is served with rice, bread and vegetables. You may make it in advance and refrigerate.

1¼ lb. smelt (small fish)
1 medium onion chopped
1 teaspoon tamarind paste mixed with 1 cup water
2 teaspoons oil

Seasonings:

½ teaspoon turmeric powder
2 teaspoons salt
1 teaspoon crushed garlic
1 teaspoon crushed ginger

1 teaspoon crushed green chilies
1 teaspoon coriander powder
½ teaspoon red chili powder
1 teaspoon each of poppy seeds,
sesame seeds and coconut flakes
(slightly roasted and ground)

Garnish: 1 tablespoon chopped green coriander

1. Remove eyes and tail of fish; rinse. Marinate in turmeric powder and 1 teaspoon salt for 15 minutes. Discard the marinade.
2. To prepare 'masala' (the spiced mixture), heat the oil in a skillet on medium-high heat. Sauté garlic and onions until translucent. Stir in ginger, green chilies, coriander powder, red chili powder, and salt. After about 30 seconds, add tamarind paste mixed with water and the remaining seasonings. Cook, while stirring for about 15 minutes.
3. Put the fish in a baking dish. Pour the prepared 'masala' over the fish. Bake at 375°F for 20 minutes (water will be absorbed). Mix gently and serve hot garnished with green coriander.

Makes about 7 servings, ½ cup each. Per serving –
Nutritive Value: 99 calories, 14 g protein, 2 g carb, 0 g fiber, 3 g fat, 57 mg chol.
Food Group Exchange: 1 Legumes/Meat, 1/8 Vegetable, 1/8 Fat.

BIRYANI (Rice with Chicken or Lamb)

This main dish, a blend of meat, rice and spices, could tickle anybody's taste-buds. It is best made fresh. Refrigerate the left–overs and warm in the microwave, covered, before serving. It goes well with yogurt and vegetables.

2½ lb. boneless chicken breast or pieces (or lamb)
4 tablespoons plain yogurt
3 cups Basmati rice
3 medium onions (chopped lengthwise)
2 tablespoons oil

Seasonings:

2 teaspoons crushed garlic
½ teaspoon crushed ginger
1 teaspoon crushed green chilies

1 tablespoon garam masala
1 teaspoon red chili powder
2 teaspoons salt

1. Cut the chicken (or lamb) into small pieces. Make a mixture of yogurt and seasonings, using 1 teaspoon salt. Marinate the chicken in the mixture for minimum 3 hours in the refrigerator.
2. Check the rice for any foreign matter; rinse. Bring the rice to a boil, in 5 cups water and 1 teaspoon salt; let it simmer on low heat, covered, about 10 minutes. Remove from the heat before completely cooked. Drain excess water if any; keep aside.
3. Heat the oil in a large pot; brown the onions and remove them from oil. To the same pot, add the marinated chicken (or lamb) along with the marinade and cook until almost done. Spread half the rice over the chicken, then browned onions, and then the remaining rice.
4. Cook, covered, on low-medium heat until the rice and chicken are done (about 20 minutes). Serve hot.

Makes about 18 servings, ½ cup each. Per serving –
Nutritive Value:197 calories, 16 g protein, 24 g carb, 2 g fiber, 4 g fat, 44 mg chol.
Food Group Exchange: ¾ Grain, ¾ Legumes/Meat, ¼ Vegetable, 1/8 Fat.

BLACK PEPPER CHICKEN

This spicy delicious chicken is served with rice, bread, and vegetables. It can be made in advance and frozen or refrigerated.

12 chicken pieces (preferably thighs)
2 medium onions (chopped in big pieces)
2 tablespoons plain yogurt
1 teaspoon lemon juice
2 tablespoons ground cashews
1 tablespoon ground almonds

Seasonings:
1 teaspoon crushed garlic
½ teaspoon crushed ginger
1 teaspoon crushed green chilies
1 teaspoon coriander powder

½ teaspoon turmeric powder
½ teaspoon red chili powder
1 teaspoon black pepper
1 teaspoon salt

To sauté and cook:
3 tablespoons oil
1 teaspoon mustard seeds
½ teaspoon cumin seeds
2 bay leaves

2 cups buttermilk
1 tablespoon chopped green coriander
1 teaspoon garam masala

1. Clean and skin the chicken. Make a mixture of all the ingredients and seasonings; marinate the chicken in the mixture for 15–20 minutes.
2. To sauté, heat a pot on medium–high heat. Add the oil. Put mustard seeds, cumin seeds, and bay leaves. As soon as they change color, add the marinated chicken along with the marinade. Keep stirring for 5–10 minutes until the spices become golden brown.
3. Add the buttermilk and green coriander. Cook the chicken, partially covered, on low-medium heat until the chicken is done (about 15 minutes). Stir in garam masala. Serve hot.

Healthy Alternative: Reduce or eliminate the oil in the sauté.

Makes about 12 servings, 1 piece each. Per serving –
Nutritive Value: 195 calories, 12 g protein, 4.6 g carb, 0.4 g fiber, 14 g fat, 49 mg chol.
Food Group Exchange: 1 Legumes/Meat, ¼ Vegetable, 1/6 Dairy, ¼ Fat.

CHICKEN-TOMATO KEEMA

This dish is made from ground meat. It is easy to mix vegetables in it. Goes well with 'Nan' and rice. It can be made in advance and frozen or refrigerated.

1¼ lb. ground chicken
1 medium onion chopped or crushed
2 large tomatoes chopped
2 teaspoons oil

Seasonings:

1 teaspoon mustard seeds	½ teaspoon turmeric powder
½ teaspoon cumin seeds	½ teaspoon red chili powder
1 teaspoon crushed garlic	1 teaspoon black pepper
½ teaspoon crushed ginger	1 teaspoon salt
1 teaspoon crushed green chilies	1 teaspoon garam masala
1 teaspoon coriander powder	1 tablespoon chopped green coriander

1. Rinse the chicken. Heat the oil in a pot on medium–high heat. Sauté mustard seeds and cumin seeds. Stir in garlic and onions; cook until translucent.
2. Add the chicken and remaining seasonings (except garam masala and green coriander). Add the tomatoes after 5 minutes. Cook, adding about one cup water as needed and stirring, for about 25 minutes.
3. Add garam masala and green coriander. Cook for another 5–10 minutes. Serve hot.

Variation: Use any other ground meat the same way. Can add ¾ cup green peas, grated cauliflower, or pureed spinach along with chicken for color and texture.

Makes about 6 servings, ½ cup each. Per serving –
Nutritive Value: 136 calories, 22 g protein, 4.4 g carb, 1 g fiber, 3.3 g fat, 54 mg chol.
Food Group Exchange: 1 Legumes/Meat, ½ Vegetable, 1/8 Fat.

CURRIED CHICKEN

This is the most popular way to prepare chicken. You can use boneless chicken or that with bones. It can be made in advance and frozen or refrigerated.

2½ lb. chicken (breast or pieces)
2 medium onions finely chopped or crushed
1 large tomato chopped
2 tablespoons oil

Seasonings:

1 tablespoon crushed garlic	1 teaspoon salt
1 teaspoon turmeric powder	1 teaspoon garam masala
½ teaspoon red chili powder	1 teaspoon black cumin seeds

Garnish: 2 tablespoons chopped green coriander

1. Rinse the chicken and cut into small pieces. Heat the oil in a pot on medium heat. Sauté the onions and garlic until translucent. Add turmeric and red chili powder. Sprinkle little water, as needed, to cook all the spices.
2. Add the chicken and salt. While stirring, add tomatoes. After 5–6 minutes, add about ½ cup water and let the chicken cook, partially covered, on low-medium heat until it is done (about 20 minutes).
3. Stir in garam masala and black cumin seeds. Serve hot garnished with green coriander.

Variation: To make it richer, use boneless chicken. Add ½ cup heavy cream when chicken is almost cooked. Cook for only 5 minutes after adding heavy cream.

Healthy Alternative: Add 1 large chopped potato and 1 cup green peas along with chicken. Reduce or eliminate the oil in the sauté.

Makes about 12 servings, ½ cup each. Per serving –
Nutritive Value: 143 calories, 20 g protein, 2 g carb, 0.5 g fiber, 5 g fat, 66 mg chol.
Food Group Exchange: 1 Legumes/Meat, ¼ Vegetable, 1/6 Fat.

EGG CURRY

Make this curry using hard boiled eggs. It is delicious and very festive.

4 eggs, hard boiled
1 cup frozen (or fresh) green peas
½ cup tomato puree (canned or fresh)
1 tablespoon oil

<u>Seasonings</u>:

1 onion chopped
1 teaspoon grated ginger
½ teaspoon cumin powder
1 teaspoon coriander powder
½ teaspoon turmeric powder
½ teaspoon paprika

½ teaspoon ground black pepper
½ teaspoon red chili powder
½ teaspoon crushed green chili
1 teaspoon salt
1 teaspoon garam masala

<u>Garnish</u>: 1 tablespoon chopped green coriander

1. Peel the boiled eggs and make a couple of slits, without breaking the eggs.
2. Heat the oil in a pan on medium-high heat. Add chopped onion and stir until they are light brown. Add ginger, cumin powder, coriander powder and peas. Cook, while stirring, for a few minutes until the peas are little tender.
3. Add the tomatoes and remaining seasonings (except garam masala). Stir; cook for about 5 minutes, adding 1 cup water as needed.
4. Add the eggs and let them cook for another 5 minutes and absorb the flavors. Mix in garam masala. Serve garnished with green coriander.

Variation: May also add 2 boiled potatoes along with peas.

Makes 4 servings, 1 piece each. Per serving –
Nutritive Value: 144 calories, 8 g protein, 9 g carb, 2 g fiber, 8 g fat, 187 mg chol.
Food Group Exchange: 1 Legumes/Meat, 1 Vegetable, ¼ Fat.

FISH-DO-PIAZZA

This is a popular dish with lot of onions and tomatoes ('piazz' means onions). You may increase the quantity of onions.

1½ lb. cod fish or halibut
3 medium onions chopped
2 cups crushed tomatoes
2 tablespoons oil

<u>Seasonings</u>:

2 teaspoons crushed garlic
½ teaspoon crushed ginger
1 teaspoon crushed green chilies
1 tablespoon coriander powder
2 teaspoons cumin powder

½ teaspoon red chili powder
1 teaspoon salt
½ teaspoon black pepper
½ teaspoon saffron mixed in
1 tablespoon warm water

<u>Garnish</u>: 2 tablespoons chopped green coriander

1. Clean the fish and chop into small cubes. Heat the oil in a skillet on medium heat. Sauté garlic and onions until they are light brown. Stir in the remaining seasonings (except saffron and black pepper); stir for a couple of minutes.
2. Add the tomatoes and black pepper; cook until the oil seems to be separate from the cooking herbs and seasonings. Add fish; stir for 3–4 minutes.
3. Add saffron mixed with water. Cover and simmer on low-medium heat until the fish is done (about 15 minutes). Add about ½ cup water as needed.
4. Serve hot garnished with green coriander.

Note: To make **CHICKEN-DO-PIAZZA,** substitute chicken for fish. Also add 2–3 chopped potatoes along with chicken. Mash the potatoes to get thick gravy. Chicken and potatoes take about 45 minutes to cook.

Makes about 8 servings, ½ cup each. Per serving –
Nutritive Value: 156 calories, 19 g protein, 7 g carb, 2 g fiber, 5.6 g fat, 27 mg chol.
Food Group Exchange: 1 Legumes/Meat, 1 Vegetable, ¼ Fat.

HYDERABADI CHICKEN

This dish has wonderful aroma, using some regional ingredients such as coconut. It can be made in advance and frozen or refrigerated.

**4 legs and 4 thighs of chicken
1 medium onion chopped
2 tablespoons plain yogurt
3 tablespoons grated coconut
1 large tomato chopped
2 tablespoons oil**

<u>Seasonings</u>:

1 teaspoon crushed garlic
½ teaspoon crushed ginger
1 teaspoon crushed green chilies
1 teaspoon coriander powder
¼ teaspoon turmeric powder

½ teaspoon red chili powder
1 tablespoon ground poppy seeds
1 teaspoon salt
1 teaspoon garam masala

<u>Garnish</u>: 2 tablespoons chopped green coriander

1. Clean and skin the chicken. Heat the oil in a skillet on medium heat. Sauté garlic and onions until translucent. Add ginger, green chilies, coriander powder, turmeric powder, red chili powder and the chicken.
2. While stirring, after 3–4 minutes, gradually add yogurt, coconut, poppy seeds, and salt. Stir in the tomatoes. Cook everything, partially covered, on low-medium heat, adding about one cup water as needed, until the chicken is done (about 20 minutes).
3. Stir in garam masala. Serve hot garnished with green coriander.

Makes about 8 servings, ½ cup each. Per serving –
Nutritive Value: 194 calories, 18 g protein, 3 g carb, 0.7 g fiber, 12 g fat, 77 mg chol.
Food Group Exchange: 1 Legumes/Meat, ¼ Vegetable, ¼ Fat.

LAMB CURRY

This spicy delicious lamb is served with rice or bread. It can be made in advance and frozen or refrigerated.

1¼ lb. lamb (shank or leg)
1 medium onion chopped
1 cup crushed tomatoes
2 tablespoons oil

Seasonings:

2 garlic cloves
1" piece ginger
1 green chili
1 teaspoon cumin powder

1 teaspoon coriander powder
½ teaspoon turmeric powder
½ teaspoon red chili powder
2 teaspoons salt (to taste)

Garnish: 1 tablespoon chopped green coriander

1. Rinse the lamb and cut into cubes. Blend onions, garlic, ginger and green chili in the blender to make a paste.
2. Heat the oil in a pot on medium heat. Sauté the paste for 5–10 minutes until it is light brown and the oil appears to be separated. Stir in the remaining seasonings.
3. Add the lamb; cook, while stirring for about 15 minutes. Add tomatoes and about 2 cups water; cook for another 15 minutes.
4. Serve hot garnished with green coriander.

Healthy Alternative: Double the quantity of onions and garlic. Add some chopped spinach along with lamb. Reduce or eliminate the oil.

Makes about 8 servings, ½ cup each. Per serving –
Nutritive Value: 191 calories, 14 g protein, 4 g carb, 1 g fiber, 13 g fat, 47.5 mg chol.
Food Group Exchange: 1 Legumes/Meat, ¾ Vegetable, ¼ Fat.

Our body is 70% water and needs 8 to 10 glasses every day to avoid dehydration.

MEATBALLS CURRY

Serve this spicy delicious curry with rice. Meatballs can be made in advance and frozen.

1 lb. ground meat (turkey, chicken, or any other)
1 egg
½ cup bread crumbs

Seasonings:

2 teaspoons onion powder
½ teaspoon red chili powder

1 teaspoon salt (to taste)

1. Combine everything together to make a stiff mixture that can be made into small balls.
2. Place the balls in a wide skillet on medium heat. Brown them in their own fat, turning to cook on all sides. *Note:* You may bake them in 350°F oven for about 15 minutes.

To Make Curry:

2 medium size onions finely chopped or crushed
½ cup crushed tomatoes
2 tablespoons oil

Seasonings:

1 teaspoon crushed garlic
½ teaspoon cumin seeds
1 teaspoon crushed ginger
½ teaspoon turmeric powder
1 teaspoon coriander powder

1 teaspoon crushed poppy seeds
½ teaspoon paprika
½ teaspoon red chili powder
1+ teaspoon salt
1 teaspoon garam masala

Garnish: 1 tablespoon chopped green coriander

3. Heat the oil in a pan on medium–high heat. Add garlic and cumin seeds. Stir for a couple of seconds; add onions; stir until they are light brown.
4. Stir in the tomatoes and remaining seasonings (except garam masala). Cook at medium heat for about 10 minutes. Add about 2 cups water to make the curry. Cook until the curry is well mixed (about 20 minutes). Blend in garam masala.

5. To serve, arrange the meatballs in a serving dish. (If they are frozen, thaw in the refrigerator. Do not thaw in the microwave because they may break.) About 20 minutes before serving, pour very hot gravy on the meatballs. Garnish and keep warm.

Healthy Alternative: Add some green peas and potatoes to the curry.

Variation: When making meatballs, add 1 cup cooked wild rice instead of bread crumbs.

Makes about 10 servings, ½ cup each. Per serving –
Nutritive Value: 130 calories, 10 g protein, 6.4 g carb, 0.6 g fiber, 7.4 g fat, 54.5 mg chol.
Food Group Exchange: 1 Legumes/Meat, 1/3 Vegetable, ¼ Fat.

TANDOORI CHICKEN

'Tandoori' means 'from the oven'. This chicken is a specialty of Indian cuisine; it can be used as a snack or a main dish. It can be made in advance and frozen or refrigerated.

6 chicken pieces (thighs and legs)
4 tablespoons plain yogurt
2 tablespoons tomato paste
2 onions finely chopped
1 tablespoon oil

Seasonings:
2 teaspoons crushed garlic
2 teaspoons crushed ginger
1 tablespoon lemon juice

1½ teaspoons coriander powder
1½ teaspoons cumin powder
½ teaspoon red chili powder

¼ teaspoon clove powder
¼ teaspoon cinnamon powder
½ teaspoon cardamom powder or nutmeg
½ teaspoon paprika
1 teaspoon salt (to taste)

Garnish:
1 onion chopped lengthwise soaked in lemon and paprika
Few lemon wedges

1. Clean the chicken pieces; make slits 1 inch apart.
2. Blend the remaining ingredients and seasonings (except oil) in the food processor to make a thick mixture. Marinate the chicken in the mixture for minimum 6 hours in the refrigerator.
3. Put the chicken and marinade in a shallow baking pan. Spread oil over the chicken. Bake at 400°F, covered, until done (about 45 minutes), basting once with the marinade juices. Uncover and let it broil for 10–15 minutes to get a dark baked look.
4. Discard left–over marinade. Garnish and serve hot.

Note: If you use boneless chicken in this recipe, it is called Chicken Tikka.

Variation: Use 'Tandoori paste' available from Indian grocery store in place of all the spices. Also in addition to oil, spread 1 tablespoon ghee (clarified butter) over chicken before baking.

Makes 6 servings, 1 piece each. Per serving –
Nutritive Value: 190 calories, 18 g protein, 5 g carb, 0.7 g fiber, 10 g fat, 77 mg chol.
Food Group Exchange: 1 Legumes/Meat, ½ Vegetable, 1/6 Fat.

TANDOORI WHOLE CHICKEN

This roasted chicken is marinated in spices and served with 'Raita' or 'Yogurt sauce'.

2½ lb. whole broiler or fryer chicken
1 cup plain yogurt

Seasonings:

2 teaspoons crushed ginger
1 teaspoon coriander powder
½ teaspoon cumin powder
¼ teaspoon ground cinnamon
¼ teaspoon ground cardamom

1/8 teaspoon ground cloves
½ teaspoon red chili powder
2 teaspoons paprika
1 teaspoon black pepper
1 teaspoon salt (to taste)

Garnish:

1 tablespoon chopped green coriander

½ cup onion wedges (soaked in lemon juice and salt)

1. Clean and skin the chicken. Rinse well; pat dry with paper towels. Tie drumsticks to tail, twist wing under back. Place the chicken in a plastic bag, set aside.
2. Combine yogurt and all the seasonings to make the marinade. Pour it over the chicken, close the bag, and chill for about 12 hours in the refrigerator.
3. Put the marinated chicken (discard marinade), breast side up, on a shallow roasting pan. Insert a meat thermometer into the center of one of the inside thigh muscles (the bulb should not touch the bone). Bake, uncovered, at 375°F until done (about 1½ hours). The thermometer should register 185°F and the juices should run clear.
4. Garnish the chicken with green coriander and onion wedges.

Makes about 10 servings, 1 medium piece each. Per serving –
Nutritive Value: 156 calories, 19 g protein, 3.4 g carb, 0 g fiber, 7 g fat, 80 mg chol.
Food Group Exchange: 1 Legumes/Meat, 1/8 Dairy.

VINDALOO (Spicy Chicken or Fish)

This dish comes from Western and Southern India. Serve it with rice or bread. It can be made in advance and frozen or refrigerated.

1 lb. boneless chicken or salmon
2 medium onions chopped
1 large tomato chopped
2 tablespoons oil

Seasonings:

2 teaspoons garlic chopped
1 teaspoon cumin seeds
1 teaspoon ginger chopped
2 green chilies chopped
1 teaspoon coriander powder

½ teaspoon red chili powder
½ teaspoon cinnamon powder
½ teaspoon clove powder
3 tablespoons crushed coconut
2 teaspoons salt (to taste)

Garnish: 2 tablespoons chopped green coriander

1. Rinse the chicken (or salmon) and chop into pieces.
2. Heat the oil; sauté cumin seeds, garlic, and onions on medium heat until the onions are translucent. Add the remaining seasonings; cook for a couple of minutes. Add tomatoes.
3. Put the cooked mixture along with little water in the food processor or blender and make it smooth. 'Vindaloo masala' is ready. Put it back in the same pot, add one cup water, and boil. As soon as it boils, put chicken (or salmon) pieces in it. Add more water as needed. Cook until the meat is tender (about 25 minutes for chicken, only 10 minutes for fish.)
4. Serve hot garnished with green coriander.

Makes about 5 servings, ½ cup each. Per serving –
Nutritive Value: 177 calories, 22 g protein, 5.5 g carb, 1 g fiber, 7 g fat, 52.6 mg chol.
Food Group Exchange: 1 Legumes/Meat, ½ Vegetable, ¼ Fat.

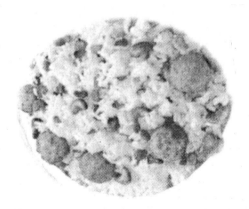

Rice and Dal (Lentils)
Comfort Foods

Rice and 'dal' (Indian lentils) are the staple foods of India, served at almost every meal. A steaming bowl of 'dal' with rice or bread, a comfort food for many, is not only delicious but also healthy and easily digestible.

There is a variety of 'dal' or Indian lentils used in Indian cooking. See the chapter *Ingredients and Terms* for different types of 'dal'. It is advisable to always pick over rice and 'dal' for discolored pieces or grit. Put them in a bowl and rinse a couple of times running your fingers through them, until water runs clear. They become 3–4 times in volume when cooked. Cook them in water or add some vegetable or chicken stock, as desired. Some general tips include:

➢ Rice is cooked in 1½–2 times of liquid. Brown rice takes 2–2½ times liquid and twice the time of white rice to cook. Pre-soaked rice takes less water and less time. Set the heat to low after the first boil.

➢ Rice cooks to dry and fluffy consistency. If there is extra liquid and rice is done, uncover it to let the water evaporate. If rice is not ready and no liquid is left, sprinkle little water, cover tightly, and leave on very low heat for few more minutes.

➤ ***To cook rice in the microwave,*** use a covered casserole dish. For 2 cups white rice and 3½ cups water, cook on high for 7 minutes, or until boiling; then on medium heat for about 10 minutes until most of the water is absorbed. Stir with a fork and let stand, covered, for 3–4 minutes.

➤ For large amount of rice, it may be easier to ***cook in the conventional oven.*** Boil rice and water on top of the stove. Then transfer to the preheated oven at 375°F and let it simmer, covered, until most of the water is absorbed (20–25 minutes). Let it stand for 15–20 minutes; stir with a fork before serving.

➤ Replace all or part of water for cooking by vegetable or chicken stock for added flavor and nutrition. Add vegetables and seasonings as desired. For additional protein, you can also stir in 2–3 tablespoons of Textured Vegetable Protein (TVP) when rice or 'dal' is half cooked.

➤ 'Dal' takes 3–4 times of liquid to cook. Pre-soaked 'dal' takes less water and less time. Cook it on medium heat until it is soft and semi–liquid consistency. When refrigerated, it absorbs all the liquid and becomes little hard. Add water as needed when re-warming.

➤ You may cook 'dal' on top of the stove, or in a pressure cooker, or a slow cooker. It is better to prepare 'whole dal' in a pressure cooker because it is faster and texture become creamier. For details of how to sauté, see page 32.

To help plan nutritious meals, each recipe gives nutritive value (calories, protein, carbohydrate (carb), fiber, fat, and cholesterol (chol)), and Food Group Exchange for a helping of the dish. Estimate is rounded off for ease of understanding. Garnishes, topping and small amounts of seasoning are not accounted for. (See page 13 for basis of estimating Food Group Exchange and nutritive value.)

Abbreviations:

carb: carbohydrate,	chol: cholesterol,	F: Fahrenheit,
g: gram,	lb: pound,	med: medium,
mg: milligram,	oz: ounce.	

BULGUR PULAO

If you are trying to include other grains in your diet, make 'pulao' (seasoned rice) with bulgur—wheat kernels that have been parboiled and dried. Serve with any vegetable and 'Raita'.

¾ cup Basmati rice (white or brown)
1 chopped onion
1 cup bulgur (coarse grind), slightly toasted in oven
2 cups mixed vegetables
(grated carrots, chopped mushrooms, cauliflower)
1 tablespoon oil

Seasonings:
1 teaspoon cumin seeds   1 teaspoon garam masala
1 teaspoon salt

Garnish: ½ cup chopped nuts or olives

1. Check, rinse and drain the rice. Heat the oil in a 3-quart pot on medium heat. Add cumin seeds; as soon as they change color, add chopped onions. Stir until the onions are translucent. Stir in the bulgur and cook for a couple of minutes.
2. Add the rice, vegetables and salt; stir for about 5 minutes.
3. Add 3¼ cups water (4 cups for brown rice). When the water starts to boil (in about 5 minutes), lower the heat, add garam masala, and let the rice simmer, covered, until cooked (15–20 minutes for white rice, 40–50 minutes for brown rice). Garnish and serve hot.

Variation: Add some wild rice for chewy texture and smoky flavor.

Makes about 8 servings, ½ cup each. Per serving –
Nutritive Value: 164 calories, 3.6 g protein, 31 g carb, 3 g fiber, 2 g fat, 0 mg chol.
Food Group Exchange: 1 Grain, 1/3 Vegetable, 1/8 Fat.

CHANA GHIYA DAL (Lentils & Squash)

'Ghiya' or 'dhudi', also called Italian squash, is pale green and long (2–4 ft), with nutty flavor. This combination of lentils and squash is especially popular in North India. Serve it cooked to semi-liquid consistency. It goes well with 'Chapati' or 'Tandoori Roti'. It can be refrigerated or frozen.

**1 cup Chana dal
2 cups chopped ghiya (long squash)
1 chopped onion
½ cup tomato puree
1 tablespoon oil**

Seasonings:

1 teaspoon salt	1 teaspoon crushed ginger
¼ teaspoon turmeric powder	1 teaspoon coriander powder
1 teaspoon cumin seeds	½ teaspoon red chili powder
½ teaspoon caraway (ajwain) seeds	1 teaspoon crushed green chili
1–2 teaspoons crushed garlic	½ teaspoon garam masala

Garnish:

1 tablespoon green chopped coriander   ½ teaspoon lemon juice

1. Pick over dry 'dal' for any grit; rinse. Bring to boil about 3 cups water in a 3-quart saucepan. Add 'dal' to hot water. Stir in salt and turmeric powder. (Water can boil over when 'dal' is added; lower heat as needed.) Partially cover and simmer on medium heat until 'dal' is half-cooked, about 45 minutes. *Note:* 'Dal' can be cooked in a slow cooker (4–5 hours) or a pressure cooker (about 15 minutes).
2. Add the chopped squash and let everything cook together for about ½ hour. (Add hot water as needed.)
3. To sauté, heat the oil in a small skillet on medium heat. Add cumin and caraway seeds; as soon as they change color (few seconds), add garlic and onions. Stir until the onions are light brown. Add tomato puree and the remaining seasonings (except garam masala); cook for a couple of minutes. Sprinkle little water if needed.
4. Mix the sautéed seasonings into the cooked dal and continue cooking on medium heat for 5–10 minutes until the dal is thickened. Add garam masala. Garnish and serve hot.

Makes about 8 servings, ¾ cup each. Per serving –
Nutritive Value: 124 calories, 6 g protein, 19 g carb, 1.4 g fiber, 3 g fat, 0 mg chol.
Food Group Exchange: ¾ Legumes/Meat, ½ Vegetable, 1/8 Fat.

DAL MAKHNI (Creamy Lentils)

The amount of cream in this delicious dish can be adjusted to your taste. Mostly served in North India, It is a must on special occasions. Serve it hot, semi-liquid consistency, with a dash of butter on top, along with rice, 'Nan' or 'Tandoori Roti' and 'Onion Salad'. It can be refrigerated or frozen.

½ cup red kidney beans
1 cup Urad whole black dal
½ cup tomato puree
1 chopped tomato
2 tablespoons heavy cream (or sour cream)
1 tablespoon oil

Seasonings:
1 teaspoon salt
¼ teaspoon turmeric powder
½ teaspoon cumin seeds
1 teaspoon crushed garlic
1 chopped onion

½ teaspoon crushed ginger
½ teaspoon coriander powder
½ teaspoon red chili powder
1 teaspoon crushed green chili
1 teaspoon garam masala

Garnish:
1 tablespoon green chopped coriander
½ teaspoon lemon juice (optional)

1. Pick over red kidney beans for any grit; rinse, and soak in about 2 cups water for 3–4 hours.
2. Check the dry 'dal' for any grit; rinse.
3. Bring to boil about 4 cups water in a 3-quart saucepan. Add the 'dal' and soaked beans to hot water. Stir in salt and turmeric powder. (Water can boil over when 'dal' and beans are added; lower the heat as needed.) Partially cover and simmer on medium heat until the beans and 'dal' are tender, about one hour. (Add hot water as needed.) *Note:* 'Dal' and beans can be cooked in a slow cooker (4–5 hours) or in a pressure cooker for about 15 minutes.
4. To sauté, heat the oil in a small skillet on medium heat. Add cumin seeds; as soon as they change color (few seconds), add garlic and onions. Stir until the onions are light brown. Add ginger, tomato, tomato puree, and the remaining seasonings (except 'garam masala'); cook for a couple of minutes. Sprinkle little water if needed.
5. Slowly add the cream; keep stirring and cook for another few minutes until the 'masala' is brownish color.

6. Mix the sautéed seasonings into the cooked 'dal' and beans; continue cooking on medium heat for 5–10 minutes until 'dal' is thickened. Add 'garam masala'. Serve hot, garnished with green coriander. Optionally sprinkle lemon juice.

Variation: Use frozen kidney beans and skip step 1. If using canned beans, drain and add them to cooked 'dal'.

Healthy Alternative: Add some vegetable stock instead of water when 'dal' is half cooked. To reduce fat, substitute yogurt for heavy cream or sour cream.

Makes about 8 servings, ¾ cup each. Per serving –
Nutritive Value: 172 calories, 9.5 g protein, 26.4 g carb, 3 g fiber, 3.7 g fat, 5 mg chol.
Food Group Exchange: 1 Legumes/Meat, ¼ Vegetable, 1/3 Fat.

GARLIC DAL (Savory Lentils)

This 'dal is the perfect accompaniment to spicy vegetables, bread and rice. One of the favorites is a mix of split green & yellow Mung and split reddish Masoor. When cooked, dry 'dal' becomes almost four times in volume. Serve it hot when well mixed and of semi-liquid consistency. It can be refrigerated or frozen.

½ cup Mung split dal with peel
½ cup Masoor split dal
½ chopped onion
1 chopped tomato
1 tablespoon oil

Seasonings:

1 teaspoon salt
¼ teaspoon turmeric powder
½ teaspoon cumin seeds
1 teaspoon crushed garlic
½ teaspoon crushed ginger

½ teaspoon coriander powder
½ teaspoon red chili powder
1 teaspoon crushed green chili
1 teaspoon garam masala

Garnish:

1 tablespoon green chopped coriander
½ teaspoon lemon juice

1. Pick over dry 'dal' for grit; rinse a couple of times and drain.
2. Bring to boil about 3 cups water in a 2-quart saucepan. Add 'dal' to hot water. Stir in salt and turmeric powder. (Water can boil over when 'dal' is added; lower the heat as needed.)
3. Partially cover and simmer on medium heat until 'dal' is tender, 30–45 minutes. (Add hot water depending on the consistency desired.) *Note:* Split 'dal' can be cooked in a slow cooker [2–3 hours] or in a pressure cooker for about 10 minutes.
4. To sauté, heat the oil in a small skillet on medium heat. Add cumin seeds; as soon as they change color (few seconds), add garlic and onions. Stir, sprinkling little water if needed, until onions are golden brown. Add ginger and remaining seasonings (except tomatoes and garam masala); stir for a couple of minutes. Add tomatoes and cook for another minute.
5. Mix the sautéed seasonings into the cooked 'dal' and continue cooking on medium heat for 5–10 minutes until 'dal' is thickened. Add garam masala.

6. Serve hot, garnished with green coriander. Optionally sprinkle lemon juice.

Variation 1: Use brown lentils, peeled yellow Mung, peeled light yellow Urad, or split dark yellow Toor (or a mix of them). They take about 3 cups of water to 1 cup of dry 'dal' and only 30–40 minutes to cook.

Variation 2: Use whole green Mung, whole black Urad, whole dark brown Masoor, whole yellow brownish Toor, or split yellow Chana (or a mix of them). They take about 4 cups of water to 1 cup of dry 'dal' and longer to cook (about 1 hour). (Takes 4–5 hours in slow cooker, 25 minutes in pressure cooker.)

Healthy Alternative: Add some vegetable stock or 3 tablespoons of Textured Vegetable Protein (TVP) when 'dal' is half cooked.

Makes about 6 servings, ¾ cup each. Per serving –
Nutritive Value: 115 calories, 6 g protein, 17.4 g carb, 4 g fiber, 3 g fat, 0 mg chol.
Food Group Exchange: 1 Legumes/Meat, 1/6 Vegetable, 1/6 Fat.

Food is the fuel that provides the human body with the nutrients and energy required for healthy functioning.

KHICHDI (Mixed Rice and Lentils)

If you want to make a complete meal and something healthy, try 'Khichdi'. It is the best meal to serve to children and people recovering from illness because it is easy to digest. Serve it with plain yogurt, butter, or 'lemon pickle'.

1 cup long–grain rice (white or brown)
1 cup split Mung dal (or split Masoor or Toor dal)
2 teaspoons butter or oil

Seasonings:

¼ teaspoon turmeric powder
¼ teaspoon crushed ginger

1½ teaspoons salt
1 teaspoon cumin seeds

1. Pick over rice and 'dal' for any grit; rinse a couple of times and drain.
2. Put everything together (except oil and cumin seeds) in a large pot with about 6 cups water. Cook on high heat, partially covered. When it starts to boil, lower the heat to medium and let it cook for about 15 minutes.
3. Lower the heat to low and simmer, covered, until rice and 'dal' are tender (about 15 minutes). Add more water as needed. It can be semi-thick or thin consistency. Mash it a little.
4. Heat the oil (or butter) in a small pot. Add cumin seeds. As soon as they change color (few seconds), add them to 'Khichdi'. Serve hot.

Healthy Alternative: Add some vegetable stock or finely chopped vegetables when 'Khichdi' is half cooked.

Makes about 12 servings, ¾ cup each. Per serving –
Nutritive Value: 113 calories, 5 g protein, 22 g carb, 3.5 g fiber, 1 g fat, 0 mg chol.
Food Group Exchange: ½ Grain, ½ Legumes/Meat, 1/12 Fat.

LEMON RICE

This is delicious and very cooling in hot summer days. It is a perfect dish to take to picnics because it can be served cold.

2 cups long–grain rice
3½ cups water to cook rice
¼ cup halved cashews or raw peanuts
4 tablespoons lemon juice
1 tablespoon oil

Seasonings:

1 teaspoon mustard seeds	½ teaspoon turmeric powder
2 teaspoons split peeled Urad dal	1 tablespoon curry leaves
1 whole red chili	¼ teaspoon red chili powder
1 teaspoon crushed ginger	1 teaspoon salt (to taste)
1 teaspoon crushed green chili	

Garnish: 1 tablespoon chopped green coriander

1. Check, rinse and soak the rice for about 10 minutes; drain.
2. Boil the rice and 3½ cups water; cook covered on low heat until tender. (To prevent the rice from sticking, uncover the pot, fluff the rice or spread them in a large bowl.)
3. Heat the oil in a skillet on medium heat. Sauté mustard seeds; stir in Urad dal and peanuts (or cashews). Add whole red chili. After a couple of seconds, add ginger, green chili, and turmeric powder. (It gives wonderful aroma.) After a few seconds, stir in curry leaves and red chili powder. Turn off the heat.
4. About ½ hour before serving, mix the sauté and cooked rice. Mix in lemon juice and salt. Keep covered. Serve warm or at room temperature, garnished with green coriander. This dish is generally not re-warmed. (You may remove the whole red chili.)

Healthy Alternative: Add some vegetables such as green peas and red bell pepper in the sauté (step 3) for color, texture, and nutrition.

Makes about 10 servings, ½ cup each. Per serving –
Nutritive Value: 173 calories, 3 g protein, 32 g carb, 1 g fiber, 3 g fat, 0 mg chol.
Food Group Exchange: 1 Grain, 1/8 Legumes/Meat, 1/8 Fat.

PULAO (Seasoned Rice)

Pulao or 'pilaf' can be served with any 'dal', yogurt or any stew like vegetable, along with 'Chapati' or bread. Basmati rice that swells lengthwise when cooked, is especially suitable for pulao.

2 cups Basmati rice (white or brown)
2¼ cups water to cook (3½ cups water for brown rice)
1 cup green peas, grated carrots, cauliflower pieces or mixed vegetables
1 chopped onion
1 tablespoon oil

Seasonings:

1 teaspoon cumin seeds	1" cinnamon stick
4 cloves	4 dried bay leaves
2 brown cardamom pods	1 teaspoon salt (to taste)

Garnish: 2 tablespoons roasted chopped peanuts and cashews or fried onions

1. Pick the rice for any foreign matter and rinse. Soak the rice for ½ hour; drain.
2. Heat the oil in a 2–quart pot on medium heat. Sauté cumin seeds, cloves, cinnamon, bay leaves; add chopped onions; stir until the onions are golden brown. Stir in the desired vegetables.
3. Add water. When the water starts to boil, add the rice and salt. When the water boils again (in about 2 minutes), set the heat to low and let the rice simmer, covered, until cooked (about 15 minutes for white rice, about 30 for brown rice).
4. Remove big pieces of seasonings. Serve hot garnished as desired.

Variation: Sprinkle 1 teaspoon butter and/or 1 teaspoon lemon juice over cooked rice; mix with a fork so that rice does not break.

Makes about 12 servings, ½ cup each. Per serving:
Nutritive Value: 123 calories, 3 g protein, 25 g carb, 2 g fiber, 1.5 g fat, 0 mg chol.
Food Group Exchange: 1 Grain, ¼ Vegetable, 1/8 Fat.

RASAM (Spicy Lentil Drink)

This healthy soup drink is prepared using a special spice mixture 'rasam powder'. It is served hot as an appetizer.

1 cup Toor split dark yellow dal
2 chopped tomatoes
1 tablespoon tamarind paste mixed with 4 cups water
1 tablespoon oil

Seasonings:
1 tablespoon rasam powder   1 teaspoon salt
½ teaspoon turmeric powder

Sauté:
1 teaspoon mustard seeds   ¼ teaspoon asafetida powder
1 tablespoon curry leaves

1. Check and rinse Toor dal. Boil with 5 cups water, salt and turmeric powder for 30–45 minutes until tender.
2. Boil together tamarind paste mixed with water, tomatoes, rasam powder, and salt until everything is blended (about ½ hour). Add to the cooked 'dal'; boil again for a couple of minutes. Add more water as needed.
3. To sauté, heat the oil in a small pan. Add mustard seeds. When they splutter, add curry leaves and asafetida powder. Stir the sauté into the cooked 'rasam'.
4. Garnish with coriander leaves, if desired, and serve.

Makes about 10 servings, one cup each. Per serving –
Nutritive Value: 88 calories, 5 g protein, 13.6 g carb, 1 g fiber, 2 g fat, 0 mg chol.
Food Group Exchange: ¾ Legumes/Meat, ¼ Vegetable, 1/8 Fat.

SAFFRON RICE

Enjoy the aroma and delicate golden color of saffron in this rice which goes with any meal. Serve it as a side dish with curried vegetables and yogurt.

2 cups Basmati rice
3¼ cups water to cook
1 teaspoon saffron threads soaked in
2 tablespoons warm milk
1½ tablespoons oil

Seasonings:

2–3 small cinnamon pieces   1 large brown cardamom
4 cloves   1 teaspoon salt (to taste)

Garnish: 2 tablespoons roasted cashew halves (optional)

1. Pick over rice for any foreign matter; rinse. Soak the rice for 10 minutes; drain when ready to use.
2. Heat the oil in a 3-quart pot with tight-fitting lid on medium heat. Add cinnamon, cloves, and cardamom. As they change color (in few seconds), add the rice. Stir rice gently for about 5 minutes until all moisture is absorbed. Add water and salt.
3. When the water starts to boil, add saffron along with milk, reduce the heat to low and let the rice simmer, covered, until it is cooked (about 20 minutes). Fluff rice with a fork and leave covered till ready to serve.
4. Remove large pieces of seasonings; serve hot garnished with nuts, if desired.

Makes about 10 servings, ½ cup each. Per serving –
Nutritive Value: 162 calories, 2.4 g protein, 30.4 g carb, 1 g fiber, 2 g fat, 0 mg chol.
Food Group Exchange: 1 Grain, 1/8 Fat.

SAMBAR (Lentils with Vegetables)

This is like soup, served hot, generally with 'Dosa', 'Idli', or rice. Add any vegetables that you like.

1 cup Toor split dark yellow dal
2 carrots
½ eggplant (or any other vegetable)
1 chopped onion
1 tablespoon tamarind paste mixed with 2 cups water
1 tablespoon oil

Seasonings:

½ teaspoon turmeric powder
2 teaspoons salt
1 tablespoon coriander seeds
1 teaspoon fenugreek seeds
1 whole red chili

3 teaspoons Chana dal
1 tablespoon un-sweetened grated coconut
¼ teaspoon asafetida powder
1 teaspoon mustard seeds

Garnish: 1 tablespoon chopped curry leaves

1. Pick over 'dal' for any foreign matter; rinse a couple of times and drain.
2. Cook the 'dal' in about 6 cups water in a large pot, adding salt and turmeric powder, until tender.
3. Roast the remaining seasonings, except mustard seeds, lightly; grind them together. Set aside. Cut the vegetables into ½" pieces.
4. Heat the oil in a medium pot. Sauté mustard seeds. Add onions and stir until light brown. Stir in carrots and eggplant (or any other vegetable). When half cooked, add the tamarind paste mixed with water; cook until the vegetables are tender (about 20 minutes).
5. Blend in the ground seasonings and curry leaves. Add everything to the cooked 'dal'; boil together for a couple of minutes. Add more water, if needed, to bring to soupy consistency.

Variation: Use 'Sambar Powder' available from Indian grocery store instead of roasting and grinding your own spices.

Makes about 12 servings, ¾ cup each. Per serving –
Nutritive Value: 80 calories, 4 g protein, 13 g carb, 1 g fiber, 1.5 g fat, 0 mg chol.
Food Group Exchange: ½ Legumes/Meat, ¾ Vegetable, 1/8 Fat.

SPINACH DAL

This 'dal', of semi-liquid consistency, is served with bread and rice. Serve it hot with a dash of butter. It can be refrigerated or frozen.

1 cup Mung split green & yellow dal with peel
½ cup Chana yellow dal
2 cups chopped spinach
1 chopped tomato
1 tablespoon oil

Seasonings:

1 teaspoon salt	½ teaspoon crushed ginger
¼ teaspoon turmeric powder	½ teaspoon coriander powder
½ teaspoon cumin seeds	½ teaspoon red chili powder
½ teaspoon caraway seeds	1 teaspoon crushed green chili
1 teaspoon crushed garlic	1 teaspoon garam masala
½ chopped onion	

Garnish: ½ teaspoon lemon juice (optional)

1. Check 'dal' for grit; rinse a couple of times and drain.
2. Bring to boil about 4 cups water in a 3-quart pan. Add 'dal' to hot water. Stir in salt and turmeric powder. (Water can boil over when 'dal' is added; lower the heat as needed.)
3. Partially cover and simmer on medium heat until 'dal' is almost cooked (about 40 minutes). (Add more hot water depending on the consistency desired.)
4. Add chopped spinach to the cooked 'dal'; let cook for about 10 minutes until everything is well mixed.
5. To sauté, heat the oil in a small skillet on medium heat. Add cumin and caraway seeds; as soon as they change color (few seconds), add garlic and onions. When the onions are golden brown, stir in tomatoes and remaining seasonings (except garam masala) and cook for a couple of minutes.
6. Mix the sautéed seasonings into the cooked 'Spinach Dal'. Continue cooking on medium heat for about 5 minutes until 'dal' is thickened. Add garam masala. Serve hot, optionally sprinkled with lemon juice.

Variation: Use peeled yellow Mung or peeled light yellow Urad dal (or a mix of them). They take little less water and only 20–30 minutes to cook.

Makes about 8 servings, ¾ cup each. Per serving –
Nutritive Value: 158 calories, 9 g protein, 25 g carb, 5 g fiber, 3 g fat, 0 mg chol.
Food Group Exchange: 1 Legumes/Meat, ½ Vegetable, 1/8 Fat.

SOOKHI DAL (Dry–look Lentils)

'Sookhi Dal' is an excellent side dish. It can be dry like rice or with some liquid.

1 cup dal (peeled Mung split or peeled Urad split)
1 medium onion (chopped lengthwise)
2 tablespoons oil

Seasonings:

¼ teaspoon turmeric powder
1 teaspoon salt
¼ teaspoon cumin seed
¼ teaspoon asafetida powder

1 teaspoon coriander powder
1 teaspoon garam masala
½ teaspoon red chili powder
1 teaspoon chopped green chili

Garnish:

1 teaspoon lemon juice

1 tablespoon chopped green coriander

1. Check 'dal' for grit, rinse a couple of times and drain.
2. Bring to boil 2 cups water in a 2-quart saucepan. Add the 'dal' to hot water. Stir in turmeric powder and salt. Reduce heat; cook half–covered until 'dal' is little tender but not too soft, about 20 minutes.
3. Heat the oil in a small skillet on medium–high heat. Stir– fry the onions until golden brown; take them out for garnish. In the same skillet, add cumin seeds. Stir for a few seconds; add the remaining seasonings. Stir for a couple of minutes; mix into cooked 'dal'.
4. Sprinkle lemon juice over 'dal'. Serve hot, garnished with green coriander and fried onions.

Makes about 6 servings, ½ cup each. Per serving –
Nutritive Value: 167 calories, 8.4 g protein, 23 g carb, 6 g fiber, 5 g fat, 0 mg chol.
Food Group Exchange: 1 Legumes/Meat, 1/6 Vegetable, 1/6 Fat.

TAHIRI (Vegetable Rice)

This rice dish is a complete meal in itself. Serve with plain yogurt, 'Raita', or chutney. It is best if made fresh; can be reheated in the microwave oven, covered.

2 cups Basmati rice
1 medium onion, chopped
1 medium size potato cut in small pieces
1 cup green peas
3 cups cauliflower cut into small pieces
½ cup Mint–Coriander chutney
3 tablespoons butter (or oil)

Seasonings:
1 teaspoon cumin seeds
½ teaspoon red chili powder
1+ teaspoon salt

½ teaspoon turmeric powder
1 teaspoon garam masala

1. Check, rinse and drain the rice.
2. Heat one tablespoon butter (or oil) in a 3-quart pot on medium heat. Sauté cumin seeds and chopped onions. Stir until the onions are translucent.
3. Add the rice and other vegetables, and the seasonings (except garam masala and chutney); stir for about 5 minutes.
4. Add 3¼ cups water. When the water starts to boil (in about 5 minutes), add chutney and let the rice simmer on low heat, covered, until the rice is cooked (15–20 minutes).
5. Stir in garam masala and the remaining butter. Serve hot.

Note: Can substitute chutney by ½ cup water + 2 tablespoons chopped green coriander + 2 tablespoons fresh chopped mint + 1 chopped tomato + 1 tablespoon lemon juice.

Healthy Alternative: Reduce or omit butter which is used for flavor.

Makes about 12 servings, ¾ cup each. Per serving –
Nutritive Value: 181 calories, 4 g protein, 32 g carb, 3 g fiber, 4 g fat, 7.5 mg chol.
Food Group Exchange: 1 Grain, ¾ Vegetable, ¼ Fat.

TAMARIND RICE

South India is known for this popular rice dish suitable for all occasions, especially to take on picnics. It is served at room temperature.

2 cups Basmati or long grain rice
¼ cup cashews, halved
2 tablespoons peanuts, halved
1 tablespoon tamarind paste mixed with ¼ cup water
4 tablespoons oil

Seasonings:

2 teaspoons mustard seeds
1 tsp. each of Chana dal, Toor dal, and split peeled Urad and Mung dal
1 whole red chili
½ teaspoon fenugreek seeds
1 tablespoon chopped curry leaves

¼ teaspoon red chili powder
½ teaspoon asafetida powder

½ teaspoon turmeric powder
1 teaspoon salt (to taste)

1. Check, rinse and soak the rice for about 10 minutes; drain. Bring the rice to boil in about 3½ cups water in a 3-4 quart pot. Reduce the heat and cook covered on low heat until rice is tender. (To prevent the rice from sticking, fluff them or spread in a large bowl.)
2. Heat the oil in a small skillet on medium heat. Sauté mustard seeds; stir in different 'dal', whole red chili, and fenugreek seeds. After a couple of seconds, add nuts, curry leaves and red chili powder. When nuts are lightly roasted, add the remaining seasonings. Mix in the tamarind mixture; cook for about 5 minutes until the mixture thickens.
3. Mix everything together with cooked rice about 6 hours before serving so that the rice absorbs the flavors. Serve warm or at room temperature. Generally, it is not reheated.

Healthy Alternative: Reduce oil that is used for moistness.

Makes about 12 servings, ½ cup each. Per serving –
Nutritive Value: 198 calories, 3 g protein, 27.5 g carb, 1 g fiber, 7.5 g fat, 0 mg chol.
Food Group Exchange: 1 Grain, 1/8 Legumes/Meat, 1/3 Fat.

TOMATO DAL

Use lentils or any of the Indian lentils for this 'Dal', made without onion or garlic. Serve it as the main dish with bread and rice.

1 cup dry dal (lentils, Mung split, Toor split, oily Toor split, Urad split, Masoor split, or a mix of 2 or more)
1 chopped tomato
1 tablespoon oil

Seasonings:
¼ teaspoon turmeric powder
1 teaspoon salt
½ teaspoon mustard seeds
½ teaspoon cumin seeds
1/8 teaspoon asafetida powder
½ teaspoon crushed ginger

1 teaspoon coriander powder
1 teaspoon garam masala
½ teaspoon red chili powder
¼ teaspoon paprika
½ teaspoon crushed green chili

Garnish: 1 tablespoon chopped green coriander

1. Check 'dal' for grit; rinse a couple of times and drain.
2. Bring about 3 cups water to boil in a 2-quart pan. Add 'dal' to hot water. Stir in salt and turmeric powder. (Water can boil over when 'dal' is added; lower the heat as needed.) Partially cover and simmer on medium heat until 'dal' is tender, 30–45 minutes. (Add more hot water depending on the consistency desired.)
3. To sauté, heat the oil in a small skillet. Add mustard seeds and cumin. As they splutter (few seconds), add asafetida powder, ginger, and the remaining seasonings. Stir for a minute. Add the tomatoes and cook until the mixture is well cooked (3–5 Minutes).
4. Stir the sautéed mixture into the cooked 'dal' and simmer for 5 minutes. Serve hot, garnished with green coriander.

Makes about 6 servings, ¾ cup each. Per serving –
Nutritive Value: 144 calories, 8.4 g protein, 22.5 g carb, 6 g fiber, 3 g fat, 0 mg chol.
Food Group Exchange: 1 Legumes/Meat, 1/6 Vegetable, 1/6 Fat.

VEGETABLE BIRYANI

You may prepare the vegetables ahead of time. It is better to mix everything together when ready to serve.

2 cups Basmati rice (white or brown)
3 cups water to cook white rice, 4 cups for brown
2 cups chopped vegetables (broccoli, cauliflower,
carrots, corn, mushrooms)
¼ cup plain yogurt
1 tablespoon oil

Seasonings:

1 teaspoon cumin seeds	1 teaspoon crushed green chili
¼ teaspoon asafetida powder	½ teaspoon red chili powder
½ teaspoon turmeric powder	1 teaspoon salt
1 teaspoon crushed ginger	1 teaspoon garam masala

Garnish: 2 tablespoons chopped green coriander

1. Check, rinse and soak the rice for about 10 minutes; drain. Bring the rice and water to boil in a 2-quart pot. Reduce the heat to low and cook covered until almost done. Fluff the rice.
2. While the rice is cooking, heat the oil in a 3-quart pot on medium heat. Add cumin seeds. As soon as they splutter, add asafetida powder. Stir in the vegetables and remaining seasonings except garam masala. Cook until the vegetables are almost done.
3. Stir in the rice, yogurt, and garam masala. Cover and let everything steam over low heat until rice is tender.
4. Garnish and serve hot.

Variation: Use about 2 teaspoons lemon juice instead of yogurt. May garnish with boiled finely sliced eggs or fried onions.

Makes about 10 servings, ¾ cup each. Per serving –
Nutritive Value: 177 calories, 3.6 g protein, 34.5 g carb, 1.7 g fiber, 1.6 g fat, 0.4 mg chol.
Food Group Exchange: 1 Grain, ¼ Vegetable, 1/8 Fat.

YOGURT RICE

This is a delicious and cooling dish anytime, especially, in the hot summer days. Generally it is served as a side dish but it can become one-pot meal if some vegetables are added to it.

2 cups Basmati or long–grain rice
2 cups plain yogurt
½ cup sour cream
1 tablespoon oil

Seasonings:

1 teaspoon mustard seeds
1 teaspoon split Urad dal
1 teaspoon crushed ginger
1 teaspoon crushed green chili

1 tablespoon chopped curry leaves
½ teaspoon red chili powder
1 teaspoon salt

Garnish: ¼ cup chopped cashews or roasted peanuts

1. Check, rinse and soak the rice for about 10 minutes; drain.
2. Add the rice and 3½ cups water in a 3-quart pot; bring to a boil. Reduce the heat to low and cook covered until tender. (To prevent the rice from sticking, fluff them or spread in a large bowl.)
3. Heat the oil in a skillet on medium heat. Add the mustard seeds and cover. As soon as they splutter, stir in Urad dal, ginger, and green chili. (It smells wonderful.) Turn off the heat; add yogurt, sour cream and the remaining seasonings (curry leaves, red chili powder and salt).
4. Mix everything together with the cold cooked rice about ½ hour before serving. (If consistency is rather hard, add some milk.)
5. Garnish with the nuts. Serve cold or at room temperature.

Healthy Alternative: Add about one cup of finely chopped vegetables such as spinach, carrots and red bell pepper in the sauté (step 3) for color, texture, and nutrition.

Makes about 8 servings, ½ cup each. Per serving –
Nutritive Value: 263 calories, 6 g protein, 43 g carb, 1 g fiber, 5.4 g fat, 13.5 mg chol.
Food Group Exchange: 1 Grain, ½ Fat, ¼ Dairy.

Breads

Breads are unexcelled in nutrition, aroma, taste and texture. For daily meals, make 'Chapati', 'Parantha', or 'Tandoori Roti'. Baking of unleavened bread on top of a flat skillet, griddle, or 'tawa' is unique. As you practice, you establish a rhythm of work so that you are rolling out the next 'Chapati' or 'Parantha' while the previous one is baking. Breads, except for 'Stuffed Potato Parantha', freeze very well.

Breads require the preparation of dough. You may knead enough dough for several days, and refrigerate or freeze. (If frozen, thaw it in the refrigerator for about 12 hours.) Take the dough out of the refrigerator and let it come to room temperature for 5–10 minutes before using. For details of how to knead dough and other techniques, refer to the chapter *Preparation Techniques. Note:* You may use a food processor to make dough and a tortilla maker (Tortilla Chef), available from Indian/Pakistani grocery stores, to make bread.

'Atta' or the flour used for Indian breads is finer and lighter than the whole-wheat flour available from grocery or health food stores. Wheat is milled almost to a powder. If you use the whole-wheat flour, the bread will be little heavier and doughier.

To help plan nutritious meals, each recipe gives nutritive value (calories, protein, carbohydrate (carb), fiber, fat, and cholesterol (chol)), and Food Group Exchange for a helping of the dish. Estimate is rounded off for ease of understanding. Garnishes, topping and small amounts of seasoning are not accounted for. (See page 13 for basis of estimating Food Group Exchange and nutritive value.)

Abbreviations:

carb: carbohydrate,	chol: cholesterol,	F: Fahrenheit,	g: gram,
lb: pound,	med: medium,	mg: milligram,	oz: ounce.

BHATURE (Fried Sour Bread)

'Bhature' are generally served with 'Chhole' at special occasions. Serve them hot. If cold, reheat in stacks of 8–10 in the oven at 350°F, wrapped in foil, or in the microwave oven in plastic wrap or paper towel.

2 teaspoons yeast
1 teaspoon sugar
5 cups all-purpose flour + ½ cup for dusting
2 cups plain yogurt
Oil to deep–fry (about 2" deep in a wok)

<u>Seasonings:</u> ½ teaspoon salt

1. Mix the yeast in ¼ cup warm water. Add the sugar and let it stand for 5–10 minutes until it rises.
2. Mix together 5 cups flour, yogurt, salt, and the yeast mixture in a deep bowl. Knead the dough, adding water as needed, until it becomes smooth and supple. Cover with a kitchen towel and let it rise for 3–5 hours in a warm place. Press it down and let it rise for another hour.
3. Break the dough into small pieces. Moisten hands with little oil if needed to make the balls and flatten them into 2" patties. Dip each patty in flour to coat, cover and leave for another 15 minutes to rise.
4. Roll each patty on flat surface with a rolling pin, turning as needed, using oil to avoid sticking, in round or oval shape, about ¼" thick.
5. **Deep-fry:** Heat the oil in a deep skillet or wok on medium–high heat. (Test fry a tiny piece of dough to make sure the oil is right temperature.) Put one 'Bhatura' at a time in hot oil. Turn after a few seconds with a slotted flat spatula; press gently on sides and center with the back of the spatula to make it puff up. Turn again; take out when light brown on both sides. (You may have to increase the heat at times; regulate as needed.)
6. Drain on paper towels. Serve immediately or stack and wrap in aluminum foil.

Healthy Alternative: Substitute all–purpose flour partially by whole–wheat flour.

Variation: May use frozen bread dough available from the grocery store instead of making your own dough. Thaw the dough, preferably in refrigerator, for 24 hours before using.

Makes about 15 servings, one piece each. Per serving –
Nutritive Value: 280 calories, 5.6 g protein, 34 g carb, 1 g fiber, 13.5 g fat, 2 mg chol.
Food Group Exchange: 1 Grain, 1/8 Dairy, 1 Fat.

CHAPATI (Unleavened Flat Bread)

'Chapati' is every day food, served with vegetables, 'dal', and other dishes. People have developed the skill over years to make a perfect round 'Chapati', all of the same size and thickness. You can freeze 'Chapati' and warm in the oven before eating.

2 cups whole–wheat flour (+½ cup for dusting)
Butter, if desired

1. Put 2 cups flour in a wide bowl. Knead the dough, adding water (or any other liquid such as milk or vegetable stock) as needed, until it becomes smooth and supple. Cover with a kitchen towel and set aside for about an hour in a warm place. Refrigerate for a couple of hours for easier handling.
2. Break a small piece of the dough and make into a smooth ball, working between your palms, using flour as needed, and flatten into about 2" patty. Make several patties and cover with a towel. Roll each patty on floured surface, turning as needed, into a thin round, 6–7" in diameter.
3. **Bake on a griddle**: Heat a griddle (or flat heavy skillet or 'tawa') on medium-high heat. Slap the 'Chapati' to remove excess flour and slide it to the griddle. After few seconds the top will change color and the bottom will have few light brown specks. Turn over with a flat spatula and cook the other side also until it has some light brown specks.
4. Remove from the skillet with a folded kitchen towel in your hand and put the first side on gas flame or electric ring (with a protector). Hold it about ¼ inch above the burner with tongs to prevent from burning. 'Chapati' will now fill up with steam and puff up. Taking care not to burn, slightly heat the other side also. *Note:* You can puff up the 'Chapati' on top of griddle also by applying light pressure on all sides with a folded towel.
5. Brush little butter on one side of 'Chapati', if desired. Serve immediately or stack and wrap them in aluminum foil lined with paper towel.

Healthy Alternative: For texture and nutrition, add ½–1 cup of wheat germ, gram flour, soy flour, or oatmeal (or a mixture) to the flour when making the dough.

Makes about 8 servings, one piece each. Per serving –
Nutritive Value: 120 calories, 5 g protein, 22 g carb, 4 g fiber, 1 g fat, 0 mg chol.
Food Group Exchange: 1 Grain.

KACHORI (Fried Stuffed Bread)

'Kachori' are often served as a breakfast meal with 'Alu Bhaji (Curried Potatoes)'. They can be made in advance and refrigerated or frozen. Before serving, reheat in the oven at 350°F, wrapped in foil in stacks of ten, or in the microwave oven wrapped in plastic wrap or paper towel.

1 cup peeled split Urad dal
2 cups whole–wheat flour (+ ¼ cup for dusting)
Oil to deep fry (about 2" deep in a wok)

Seasonings:
½ teaspoon salt   ½ teaspoon red chili powder
1 teaspoon coriander powder

1. Rinse and soak the 'dal' for 5–6 hours in warm water. Drain; grind finely with as little water as possible to make a thick consistency paste to be used for filling. (Add some Urad dal flour if the paste is not thick enough.) Refrigerate the filling for 2–3 hours to make it easier to handle. (The filling can also be frozen.)
2. Mix 2 cups flour and some water, and knead the dough until it becomes smooth and supple. Make small patties (8–10) out of the dough, dusting with flour as needed. Keep them covered.
3. On a flat oiled surface, roll each patty with a rolling pin, turning as needed, into a 4" round. (You may instead use a tortilla maker to roll 'Kachori'.)
4. Add all the seasonings to the filling. Place 1–2 tablespoons of the filling in each round and press the ends together to hold the filling securely. Press down with your hand and make a patty again and roll to make a 6" round on oiled surface, about 1/6" thick.
5. Heat the oil in a deep skillet or wok on medium-high heat and fry (see 'Deep-Fry' on page 205). Put one 'Kachori' at a time in hot oil. Turn after a few seconds with a slotted spatula, and press gently on sides and center with the back of the spatula to make it cook evenly. (They may not fluff up as 'Puri' or 'Bhature'.) Turn again; remove when light brown on both sides.
6. Drain on paper towels lined with plastic underneath. Serve immediately or stack and wrap in aluminum foil.

Variation: To make it easier, instead of filling each patty (step 5), knead the dough with the filling mixture.

Makes about 10 servings, one piece each. Per serving –
Nutritive Value: 257 calories, 7 g protein, 24.4 g carb, 5 g fiber, 14.6 g fat, 0 mg chol.
Food Group Exchange: 1 Grain, 1/3 Legumes/Meat, 1 Fat.

Khatti Roti (Sour Dough Flat Bread)

Served normally for breakfast, spice it up as you like. Plan for it a day or two in advance. You can refrigerate or freeze prepared 'Roti'; warm in the oven just as any piece of bread before serving.

2 cups whole-wheat flour (+ ½ cup for dusting)
Butter, if desired

Seasonings:

½ teaspoon salt

½ teaspoon red chili powder

½ teaspoon coriander powder

½ teaspoon cumin powder

1. Knead 2 cups flour, adding water as needed, until the dough becomes smooth and supple. Cover with a kitchen towel and set aside at room temperature for 24–36 hours until it rises and develops a tangy aroma.
2. When ready to use, work the dough again, adding all the seasonings and little flour, if needed. Break a small piece of the dough and make into a smooth ball, working between your palms, using extra flour as needed, and flatten into about 2" patty. Make all the patties and cover with a towel.
3. Dust a flat surface with little flour. Roll each patty with a rolling pin into a round, 6-7" across, about 1/6" thick.
4. Heat a griddle (or heavy flat skillet or 'tawa') on medium-high heat. Slap the 'Roti' to remove excess flour and slide it to the griddle. After few seconds the top will change color and the bottom will have few light brown specks. Turn over with a flat spatula and cook the other side a little longer, which should have light brown specks too.
5. Remove from the griddle with a folded kitchen towel in your hand. Bake it on a gas flame or electric ring (with a protector). Hold it about ¼ inch above the burner to prevent from burning. Slightly heat the other side also.
6. Brush little butter on top, if desired. Serve hot.

Variation: Before putting on gas flame, pinch the top layer between your thumb and first finger at 3–4 places, making it crispier and giving it a high and low effect.

Makes about 8 servings, one piece each. Per serving –
Nutritive Value: 120 calories, 5 g protein, 22 g carb, 4 g fiber, 1 g fat, 0 mg chol.
Food Group Exchange: 1 Grain.

NAN (Baked Flat Bread)

'Nan' are served with vegetables, legumes or meat dishes. Traditionally they are made in coal or wood fired clay 'tandoor' or oven that gives a wonderful smoky flavor. This is an easier way to make them. They can be made in advance and frozen. Cut them into two halves, if desired, and warm in the oven before serving.

5 cups all–purpose flour + ½ cup for dusting
2 teaspoons yeast
1 teaspoon sugar
2 cups plain yogurt

Seasonings: 1 teaspoon salt

Garnish:
2 tablespoons milk   1 tablespoon poppy seeds or sesame seeds
                                                  Butter

1. Mix the yeast in ¼ cup warm water. Add the sugar and let it stand for 5–10 minutes until it rises. Mix with 5 cups flour, yogurt, and salt in a deep bowl, and knead into a smooth dough. Add more water as needed. Let it rise and make patties, same as for 'Bhature' on page 205.
2. Put a cookie sheet on top or middle shelf in an oven, preheat at 'broil'. (Can also preheat the oven to 500°F.)
3. Roll each patty on floured surface, turning as needed, in round or oval shape, about 1/8" thick. Optionally brush each 'Nan' with little milk and sprinkle a few poppy (or sesame) seeds; press gently. ***Note:*** Roll 5–6 'Nan' and start baking. With practice, you'll be able to roll the next batch of 'Nan' while the previous one is baking.
4. **Broil:** Slide 4–6 'Nan' on the baking sheet in the pre-heated oven. Make sure that the oven stays hot; open the oven door a little if the oven turns off. When light brown specks appear on the top (after 1–2 minutes), turn each 'Nan' to bake the other side. It should become fluffy and crisp with light brown patches on both sides. (Do not over-brown because that makes the 'Nan' hard.) Bake all 'Nan' this way.
5. Spread little butter on each 'Nan', if desired. Stack them and wrap in aluminum foil to keep them warm and soft. Serve warm.

Recipes with a Spice

Variation 1: When a 'Nan' is half rolled (step 3), fold in mashed potatoes, grated broccoli, cauliflower, onions, 'paneer' (fresh cheese), or a combination with some spices. Press the edges together to hold the filling securely; press down with your hand, make the patty again and roll; proceed as usual.

Variation 2: May use the frozen bread dough available from the grocery store instead of making your own dough. Thaw the dough, preferably in the refrigerator, for 24 hours before using.

Healthy Alternative: For texture and nutrition, substitute all–purpose flour partially by whole–wheat flour. Also mix about 1 cup of any of other flour such as wheat germ, gram flour, soy flour, or oat bran when making the dough. Can also add pureed spinach.

Makes about 15 servings, one piece each. Per serving –
Nutritive Value: 161 calories, 5.5 g protein, 32 g carb, 1 g fiber, 1.4 g fat, 4 mg chol.
Food Group Exchange: 1.3 Grain, 1/8 Dairy.

Strange to see how a good dinner and feasting reconciles everybody.
Samuel Pepys

PARANTHA (Unleavened Griddle-Fried Bread)

It is fun making a 'Parantha', rolling and folding, making into a triangle or round. They stay soft and go very well in lunch box along with any dry vegetable or pickle. You can also cut them into quarter pieces, top with cheese or a fruit jam, and use as snacks. You can freeze prepared 'Parantha'; warm in the oven just as any piece of bread.

2 cups whole-wheat flour (+ ½ cup for dusting)
Water, milk or yogurt for making dough
Oil to pan–fry

<u>Seasonings:</u> ½ teaspoon salt

1. Knead 2 cups flour, adding water (or any other liquid) as needed, until the dough becomes smooth and supple. Cover with a kitchen towel and rest the dough for about an hour in a warm place.
2. Break a small piece of the dough and make into a smooth ball, working between your palms, using extra flour as needed, and flatten into about 2" round patty. Make several patties and cover with a towel.
3. Dust a flat surface with little flour. Roll each patty into a round 5–6" across; brush lightly with ¼ teaspoon oil with back of a spoon. Fold it into half, brush little oil, and fold again to make a triangle. Press with your hand and cover with dry flour.
4. Roll the layered patty, turning as needed, into a round or triangle, fairly thin (about 1/6" thick). Use as little dry flour as possible because the flour burns on the greased griddle.

5. **Pan-fry:** Heat a griddle (or heavy skillet or 'tawa') on medium-high heat. Slap the 'Parantha' to remove excess flour and slide it to the griddle. After a few seconds the top will change color and the bottom will have few light brown specks. Turn over with a flat spatula.
6. Spread ¼ teaspoon oil on the 'Parantha' while the second side cooks and gets a few light brown specks. Turn with the spatula again. Spread oil on the second side too. Press the corners with the spatula to make the 'Parantha' crisp. (Take care not to burn the 'Parantha'; regulate heat as needed.) When the first side gets more brown flecks, turn again to make it crispy on the second side too.
7. Transfer to a plate lined with paper towel. Cover loosely with aluminum foil wrap to keep them warm. Continue with the remaining 'Parantha' the same way.

Variation: Sprinkle some salt and red chili powder before folding the 'Parantha' in step 3. You may make sweet 'Parantha' by sprinkling sugar.

Healthy Alternative: Skip brushing oil inside the 'Parantha'. Make them using minimum oil on a heavy griddle.

Makes about 8 servings, one piece each. Per serving –
Nutritive Value: 155 calories, 5 g protein, 22 g carb, 4 g fiber, 5 g fat, 0 mg chol.
Food Group Exchange: 1 Grain, ½ Fat.

POTATO PARANTHA (Stuffed Griddle–Fried Bread)

Stuffed 'parantha' served with yogurt and chutney, make a great snack or breakfast meal. You can use different stuffing such as grated cauliflower or radish (preferably white radish), or finely chopped onions, or 'paneer'. You may refrigerate them and re–warm in the oven or skillet before serving. Except those with potato stuffing, they can be frozen. Serve hot.

2 cups whole–wheat flour (+ ½ cup for dusting)
½–¾ cup water, milk or vegetable stock
¼ cup oil to cook

Stuffing:

3–4 boiling potatoes, boiled, peeled and mashed
½ onion, finely chopped

Seasonings:

1 teaspoon grated ginger	¼ teaspoon black pepper
1 teaspoon crushed green chili	¼ teaspoon caraway seeds
½ teaspoon red chili powder	1 tablespoon chopped green coriander
½ teaspoon mango powder	1 teaspoon salt
½ teaspoon coriander powder	

1. Knead 2 cups flour, adding water (or any other liquid) as needed, until the dough becomes smooth and supple. Let it stand for ½ hour, covered.
2. Mix the stuffing and seasonings. Add salt when ready to make the 'Parantha' because salt makes the stuffing watery.
3. Dust a flat surface with flour. For each 'Parantha', make two small patties and roll them into thin rounds (about 1/6" thick). Brush one side with ¼ teaspoon oil and spread about 2 tablespoons of the filling. Cover with another round, pat the ends, and roll gently to make a thin round. (Another way is to roll one patty, about 5" across; brush with oil, place filling in center, and fold and press the edges over it to hold the filling securely. Make a patty and roll on floured surface to make about 1/6" thick round.)
4. Put the 'Parantha' on a hot griddle (or heavy skillet or 'tawa') on medium heat. Pan-fry the same way as for 'Parantha' on page 211.

Healthy Alternative: Skip brushing oil inside the 'Parantha'. Make them using minimum oil on a heavy griddle.

Variation: Use another stuffing such as grated ½ head cauliflower, or 1½ cups grated white radish (daikon). (Squeeze excess water from radish which can be used to knead the flour.)

Makes about 10 servings, one piece each. Per serving –
Nutritive Value: 168 calories, 5 g protein, 25 g carb, 4 g fiber, 5.4 g fat, 0 mg chol.
Food Group Exchange: 1.3 Grain, ½ Fat.

213

PURI (Fried Puffed Bread)

'Puri' are delicious served with any vegetable, especially with potatoes or 'Chhole'. They make a great picnic food and are liked by all. You can freeze them if desired; warm in the oven just as any piece of bread before eating.

2 cups whole-wheat flour (+ ¼ cup for dusting)
Water (or milk or yogurt) for dough
Oil to deep fry (about 2" deep in a wok)

Seasonings:
½ teaspoon salt   ¼ teaspoon caraway seeds (ajwain)

1. Mix 2 cups flour and the seasonings. Knead the dough, adding water (or any other liquid) as needed, until it becomes smooth but stiffer than that for other types of breads.
2. Make small patties (about 12) out of the dough, using flour as needed. Keep them covered. Roll each patty, turning as needed, into round thin 'Puri' on a flat surface with a rolling pin. Use a little oil to avoid sticking. (You may instead use a tortilla maker to make 'Puri'.)
3. Heat the oil in a deep skillet or wok. Deep-fry the same way as for 'Bhature' on page 205.

Variation: When making the dough, mix in ½ cup chopped spinach or fenugreek leaves.

Makes about 12 servings, one piece each. Per serving –
Nutritive Value: 161 calories, 3.3 g protein, 14.7 g carb, 3 g fiber, 9.8 g fat, 0 mg chol.
Food Group Exchange: ¾ Grain, 1 Fat.

ROTI 2000 (Unleavened Baked Vegetable Bread)

This bread is unexcelled in nutrition and aroma; a favorite with many. You'll see everybody waiting for them as they come hot from the oven. Use any vegetable that you like. You can freeze them if desired; warm in the oven just as any piece of bread before eating. You may serve them cut into two halves.

1 cup chopped vegetables such as onion, spinach, carrots, scallions
1 cup plain yogurt
2 cups whole–wheat flour (+ ½ cup for dusting)
½ cup soy flour
½ cup gram flour (besan)
¼ cup wheat germ
¼ cup oat bran

<u>Seasonings:</u> ½ teaspoon salt

1. Puree the vegetables and yogurt in a blender until smooth. Mix with all the flours and salt and knead the dough, adding water as needed, until it becomes smooth and supple. Cover with a kitchen towel and rest the dough for about an hour in a warm place. Refrigerate for a couple of hours or overnight before using.
2. Put a cookie sheet on top or middle shelf in the oven, preheat at 'broil'. (Can also preheat the oven to 500°F.)
3. Divide the dough in about 12 pieces and make smooth balls, working between your palms, using flour as needed, and flatten into about 2" round patties. Make all the patties and cover with a towel.
4. Dust a flat surface with little flour. Roll each patty into a round 5–6" across, about 1/8" thick. **Note:** Roll 5–6 'Roti' and start baking. With practice, you'll be able to roll the next batch of 'Roti' while the previous one is baking.
5. Broil the same way as for 'Nan' on page 209.
6. Spread little butter on one side of each 'Roti', if desired. Stack them and wrap in aluminum foil to keep them warm and soft. Serve warm.

Makes about 15 servings, one piece each. Per serving –
Nutritive Value: 108 calories, 6 g protein, 19 g carb, 3 g fiber, 1.5 g fat, 1 mg chol.
Food Group Exchange: 1 Grain, ¼ Legumes/Meat, ¼ Vegetable, 1/8 Dairy.

Recipes with a Spice

TANDOORI ROTI (Unleavened Baked Bread)

This is a quick and easy way to make fresh unleavened bread that is little thicker than 'Chapati'. Dough is also more elastic and rested than that for 'Chapati'.

2 cups whole-wheat flour (+ ½ cup for dusting)
Water (or milk or yogurt) for dough

<u>Seasonings:</u> 1/8 teaspoon salt

1. Mix the flour, salt and preferred liquid and knead the dough until it becomes smooth and supple. Cover with a kitchen towel and rest the dough for about an hour in a warm place. Refrigerate for couple of hours or overnight before using.
2. Break a small piece of the dough and make into a smooth ball, working between your palms, using extra flour as needed, and flatten into about 2" round patty. Make all the patties and cover with a towel.
3. Dust a flat surface with little flour. Roll each patty into a round 5-6" across, about 1/8" thick. **Note:** Roll 5–6 'Roti' and start baking. With practice, you'll be able to roll the next batch of 'Roti' while the previous one is baking.
4. Put a cookie sheet on top or middle shelf in an oven, preheat at 'broil'. (Can also preheat the oven to 500°F.) Broil the same way as for 'Nan' on page 209.

Healthy Alternative: When making the dough, add about ½ cup of any flour such as wheat germ, gram flour, soy flour, or oat bran (or a mixture), for texture and nutrition.

Makes about 8 servings, one piece each. Per serving –
Nutritive Value: 120 calories, 5 g protein, 22 g carb, 4 g fiber, 1 g fat, 0 mg chol.
Food Group Exchange: 1 Grain.

Essential Accompaniments
Yogurt, Dips, And Salads

Yogurt and some type of salad are a must in any meal. For everyday meals, plain yogurt is used seasoned with salt, pepper, or sugar. Make it to your taste by modifying the ingredients and seasonings; it is fun. For details of how to make yogurt and other techniques, refer to the chapter *Preparation Techniques*.

To help plan nutritious meals, each recipe gives nutritive value (calories, protein, carbohydrate (carb), fiber, fat, and cholesterol (chol)), and Food Group Exchange for a helping of the dish. Estimate is rounded off for ease of understanding. Garnishes, topping and small amounts of seasoning are not accounted for. (See page 13 for basis of estimating Food Group Exchange and nutritive value.)

Abbreviations:

carb: carbohydrate,	chol: cholesterol,	F: Fahrenheit,
g: gram,	lb: pound,	med: medium,
mg: milligram,	oz: ounce.	

BEAN DIP

It is a protein rich dip that can be served with crackers or vegetables. It can also be used as a spread in sandwiches. Use any beans. You can make the bean mixture several days in advance and freeze. Heat, garnish and serve at room temperature. Makes about 3 cups.

2 cups boiled, drained cannelloni or lima beans
(frozen, canned or made from dry beans)
½ cup plain yogurt
¼ cup thinly sliced scallions
1 tablespoon grated Parmesan cheese

Seasonings:
½ teaspoon red chili powder   1 teaspoon salt
¼ teaspoon black pepper

Garnish:
1 teaspoon chopped green chilies   ¼ teaspoon roasted (dark) cumin
                                        powder
1 teaspoon chopped green coriander ¼ teaspoon paprika

1. Process the beans, yogurt, and seasonings in a food processor or blender, until smooth. Add little water or yogurt to make spreadable consistency. *Note:* You may freeze the mixture at this time. If frozen, thaw in the refrigerator overnight, or in the microwave oven for 5–6 minutes.
2. Mix in the scallions and cheese. Garnish and serve warm or at room temperature.

Variation: Add 1/3 cup heavy cream or cream cheese in place of yogurt for creamier taste.

Makes about 12 servings, ¼ cup each. Per serving –
Nutritive Value: 50 calories, 4 g protein, 8 g carb, 2 g fiber, 0.4 g fat, 1 mg chol.
Food Group Exchange: 1/3 Legumes/Meat.

BOONDI RAITA (Yogurt with Tiny Nuggets)

This tasty crunchy way to serve yogurt is very popular. "Boondi' can be made in advance and frozen. Soak it in hot water before use.

½ cup 'Boondi' *(see recipe below)*
2 cups plain yogurt

Seasonings:

¼ teaspoon roasted cumin powder   ½ teaspoon sugar
¼ teaspoon red chili powder   1 teaspoon salt
¼ teaspoon black pepper

Garnish:

1 teaspoon chopped green chilies   ¼ teaspoon roasted (dark) cumin powder
1 teaspoon chopped green coriander   ¼ teaspoon paprika

1. Soak the 'Boondi' in warm water until soft (about 5 minutes). Drain; press between your palms to remove excess water.
2. Beat the yogurt and mix in the seasonings, to taste. Add the drained 'Boondi'. Garnish with green chilies and green coriander. Decorate with roasted cumin powder and paprika.

BOONDI

Makes 2 cups of dry 'Boondi'.

1 cup gram flour (besan), sifted
1 cup water
Oil for deep frying

Seasonings:
½ teaspoon caraway (ajwain) seeds   ½ teaspoon salt

1. Mix everything together to make a thin consistency batter, adding water as needed. Whisk it well to make it smooth.
2. Heat the oil on medium heat in a deep skillet or wok for deep-frying. Hold a flat metal sieve (available from specialty stores) on top of the skillet. Drop 1 tablespoon of the batter through the sieve (makes tiny drops), rubbing gently, just enough to make one layer on top of oil.
3. Turn with a slotted flat spatula; fry until golden brown. Drain 'Boondi' on paper towels. Repeat with the remaining batter. Store in the refrigerator or freeze.

Makes about 6 servings, ¾ cup each. Per serving –
Nutritive Value: 153 calories, 5 g protein, 9 g carb, 0.4 g fiber, 10 g fat, 5 mg chol.
Food Group Exchange: ½ Dairy, ¼ Fat, 1/8 Legumes/Meat.

CARROT SALAD

A nice colorful salad, serve it anytime as an accompaniment to spicy foods. It can be made in advance and refrigerated.

4 grated carrots

Seasonings:

1 tablespoon raisins   ¼ teaspoon salt
1 tablespoon lemon juice

Mix everything together and cover. Leave for 1 hour before ready to use.

Variation: Add about 1 tablespoon roasted sesame seeds. May omit the raisins.

Makes about 8 servings, ¼ cup each. Per serving –
Nutritive Value: 17 calories, 0.4 g protein, 4 g carb, 1 g fiber, 0 g fat, 0 mg chol. Food Group Exchange: ½ Vegetable.

GARLICY VINAIGRETTE

This vinaigrette can be tossed into any salad. It can be refrigerated for several days.

1 cup balsamic vinegar
¼ cup olive oil
6 cloves garlic, chopped

Seasonings:
½ teaspoon black pepper   ½ teaspoon salt

Mix everything together in a blender until smooth. Store in a small bottle to use as salad dressing.

Variation: Add about 2 teaspoons Dijon mustard.

Makes about 10 servings, 2 tablespoons each. Per serving –
Nutritive Value: 84 calories, 0 g protein, 7 g carb, 0 g fiber, 5.5 g fat, 0 mg chol. Food Group Exchange: ½ Fat, 1/8 Vegetable.

GUJIA DAHIBARA (Stuffed Lentil Patties in Yogurt)

It is a decorative tasty dish served often in parties. Gujia can be made in advance and frozen. Soak them in hot water before use.

For Gujia

1¼ cups peeled split Urad dal
Oil for deep–frying

<u>Seasonings</u>: ½ teaspoon baking powder

<u>Stuffing</u>:

1 tablespoon crushed ginger	50 raisins
1 tablespoon crushed green chili	1 tablespoon chopped green coriander

1. Soak the 'dal' overnight in warm water. Drain; grind finely with as little water as possible to make it like thick consistency paste. Blend in the baking powder. Refrigerate the batter for 6-7 hours to make it easier to handle.
2. Spread a thin wet cloth on counter top. Sprinkle water. Whip the batter to make it light and fluffy. Take a small piece of batter (size of a golf ball), make a round and flatten on the wet cloth. (Make a few of them at one time.) Put little bit of stuffing with 2-3 raisins, in each; fold in half; press the ends.
3. Heat the oil on medium-high heat in a deep skillet or wok. Deep-fry a few 'Gujia' at a time that can fit the wok. Turn with a flat slotted spatula; fry until golden brown on all sides. Drain on paper towels. At this point you can freeze them if desired.
4. When ready to use, soak 'Gujia' in salted warm water (2 teaspoons salt to 6 cups of water) until soft (15-20 minutes). Drain; squeeze between your palms to remove excess water.

For Yogurt:

2 lb. plain yogurt

<u>Seasonings</u>:

¼ teaspoon roasted cumin powder	½ teaspoon sugar
¼ teaspoon red chili powder	1 teaspoon salt
¼ teaspoon black pepper	

Garnish:

2 teaspoons chopped green chilies   ½ teaspoon roasted (dark) cumin
powder

2 teaspoons chopped green coriander   ½ teaspoon paprika

1. Beat the yogurt and mix in the seasonings to taste. It should be rather thin consistency because 'Gujia' absorb the liquid; add milk if needed. Spread soaked and drained 'Gujia' in a wide serving dish in single layer. Top completely with the seasoned yogurt. Cover and let the 'Gujia' soak for 3–4 hours in the refrigerator.
2. Garnish with green chilies and green coriander. Decorate with roasted cumin powder and paprika.

Makes about 20 servings, one piece each. Per serving –
Nutritive Value: 158 calories, 5 g protein, 10 g carb, 1.5 g fiber, 11 g fat, 2 mg chol.
Food Group Exchange: 1/3 Legumes/Meat, ¼ Dairy, ½ Fat.

MARINATED GINGER

It is customary to serve a teaspoon of marinated ginger with meals. Now many people are catching on to it as they learn of the therapeutic values of ginger. It can be made in advance and refrigerated.

½ lb. ginger–root
4 chopped green chilies (to taste)

Seasonings:

2 teaspoons lemon juice   ½ teaspoon salt

1. Break the ginger–root, rinse, and gently scrape the thin beige skin. The flesh under the skin is the most flavorful. Grate or slice the ginger.
2. Mix everything together in a small bowl or jar. Leave covered for 2–3 hours before ready to use.

Makes about 10 servings, 1 tablespoon each. Per serving –
Nutritive Value: 24 calories, 1 g protein, 5 g carb, 0.8 g fiber, 0 g fat, 0 mg chol.
Food Group Exchange: 1/3 Vegetable.

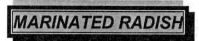
MARINATED RADISH

In India, white radish (daikon or 'mooli') is used widely. To eat white long radish with lemon, salt and pepper is a sweet reminder of sunny winters in North India. You may use white or red radish. It should preferably be made fresh or one day in advance and refrigerated.

1 lb. grated or finely chopped radish
4 chopped green chilies (to taste)

Seasonings:
1 teaspoon lemon juice   ½ teaspoon salt

1. Mix everything together except salt in a small bowl or jar. Let it marinate, covered, for about 1 hour.
2. Mix the salt few minutes before serving.

Makes about 15 servings, 1 tablespoon each. Per serving –
Nutritive Value: 11 calories, 0.4 g protein, 2 g carb, 0.6 g fiber, 0 g fat, 0 mg chol.
Food Group Exchange: ¼ Vegetable.

MUNG PAKORI (Lentil Balls in Yogurt)

It is a tasty dish served often in parties, either soaked in yogurt or 'tamarind chutney'. 'Pakori' can be made in advance and frozen. Soak them in hot water before use.

To Make Pakori

1¼ cups peeled split Mung dal
Oil for deep–frying

1. Soak the 'dal' overnight in warm water. Drain; grind finely with as little water as possible to make a thick consistency paste like batter. Whip to make it smooth and fluffy. (You may refrigerate the batter for 2-3 hours to make it easier to handle.)
2. Drop little rounds of batter (half the size of a walnut) and deep fry in hot oil on medium-high heat in a deep skillet or wok. Turn with a flat spatula; fry until golden brown on all sides. Drain extra oil on paper towels. At this point you can freeze them if desired.
3. When ready to use, soak the 'Pakori' in salted warm water (2 teaspoons salt to 6 cups of water) until soft (15–20 minutes). Drain; squeeze gently between your palms to remove excess water.

With Yogurt:

2 lb. plain yogurt

Seasonings:
¼ teaspoon roasted cumin powder
¼ teaspoon red chili powder
¼ teaspoon black pepper

½ teaspoon sugar
1 teaspoon salt

Garnish:
2 teaspoons chopped green chilies
2 teaspoons chopped green coriander

½ teaspoon roasted (dark) cumin powder
½ teaspoon paprika

1. Beat the yogurt and blend in the seasonings, to taste. Mix little milk if the yogurt mixture is thick. Spread the soaked and drained 'Pakori' in a wide serving dish in single layer. Top with the seasoned yogurt; cover well so that Pakori soak for 3-4 hours.
2. Garnish with green chilies and green coriander. Decorate with roasted cumin powder and paprika.

With Chutney:

1. Make Tamarind Chutney (see page 251). Dilute with extra water.
2. Dip soaked and drained Pakori in the tamarind solution (instead of yogurt) and serve in a wide serving dish.

Makes about 15 servings, ½ cup each. Per serving –
Nutritive Value: 141 calories, 6 g protein, 12 g carb, 2 g fiber, 8 g fat, 2.7 mg chol.
Food Group Exchange: ½ Legumes/Meat, ¼ Dairy, ½ Fat.

This is the basic salad served with any meal.

2 onions
½ cucumber
1 tomato
4 green whole or halved chilies (to taste)

Seasonings:
2 teaspoons lemon juice   ½ teaspoon salt

½ teaspoon black pepper

1. Slice onions, cucumber and tomato in round thin slices.
2. Decorate the onion slices on a plate. Top with cucumber and tomato slices, and green chilies. Sprinkle the seasonings and serve.

Makes about 8 servings, ½ cup each. Per serving –
Nutritive Value: 16 calories, 0.6 g protein, 4 g carb, 0.8 g fiber, 0 g fat, 0 mg chol.
Food Group Exchange: 1/3 Vegetable.

RAITA (Seasoned Yogurt)

It is very refreshing and goes well with spicy food. Some form of yogurt is a must in every meal. There is a wide choice for what to add to yogurt. 'Raita' can be refrigerated for a couple of days.

2 cups plain yogurt
1 cup grated (or chopped) cucumbers, carrots, onions, tomatoes, or a mix

Seasonings:
1 teaspoon crushed garlic
¼ teaspoon roasted cumin powder
¼ teaspoon red chili powder

¼ teaspoon black pepper
½ teaspoon sugar
1 teaspoon salt

Garnish:
1 teaspoon chopped green chilies

1 teaspoon chopped green coriander

¼ teaspoon roasted (dark) cumin powder
¼ teaspoon paprika

1. Beat the yogurt and mix in the seasonings, to taste. Mix the desired vegetable. (If using grated cucumbers, squeeze to remove excess water.) Cover tightly and refrigerate for at least 1 hour before serving.
2. Garnish with green chilies and green coriander. Decorate with thin lines of roasted cumin powder and paprika.

Variation: Instead of vegetables, add 2 tablespoons of fresh chopped mint (or 1 tablespoon crushed dry mint) along with other seasonings. May also add boiled chopped red potatoes.

Makes about 5 servings, ¾ cup each. Per serving:
Nutritive Value: 63 calories, 5 g protein, 7 g carb, 0.2 g fiber, 1.5 g fat, 4 mg chol.
Food Group Exchange: ½ Dairy, 1/6 Vegetable.

TOSSED VEGGIE TOFU SALAD

It is a great salad with ginger flavored seasoning. Check out the different types of lettuces that are available and use them in this salad.

**1 cucumber
1 green pepper
1 red pepper
1 small red onion
1 tomato
1 cup spinach leaves in byte-size pieces
½ lb. radish
1 carrot
8 oz. (about 1 cup) tofu, mashed or cubed**

Seasonings:

1 crushed green chili

½ teaspoon crushed ginger

2 teaspoons lemon juice (or ¼ cup plain yogurt lightly whipped with 1 teaspoon olive oil)

¼ teaspoon red chili powder

½ teaspoon black pepper

½ teaspoon salt

1. Wash and prepare the vegetables. Chop them in small cube like pieces.
2. Mix everything together in a salad bowl and cover. Let it marinate for about half hour before serving.

Variation: Add some cooked pasta or beans. May also add some broccoli that has been blanched in boiling water for 20 seconds.

Makes about 10 servings, one cup each. Per serving –
Nutritive Value: 36 calories, 2.5 g protein, 5.5 g carb, 2 g fiber, 1 g fat, 0 mg chol.
Food Group Exchange: 1 Vegetable, 1/8 Legumes/Meat.

VEGETABLE FINGER SALAD

Choose fresh and tender vegetables that you like to make a cool and colorful medley of vegetables. Serve it with a dip.

1 cucumber
1 red or yellow pepper
1 stalk celery
½ cup cherry or grape tomatoes
½ lb. radish
½ lb. daikon (white radish)
½ lb. carrots (or baby carrots)

Seasonings:

2 teaspoons lemon juice
½ teaspoon black pepper

¼ teaspoon red chili powder
½ teaspoon salt

1. Wash and trim the vegetables; cut them in round and long shapes that you desire. Decorate them in a platter.
2. Sprinkle the lemon juice and other seasonings, to taste.

Variation: Use pickling cucumbers that are crunchier.

Makes about 10 servings, one cup each. Per serving –
Nutritive Value: 26 calories, 1 g protein, 6 g carb, 1.7 g fiber, 0 g fat, 0 mg chol.
Food Group Exchange: ¾ Vegetable.

YOGURT ONION SAUCE

Use this sauce over plain vegetables, meat dishes or rice. Make the onion–garlic mixture ahead of time and mix with yogurt when ready to serve. It can be refrigerated for a couple of days. Makes about 2 cups.

2 medium chopped onions
1 cup plain yogurt
½ cup finely chopped cucumber
2 teaspoons oil

Seasonings:

½ teaspoon crushed garlic
½ teaspoon coriander powder
¼ teaspoon cumin powder
½ teaspoon garam masala

¼ teaspoon red chili powder
1 teaspoon paprika
¼ teaspoon salt

1. In a small saucepan, heat the oil on medium heat. Sauté the garlic and onions until golden brown. Add all the seasonings and stir for 1–2 minutes. Add about ¼ cup water and cook covered, for 5 minutes.
2. When completely cool; stir in the yogurt and cucumber. Cover and chill.

Makes about 4 servings, ½ cup each. Per serving –
Nutritive Value: 81 calories, 4 g protein, 9 g carb, 1 g fiber, 3 g fat, 2.5 mg chol.
Food Group Exchange: ¾ Vegetable, ¼ Dairy, 1/6 Fat.

YOGURT SALAD DRESSING

Use this dressing on any salad. It can also be used to marinate vegetables, tofu, or meat before baking or grilling them. It can be refrigerated for a couple of days. Makes little more than a cup.

1 cup plain yogurt
1 tablespoon olive oil
2 tablespoons balsamic vinegar

Seasonings:

½ teaspoon crushed garlic
1 teaspoon minced onions
½ teaspoon minced ginger

½ teaspoon chopped green chili
½ teaspoon black pepper
½ teaspoon salt

Whisk together everything, preferably in a blender.

Healthy Alternative: Omit oil. Increase the amount of vinegar or add 1 tablespoon lemon juice. May also add chopped cucumber or tomato.

Makes about 8 servings, 2 tablespoons each. Per serving –
Nutritive Value: 34 calories, 1 g protein, 3 g carb, 0 g fiber, 2 g fat, 1 mg chol.
Food Group Exchange: 1/8 Dairy, 1/8 Fat.

Tentalizing Spicing
Pickles and Chutney

Pickles (called 'achar' in Hindi) and chutney add zest to food. Chutney is a smooth blend of some fruit or vegetable, herbs, and spices. Generally, it cannot be preserved as long as pickles. You can make pickles and chutney as spicy and hot as you like by modifying the quantity and type of seasonings, especially green chilies and red chili powder. Serve them cold or at room temperature as condiments with any snack or meal. They also make excellent sandwich spreads. Some of them can be stored for more than a year. Always use a non-metallic container to prepare and store them.

To help plan nutritious meals, each recipe gives nutritive value (calories, protein, carbohydrate (carb), fiber, fat, and cholesterol (chol)), and Food Group Exchange for a helping of the dish. Estimate is rounded off for ease of understanding. Garnishes, topping and small amounts of seasoning are not accounted for. (See page 13 for basis of estimating Food Group Exchange and nutritive value.)

Note: Since pickles and chutney are served as condiments in small quantities, their Food Group Exchange value is not analyzed. In general, they are high in sodium.

Abbreviations:

carb: carbohydrate,	chol: cholesterol,	F: Fahrenheit,
g: gram,	lb: pound,	med: medium,
mg: milligram,	oz: ounce.	

BASIL CHUTNEY

This chutney is especially good as a dip with vegetables or mixed with pasta. It can be easily made in advance and frozen or refrigerated.

1 bunch (5–6 oz.) fresh basil
2 tomatoes, cut
2 tablespoons peanuts (or any other nuts)
1 tablespoon olive oil

Seasonings:

4 cloves garlic	¼ teaspoon chili powder
2 green chilies	1 teaspoon salt

1. Snip and wash the basil, removing any hard stems.
2. Grind everything together in a blender to make a semi-liquid smooth mixture. Add little water or more oil if needed. Store in the refrigerator in a nonmetallic container.

Makes about 10 servings, 2 tablespoons each. Per serving –
Nutritive Value: 22 calories, 1 g protein, 3 g carb, 1 g fiber, 1 g fat, 0 chol.

CARROT-CHILI PICKLE

Mixing chilies with carrots diminishes the fire of the chilies. This pickle can generally be stored, without refrigeration, for a long time. It is however better to refrigerate.

1 cup chopped carrots (in cubes or grated)
1 cup chopped green chilies (hot, mild, or mixed)
2 tablespoons oil
1 tablespoon white vinegar

Seasonings:

2 tablespoons coarsely crushed mustard seeds

3 teaspoons salt

1. Mix everything together; put in a glass or plastic jar.
2. Leave in the sun or a warm place for 2–3 days; stir the pickle everyday. Store preferably in the refrigerator. Serve cold or at room temperature.

Variation: Also add 10–15 cloves of garlic to the pickle.

Makes about 30 servings, 2 teaspoons each. Per serving –
Nutritive Value: 12 calories, 0 g protein, 1 g carb, 0 g fiber, 1 g fat, 0 mg chol.

CHILI PICKLE (without oil)

Use jalapin pepper or any other green chili for this pickle. It can be stored for a long time.

1 cup chopped green chilies (hot, mild, or mixed)

Seasonings:
1 tablespoon crushed mustard seeds   1 teaspoon salt
1 tablespoon lemon juice

1. Mix everything together; put in a plastic or glass jar.
2. Leave in sun or a warm place for 2–3 days; stir the pickle everyday. Store preferably in the refrigerator. Serve cold or at room temperature.

Variation: Mix ½–1 cup grated carrots with chilies to diminish the fire of the chilies.

Makes about 12 servings, 2 teaspoons each. Per serving –
Nutritive Value: 5 calories, 0 g protein, 1 g carb, 0 g fiber, 0 g fat, 0 mg chol.

CHUTNEY POWDER

Many families keep this powder (also called Mulagai powder) ready in the house to be used with any meal. It is especially served with 'Dosa' and 'Idli'. It can be refrigerated for several days. Makes about ¾ cup.

2 tablespoons Chana dal
2 tablespoons Urad peeled split dal
10 red whole chilies
1 tablespoon tamarind pulp
2 tablespoons grated un-sweetened coconut

Seasonings:
¼ teaspoon fenugreek seeds (methi)   1 teaspoon curry leaves
1/8 teaspoon asafetida powder   1½ teaspoons salt

To Sauté:
1 teaspoon oil   1 teaspoon mustard seeds

1. Roast the fenugreek seeds, asafetida powder, and curry leaves in the oven or a skillet on medium–high heat. Also roast the Chana dal, Urad dal, and red chilies.
2. Mix in the tamarind pulp, coconut and salt. Grind everything together to a coarse powder.
3. To sauté, heat the oil in a small pan on medium-high heat. Add mustard seeds and cover. Turn off the heat as soon as they splutter. Add the sauté to the powder.

Healthy Alternative: Omit the sauté. Add 2 teaspoons roasted sesame seeds instead of coconut.

Makes about 12 servings, 1 tablespoon each. Per serving –
Nutritive Value: 29 calories, 1 g protein, 4 g carb, 1 g fiber, 1 g fat, 0 mg chol.
Food Group Exchange: 1/12 Legumes/Meat, 1/12 Fat.

COCONUT CHUTNEY

This chutney is traditionally served with 'Dosa' and 'Idli'. It can be made in advance and frozen.

1 cup grated un-sweetened coconut
¼ cup roasted peanuts
½ cup plain yogurt

Seasonings:

¼" piece ginger (peeled and washed)
6 (or more) green chilies

1+ teaspoon salt
¼ bunch of green coriander (snipped, washed, and chopped)

To Sauté:

1 teaspoon oil
1 teaspoon mustard seeds

½ teaspoon Urad peeled split dal
¼ teaspoon fenugreek seeds (methi)

1. Mix all the ingredients and seasonings and grind to a semi-thick paste in a blender. Add more yogurt or little water if needed.
2. To sauté, heat the oil in a small pan on medium-high heat. Add mustard seeds and cover. As soon as they splutter, add Urad dal and fenugreek seeds, and stir for a few seconds. Add the sauté to the chutney.

Healthy Alternative: Reduce the amount of coconut and increase that of coriander. Use minimum oil for the sauté.

Makes about 16 servings, 2 tablespoons each. Per serving –
Nutritive Value: 38 calories, 1 g protein, 2 g carb, 0.5 g fiber, 3 g fat, 0 mg chol.

DATES (Khajoor) CHUTNEY

Dates are delicious in any form. This makes an excellent sandwich spread. This chutney can generally be stored without refrigeration, though it is better to refrigerate if it is to be kept for a long time.

20 oz. fresh dates pitted and chopped finely
½ cup sugar
¼ cup lemon juice
1 cup white vinegar

Seasonings:
2 tablespoons red chili powder
1 tablespoon garam masala

¼ cup salt

1. Mix the dates, other ingredients and seasonings to your taste. Put in a glass or plastic jar with a lid.
2. Leave in sun or a warm place for 2–3 days; stir the pickle everyday. Serve cold or at room temperature.

Makes about 40 servings, 1 tablespoon each. Per serving –
Nutritive Value: 50 calories, 0.3 g protein, 13 g carb, 1 g fiber, 0 g fat, 0 mg chol.

GARLIC PICKLE

This pickle keeps well in the refrigerator. It can be used as a spread on bread or mixed with any dish to add a punch.

2 heads (about 6 oz.) garlic

<u>Seasonings</u>:

2 teaspoons cumin powder

1 teaspoon red chili powder

2 tablespoons lemon juice

1½ teaspoons salt

1. Separate the garlic cloves and peel them.
2. Puree the cloves and the seasonings in a food processor. Put in a plastic or glass jar and store in the refrigerator. Serve cold or at room temperature.

Variation: Add 1 tablespoon olive oil that helps to preserve the garlic longer.

Makes about 15 servings, 1 tablespoon each. Per serving –
Nutritive Value: 17 calories, 1 g protein, 4 g carb, 0.3 g fiber, 0 g fat, 0 mg chol.

GRAM FLOUR CHILIES

These chilies are served as side dish or as topping especially for 'Dhokla'. They can be refrigerated for several days.

**1 lb. green (hot, mild or mixed) chilies,
cut in halves lengthwise
½ cup gram flour (besan)
3 tablespoons oil**

Seasonings:

1½ teaspoons mustard seeds
¼ teaspoon caraway (ajwain) seeds
2 teaspoons coriander powder
1 teaspoon mango powder

½ teaspoon turmeric powder
2 teaspoons salt
1 tablespoon lemon juice

1. Heat the oil in a skillet on medium heat. Add the mustard seeds and cover. As soon as they start to pop (few seconds), add the caraway seeds and green chilies; stir together for 5 minutes.
2. Reduce the heat. Add the gram flour and the remaining seasonings, except lemon juice. Keep on stirring until the gram flour is roasted (5–10 minutes). Add more oil as needed. Take care not to burn the flour. Add lemon juice.
3. Serve cold or at room temperature.

Healthy Alternative: To reduce oil, roast the gram flour in the oven or microwave until golden brown. Mix the gram flour with green chilies and add little water for everything to mix.

*Makes about 16 servings, 1 tablespoon each. Per serving –
Nutritive Value: 45 calories, 1 g protein, 4 g carb, 0.7 g fiber, 3 g fat, 0 mg chol.*

LEMON PICKLE

This pickle, made without oil, can be stored for a long time.

10 lemons

Seasonings:

2 tablespoons sugar
1 teaspoon chili powder
2 teaspoons garam masala

1 teaspoon black pepper
2 tablespoons salt

1. Rinse and dry the lemons. Cut 7 lemons into 4–6 slices. Mix with the seasonings and put in a glass or plastic jar.
2. Pour lemon juice from the remaining 3 lemons. Cover tightly and keep in the sun (or a warm place) for a week, shaking the jar every day, until the lemon skin is little tender. Store in a cool dry place or refrigerate.

Makes about 20 servings, ½ lemon each. Per serving –
Nutritive Value: 16 calories, 0.7 g protein, 7 g carb, 2.5 g fiber, 0 g fat, 0 mg chol.

MANGO–ASAFETIDA PICKLE

Make this spicy pickle without oil. It does not need to be refrigerated unless you want to keep it for a long time. Fills a 1–2 lb. jar.

2 lb. raw green mangoes

Seasonings:
2 tablespoons salt
1 tablespoon red chili powder

2 teaspoons asafetida powder
2 tablespoons sugar

1. Wash the mangoes and pat–dry them. Peel and cut them into long thin slices; discard the pit. Mix the mango slices and salt in a wide stainless steel container and leave for 4–5 hours until they release water.
2. Remove the slices, squeezing out extra moisture, and spread them on an absorbent cloth for 3–4 hours. Save the water.
3. Mix the dried mango slices and remaining seasonings. Add the salted water just enough to wet the mixture. Adjust the seasonings. Put the pickle in a jar, cover, and store in a warm place for a few days. Shake everyday. Pickle may be refrigerated if it is to be kept long.

Makes about 32 servings, 2 tablespoons each. Per serving –
Nutritive Value: 21 calories, 0 g protein, 6 g carb, 0.5 g fiber, 0 g fat, 0 mg chol.

It takes about 20 minutes for your brain to notice that you have eaten.

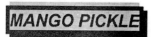

MANGO PICKLE

This is the most popular pickle in India. Almost everybody makes this pickle when mangoes are abundant and easily available. It does not need to be refrigerated unless you want to keep it for a long time. Fills a 1–2 lb. jar.

**2 lb. raw green mangoes
2 cups oil (preferably mustard oil)**

<u>**Seasonings**</u>:

2 tablespoons fennel seeds
2 tablespoons fenugreek seeds
1 tablespoon onion seeds (kalonji)
1 tablespoon red chili powder

1 tablespoon turmeric powder
2 tablespoons salt
1 teaspoon asafetida powder

1. Wash the mangoes and pat–dry them. Without peeling, cut them into long thin slices; discard the pit. Dry the slices in sun for 10–12 hours spread on an absorbent cloth.
2. Heat half of the oil in a large skillet on medium heat. Add the seasonings except salt and asafetida powder. As soon as they sizzle, add the dried mango pieces. Stir together for 5–10 minutes. Turn off the heat. Mix in the salt and asafetida powder when the mixture is cold.
3. Heat the remaining oil separately. Pour the hot oil over the spiced mango slices and adjust the spices, as needed.
4. Put the pickle in a jar, cover, and store in a warm place for a few days. Shake everyday. Pickle may be refrigerated if it is to be kept long.

Variation: Peel the mangoes before cutting. Reduce the oil by half and adjust the seasonings.

*Makes about 32 servings, 1 tablespoon each. Per serving –
Nutritive Value: 140 calories, 0 g protein, 5 g carb, 0.5 g fiber, 14 g fat, 0 mg chol.*

MANGO Spicy SALSA

You may use any other fruit such as plums, apricots, or peaches, to make this salsa. Adjust the seasonings depending on the tartness of the fruits. It can be refrigerated for several weeks.

2 mangoes peeled and chopped
2 tablespoons lemon juice
¼ cup cider vinegar

Seasonings:

1 tablespoon chopped green chilies
2 tablespoons coarsely cut green coriander

¼ teaspoon red chili powder
1 teaspoon salt

1. Mix everything together in a food processor, just enough to chop and mix (3–5 rounds). Add little water if needed.
2. Refrigerate for 2 hours before serving.

Makes about 8 servings, 2 tablespoons each. Per serving –
Nutritive Value: 35 calories, 0 g protein, 9.5 g carb, 1 g fiber, 0 g fat, 0 mg chol.

Recipes with a Spice

MANGO Sweet SALSA

You may use any sweet fruit to make this salsa. Adjust the seasonings to your taste. It can be refrigerated for several weeks.

2 mangoes peeled and chopped
1/3 cup white or brown sugar
1 tablespoon lemon juice

Seasonings:
1 teaspoon chopped green chilies
1 tablespoon coarsely cut green coriander

¼ teaspoon red chili powder
¼ teaspoon salt

1. Mix everything together in a food processor, just enough to chop and mix (3–5 rounds). Add little water if needed.
2. Refrigerate for about 2 hours for flavors to mix.

Makes about 8 servings, 2 tablespoons each. Per serving –
Nutritive Value: 66 calories, 0 g protein, 17 g carb, 1 g fiber, 0 g fat, 0 mg chol.

MINT-CORIANDER CHUTNEY

This chutney is generally served with 'Samosas', 'Pakoras' and other salty snacks. You have a number of options as to what to add to this chutney; use your taste buds. It can be easily made in advance and frozen or refrigerated.

1 small bunch fresh mint or green coriander (or mixed)
1 apple (or ½ avocado)
1 small tomato
2 tablespoons peanuts (optional)
2 tablespoons lemon juice

Seasonings:

4 green chilies
¼" piece of ginger
¼ teaspoon red chili powder
½ teaspoon ground pomegranate seeds

1 teaspoon mango powder
½ teaspoon black salt
1 teaspoon salt

1. Snip and wash the mint and coriander. Remove hard mint stems. Peel and cut the apple (or avocado), and tomato to be used.
2. Grind everything together, using about ½ cup water as needed for semi-liquid consistency. The ingredients must be ground completely. (May use a food processor to chop everything and then a blender to grind.)
3. Store in a nonmetallic container in the refrigerator.

Variation: Instead of using an apple, add some onion and garlic.

Makes about 15 servings, 1 tablespoon each. Per serving –
Nutritive Value: 10 calories, 0 g protein, 2 g carb, 0.6 g fiber, 0 g fat, 0 mg chol.

PICKLED ONIONS

Onions go with any kind of meal, formal or informal.

20 small even sized white onions
1 cup red wine vinegar

<u>**Seasonings**</u>:

1 tablespoon salt   1 teaspoon paprika

1. Peel the onions; put 2 half-cuts in each onion top. Put them in a wide mouth glass jar and cover with salt, paprika, and vinegar. Shake the jar occasionally. When the pickle is ready (in 2-3 days), refrigerate.
2. Remove the onions from vinegar when serving.

Variation: To soften the onions, boil them in vinegar and seasonings for 5–10 minutes.

Makes about 10 servings, 2 pieces each. Per serving –
Nutritive Value: 31 calories, 1 g protein, 6.5 g carb, 1 g fiber, 0 g fat, 0 mg chol.

SWEET and SOUR CHILIES

This can be served as a side dish with any meal.

2 chopped onions
1 lb. green chopped chilies (hot, mild, or mixed)
3 tablespoons oil

Seasonings:

2 tablespoons sugar   3 teaspoons salt
4 teaspoons mango powder

1. Heat the oil in a skillet on medium heat. Sauté the onions until translucent.
2. Add the green chilies; stir together for 5 minutes. Add the seasonings to taste. Stir for another 5 minutes.
3. Store in the refrigerator. Serve cold.

Healthy Alternative: Reduce the amount of oil; may increase the amount of onions, and add some garlic if desired.

Makes about 36 servings, 2 teaspoons each. Per serving –
Nutritive Value: 20 calories, 0 g protein, 2.4 g carb, 0 g fiber, 1 g fat, 0 mg chol.

SWEET VEGETABLE PICKLE

This pickle does not need to be refrigerated. You may modify the proportion of different vegetables as you like.

3 lb. vegetables (cauliflower, carrots, and turnips)
10 chopped garlic cloves
2 tablespoons chopped ginger
1 cup packed brown sugar
(preferably gur (Indian jaggery))
¾ cup vinegar
1 cup oil (preferably mustard oil)

Seasonings:

2 teaspoons chili powder
2 teaspoons garam masala

1 tablespoon crushed mustard seeds
2+ teaspoons salt

1. Wash and cut the vegetables into bite–size pieces. Put the cut vegetables in boiling water for 1 minute only. Vegetables must remain crunchy. Drain and dry the vegetables for 4–6 hours spread on an absorbent cloth. (Instead of boiling, you may microwave the vegetables on high, covered, for 6–8 minutes.)
2. Heat the oil in a large skillet on medium heat. Sauté the garlic until light brown. Stir in ginger. Add half–cooked vegetables, chili powder and garam masala. Stir together for 5–10 minutes. Turn off the heat.
3. In a separate pot, boil the brown sugar and vinegar together. Pour it on the vegetables. Also add salt and crushed mustard seeds, to taste. Vegetables should be coated by the semi-thick mixture. If necessary, add more oil and vinegar.
4. Put the pickle in a jar, cover, and store in a warm place for a few days. Shake everyday. Pickle may be refrigerated if it is to be kept long.

Healthy Alternative: You may reduce the amount of oil. Keep the pickle refrigerated after it is ready in a day or two.

Makes about 48 servings, about 2 tablespoons each. Per serving –
Nutritive Value: 63 calories, 0.4 g protein, 6 g carb, 0.7 g fiber, 5 g fat, 0 mg chol.

TAMARIND CHUTNEY

This sweet and sour chutney is generally served with yogurt dishes. This can be made in advance and frozen or refrigerated.

½ lb. tamarind block (or 4 tablespoons tamarind paste)
¼ cup sugar (or brown sugar)

Seasonings:

1 teaspoon chili powder
1 tablespoon roasted cumin powder
½ teaspoon paprika

1 teaspoon salt
½ teaspoon black salt

1. If using tamarind block, rinse; soak in about 2 cups water for 1–2 hours. If using tamarind paste, mix it with water. Boil soaked tamarind block or paste until it becomes soft (about 15 minutes). Add more water if needed. Let it cool. If using tamarind block, mash and strain through a colander to remove seeds and roughage.
2. Add the seasonings to taste. Refrigerate and serve cold.

Variation: May add some golden raisins and chopped dates to the chutney.

Makes about 10 servings, 2 tablespoons each. Per serving –
Nutritive Value: 73 calories, 0.6 g protein, 19 g carb, 1 g fiber, 0 g fat, 0 mg chol.

TAMARIND–TOMATO CHUTNEY

This chutney is similar to 'Tamarind Chutney' above. Use of the tomatoes gives it a little different taste. It can be made in advance and refrigerated or frozen.

4 tablespoons tamarind paste
6 plum tomatoes, peeled and crushed
3 tablespoons brown sugar

<u>Seasonings</u>:

1 tablespoon crushed ginger
2 green crushed mild chilies
1 teaspoon chili powder

1 teaspoon roasted cumin powder
½ teaspoon paprika
2 teaspoons salt

1. Boil the tamarind paste, tomatoes, ginger and chilies for about ½ hour. Add little water if too thick.
2. Add sugar and the remaining seasonings to taste; cook for another 5 minutes. Refrigerate and serve cold.

Makes about 10 servings, 2 tablespoons each. Per serving –
Nutritive Value: 26 calories, 0.4 g protein, 6 g carb, 0.6 g fiber, 0 g fat, 0 mg chol.

TOMATO SALSA

Make this salsa, rich in vitamin C and minerals, to your taste—hot or mild. It can be refrigerated for several days.

4 chopped red tomatoes
1 chopped red onion
1+ tablespoon lemon juice

Seasonings:

2 teaspoons chopped ginger
2 teaspoons chopped green chilies
¼ teaspoon red chili powder

¼ teaspoon ground mustard seeds
1 teaspoon salt

1. Mix everything together in a food processor, just enough to chop and mix (3–5 rounds). Do not puree.
2. Refrigerate for a couple of hours before you serve it.

Makes about 8 servings, ½ cup each. Per serving –
Nutritive Value: 13 calories, 0.4 g protein, 3 g carb, 0.6 g fiber, 0 g fat, 0 mg chol.

VEGETABLE CHUTNEY

Make this chutney from any vegetable such as zucchini, cabbage or green tomatoes. Serve it with any meal or as a sandwich spread. It can be made in advance and frozen. Makes about 2 cups.

2 cups chopped eggplant
½ tablespoon tamarind paste mixed with water
2 teaspoons oil

Seasonings:
1 teaspoon cumin seeds
2 cloves garlic
¼" piece ginger

2 (or more) green chilies
1 teaspoon salt
¼ bunch of green coriander
(snipped and chopped)

To Sauté:
1 teaspoon oil
1 teaspoon mustard seed

½ teaspoon Urad peeled split dal

1. Heat 2 teaspoons oil in a small skillet. Add cumin seeds and garlic. As they start to brown, add chopped eggplant, ginger, chilies and salt. Cook for 5–10 minute until the eggplant is lightly roasted. Add the tamarind.
2. When little cold, grind along with green coriander, to a semi-thick paste in a blender. Add little water if needed.
3. To sauté, heat 1 teaspoon of oil in a small pan on medium-high heat. Add mustard seeds and cover. As soon as they splutter, add Urad dal and stir for a few seconds. Add the sauté to the chutney.

Variation: May add a tomato when cooking the vegetable.

Makes about 12 servings, 2 tablespoons each. Per serving –
Nutritive Value: 14 calories, 0.2 g protein, 1 g carb, 0.4 g fiber, 1 g fat, 0 chol.

VEGETABLE PICKLE

Use any vegetables such as squash, turnips or beans for this pickle. It makes an excellent side dish.

1 lb. vegetables (cauliflower and carrots)
½ cup vinegar
2 teaspoons oil (preferably mustard oil)

Seasonings:

½ teaspoon turmeric powder
½ teaspoon sugar
1 teaspoon red chili powder

1 tablespoon crushed mustard seeds
1 teaspoon salt

1. Wash and cut the vegetables into medium size pieces. Put the vegetables in boiling water for 1 minute only so that they remain crunchy. Drain and dry the vegetables spread on an absorbent cloth for 4–6 hours. (Instead of boiling, you may microwave the vegetables on high, covered, for about 4 minutes.)
2. Heat the oil in a large skillet on medium heat. Add the turmeric powder, sugar and vinegar. Turn off the heat. Stir in half–cooked dry vegetables and the remaining seasonings.
3. Put the pickle in a jar, cover, and store in a warm place for 2–3 days until the pickle is ready. Shake everyday. Refrigerate the pickle for use as needed.

Makes about 12 servings, 2 tablespoons each. Per serving –
Nutritive Value: 19 calories, 0.5 g protein, 3 g carb, 1 g fiber, 1 g fat, 0 chol.

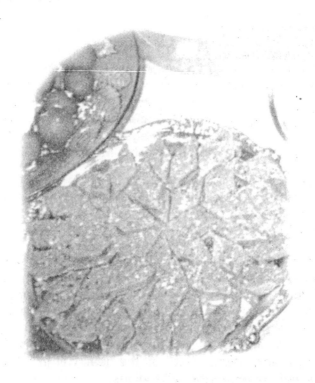

Scrumptious and Tasty

Desserts

Milk and milk products are the prime ingredients in many Indian desserts. Some recipes have been adapted to use Ricotta cheese instead of milk. Popular and delicious desserts include Carrot Halva, Gulabjamun (Rose Munchkins), Rasmalai (Milk Cakes), and Ricotta Cheese Burfi. Most of the desserts can be made in advance and frozen. Thaw and serve them at room temperature.

The ingredients used in the desserts are readily available in supermarkets. **Cardamoms and saffron** (kesar) add wonderful flavor and color. Use fresh green cardamom pods. Peel the pods, and crush the seeds coarsely using a mortar and pestle or mini processor, for use in different delicacies. Cardamom powder kept for a long time loses the essential oils and hence the flavor. Saffron flakes are generally soaked in warm water or milk before use.

Some recipes use **rose water or kewra water,** an infusion of flowers, for delicious scent. Nuts can be added in any amount for "nut nuts" and of course for taste and texture. Use unsalted butter or clarified butter (ghee) when specified.

A special decorative ingredient is **varak** or very fine edible silver film attached to a fine tissue paper. Place the tissue paper with silver side on dessert and pat gently. Remove the tissue paper; silver film stays on the dessert.

Some types of 'burfi' require making **syrup of single-thread consistency.** This refers to a test done as follows: Boil the sugar and water together, stirring often, to 200°F. Turn off the heat. Take about ¼ teaspoon of syrup, let it cool a few seconds, and tilt the spoon so that the syrup falls in drops. The droplets should make a small thread as they fall. If the syrup is too thin, cook it a little longer; if too thick, add a little water to it and give a quick boil.

To help plan nutritious meals, each recipe gives nutritive value (calories, protein, carbohydrate (carb), fiber, fat, and cholesterol (chol)), and Food Group Exchange for a helping of the dish. Estimate is rounded off for ease of understanding. Garnishes, topping and small amounts of seasoning are not accounted for. (See page 13 for basis of estimating Food Group Exchange and nutritive value.)

Abbreviations:

carb: carbohydrate,	chol: cholesterol,	F: Fahrenheit,
g: gram,	lb: pound,	med: medium,
mg: milligram,	oz: ounce.	

ALMOND BURFI (Fudge)

This fudge is delicious. You can also make a cashew fudge the same way by substituting cashews for almonds. It freezes well and can be refrigerated for several weeks. Serve at room temperature. Makes about 30 pieces.

2 cups blanched almonds
4 tablespoons (2 oz.) unsalted butter
½ cup non-fat dry milk

Seasonings:
½ teaspoon rose essence (optional) 1 tsp. coarsely crushed cardamom seeds

For Syrup:
1 cup sugar ¾ cup water

Garnish: 4 varak heets (optional)

1. Grind the blanched almonds (or cashews) into coarse powder.
2. Make the syrup by boiling the water and sugar together. Stir and simmer for 1 minute to make it single-thread consistency (see page 257).
3. In a skillet on medium heat, stir the crushed almonds and butter (added for moistness) for a few minutes. Add the syrup, rose essence and cardamoms. Reduce heat and keep stirring until the mixture is thick like dough. Add ½ cup (or more) of non-fat dry milk if the mixture is not thick enough.
4. Grease a board or counter and a rolling pin. Roll the mixture to ¼ inch thickness. If desired, spread 'varak' sheets on top for decoration.
5. Let it dry for 15 minutes; cut into diamond shape or square pieces and store in the refrigerator.

Variation: Instead of using 'varak' sheets, place chopped blanched almonds on each piece.

Healthy Alternative: Use un-blanched almonds and omit butter. Add grated apples, figs, or dates to the mixture when cooking.

Makes about 15 servings, 2 pieces each. Per serving –
Nutritive Value: 205 calories, 6 g protein, 19 g carb, 2 g fiber, 13 g fat, 9 mg chol.
Food Group Exchange: 1 Sugar, ½ Legumes/Meat, ¼ Fat.

ATTA BURFI (Whole-Wheat Fudge)

Wheat flour is considered the easiest to digest. This fudge therefore is generally served to nursing mothers. It is better to use stone ground flour. Serve warm or at room temperature. It freezes well and can be refrigerated for several weeks. Makes about 45 pieces.

3 cups whole wheat flour
1¾ cups (14 oz.) unsalted butter
1 cup non-fat dry milk

Seasonings:

1 cup coarsely crushed almonds

1 teaspoon coarsely crushed cardamom seeds

For Syrup:

1¾ cups sugar

1 cup water

Garnish: 8 varak sheets or ¼ cup chopped unsalted pistachio

1. Make the syrup by boiling the sugar and water together. Keep it aside. When ready to use, stir and simmer for 2–3 minutes to make single-thread consistency syrup. (See page 257. It is better to keep the syrup a little soft because overcooked syrup will make the 'burfi' hard.) Use it hot.
2. Grease a 9x13" cookie sheet.
3. Soften the butter in a wide pot or deep skillet on medium heat. (May reduce butter by ¼ cup if stirring on low heat.) While stirring, slowly add the flour. Keep stirring till the flour turns light brown (30-35 minutes). Regulate the heat to make sure that the mixture does not burn. It should give wonderful aroma and the butter appears separated.
4. Add the almonds; stir for a couple of minutes. Add cardamoms. Mix in dry milk. Turn off the heat.
5. Add hot syrup and mix quickly. It should be like very thick batter that will easily set. (Add more dry milk and cook a little bit more if the mixture is not thick enough.) Immediately spread it on the greased cookie sheet, about 1/3" thick. Pat gently with wax paper to make it even.
6. Garnish as desired. When cold, cut into diamond shape or square pieces and store.

Makes about 22 servings, 2 pieces each. Per serving –
Nutritive Value: 306 calories, 6 g protein, 31 g carb, 2.6 g fiber, 18.5 g fat, 41 mg chol.
Food Group Exchange: 1 Sugar, 1 Fat, ½ Grain, 1/8 Dairy, 1/8 Legumes/Meat.

BALUSHAHI (Royal Rounds)

Almost looking like a donut without a hole, these can be served as a dessert or a snack. They freeze well and can be refrigerated for couple of weeks. Serve at room temperature.

2½ cups all-purpose flour
½ cup (4 oz.) butter or shortening, melted
½ teaspoon baking soda
½ teaspoon baking powder
¾ cup plain yogurt
Oil for frying, 2–3" deep in a wok

For Syrup: 1¼ cups sugar, ¾ cup water
Garnish: Chopped unsalted pistachio (about 10)

1. Make the syrup by boiling the water and sugar together for 1 minute, stirring often, to make it single-thread consistency (see page 257). Set aside.
2. Mix the flour, butter or shortening, and baking soda. Add yogurt and knead the dough until it becomes smooth and supple. (Add yogurt, as needed.) Cover and leave the dough for about one hour.
3. Break the dough with greased hands and make small balls. Flatten each ball like a donut and press in center with your thumb to make an indent.
4. Heat the oil in a wok or deep skillet on medium heat. Fry 4-6 balls 'Balushahi' at a time on low-medium heat until they puff up and are golden brown on all sides. (It is a good idea to test fry one small 'Balushahi' to make sure that the heat is set right.)
5. Drain them on a paper towel and immerse in the syrup. Soak for 5 minutes and take them out on a plate. Fry the remaining 'Balushahi' and soak in the same way.
6. Garnish with chopped pistachio. As they cool down, they will get a glazed look. Serve at room temperature.

Makes about 16 servings, 2 pieces each. Per serving –
Nutritive Value: 251 calories, 2.5 g protein, 24 g carb, 0.5 g fiber, 16 g fat, 16 mg chol.
Food Group Exchange: 1.5 Fat, 1 Sugar, ¾ Grain.

BANANA BURFI (Fudge)

This is an excellent way to use bananas. It can be refrigerated for couple of weeks. Serve at room temperature. Makes about 35 pieces.

12 ripe bananas
1½ cups sugar
1 tablespoon unsalted butter
1 cup non-fat dry milk

Seasonings:

2 tablespoons lemon juice

1 teaspoon coarsely crushed cardamom seeds

Garnish:

½ cup chopped nuts

½ cup coconut flakes (optional)

1. Peel and cut the bananas into small pieces. Mix with sugar and keep aside for 1–2 hours.
2. Warm the butter in a skillet on medium heat. Add banana-sugar mixture and stir until all the moisture evaporates. Mash the bananas as you stir. Add the non-fat dry milk as needed to make the mixture thick.
3. Stir in the seasonings and spread on a greased cookie sheet, about ¼" thick. Garnish with the nuts and coconut.
4. Let it rest for 1–2 hours; cut into diamond shape or square pieces and store in the refrigerator.

Makes about 17 servings, 2 pieces each. Per serving –
Nutritive Value: 166 calories, 2.4 g protein, 39 g carb, 2 g fiber, 1 g fat, 3 mg chol.
Food Group Exchange: 1 Fruit, 1 Sugar, ¼ Dairy.

BEDANA (Sweet Drops)

This is considered an auspicious sweet served at happy occasions. *(Need a 'jharni' or a wide spatula with small round slots to drop the batter).* These can be kept without refrigeration for a few days. You may refrigerate or freeze them.

1 cup gram flour (besan)
2 tablespoons plain yogurt
Oil for frying, 2–3" deep in a wok

Seasonings:
¼ teaspoon turmeric powder (for color)   ½ teaspoon baking powder

For Syrup:
1 cup sugar   ¼ teaspoon saffron
¾ cup water

Garnish:
   Kewra water

1. To make the syrup, heat the water, sugar, and saffron together, stirring often, and boil for about 2–3 minutes. Keep aside.
2. Mix the flour, baking powder and turmeric with little water to make a thick batter that can be 'dropped' through the slotted spatula to make 'Bedana'. Whip it well.
3. Heat the oil in a deep skillet on medium heat. Drop the batter through the slotted spatula (jharni) into the hot oil in single layer. It will make tiny balls. Fry on all sides until 'Bedana' becomes golden and crisp. Fry in two batches if necessary.
4. Drain them on paper towels and immerse in the hot syrup. Soak for 5 minutes and take them out on a plate.
5. Serve at room temperature sprinkled with 'kewra water'.

Makes about 8 servings, ½ cup each. Per serving –
Nutritive Value: 262 calories, 4 g protein, 30 g carb, 2.5 g fiber, 15 g fat, 0 mg chol.
Food Group Exchange: 1 Sugar, ½ Grain, 1 Fat.

BESAN BURFI (Gram Flour Fudge)

This fudge-like dessert is great served with tea or coffee. Serve warm or at room temperature. It freezes well and can be refrigerated for several weeks. Makes about 54 pieces.

3 cups besan (gram flour), sifted
1½ cups (12 oz.) unsalted butter
1 tablespoon semolina (suji)
1 cup non-fat dry milk
1¾ cups sugar (finely ground)

<u>Garnish</u>:
1 teaspoon crushed cardamom seeds   4 varak sheets (optional)
½ cup chopped pistachio

1. Soften the butter in a pot or deep skillet on low heat. (May reduce butter by ¼ cup if stirring on low heat.)
2. Turn the heat to medium and add 'besan'. Stir constantly and brown the 'besan' (20-25 minutes). Make sure the mixture does not burn and regulate the heat as needed; it should be light brown.
3. Add the semolina and dry milk; stir for a couple of minutes. Turn off heat and mix in the finely ground sugar. *Note:* You may add about 4 oz. sweetened condensed milk and reduce the sugar by half.
4. Grease a 9x13" cookie sheet and spread the mixture evenly, about 1/3" thick. Pat gently with hand or wax paper. Garnish with the pistachio and cardamoms. If desired, lay varak sheets for decoration.
5. When cold, cut into diamond shape or square pieces and store.

Variation 1: Instead of spreading on a cookie sheet, take a handful of mixture in your hand and make into small smooth ball (laddu), pressing between your palms. 'Laddu' have a different texture and shape. Skip steps 4 and 5.

Variation 2: Instead of adding sugar (step 3), make single-thread consistency syrup by boiling 1¾ cup sugar and 1 cup water for 3–4 minutes. Mix the hot syrup into the flour mixture and spread immediately. Proceed with the remaining steps.

Makes about 27 servings, 2 pieces each. Per serving –
Nutritive Value: 194 calories, 4 g protein, 21 g carb, 1 g fiber, 11 g fat, 28 mg chol.
Food Group Exchange: 1 Sugar, 1 Fat, ½ Legumes/Meat.

BOONDI LADDU (Rounds with Tiny Nuggets)

This is a traditional sweet served at all happy occasions. The nuggets are very small like pearl barley. *(Need a 'jharni' or a wide spatula with tiny round holes to drop the batter)*. These can be kept without refrigeration for a few days. You may refrigerate or freeze them.

2½ cups gram flour (besan)
¼ cup milk
Oil for frying, 2–3" deep in a wok

Seasonings:

2 teaspoons coarsely crushed cardamom seeds

½ cup chopped cashews

For Syrup:

2¼ cups sugar

1¼ cups water

1. Make the syrup by heating the water and sugar together, stirring often. Boil for about 2–3 minutes to make it single–thread consistency (see page 257). Keep aside.
2. Mix the flour, milk, and about 1 cup water to make a thick batter that can be 'dropped' through the slotted spatula to make 'Boondi'. Whip it well.
3. Heat the oil in a deep wide skillet on medium heat. Place about 1 tablespoon batter on the slotted spatula (jharni) and hold it over the wok. Rub the batter with the other hand so that it drops into the hot oil in single layer. It will make tiny balls. Fry until 'Boondi' becomes golden and crisp. (Fry in two batches if necessary.)
4. Remove 'boondi' with another slotted spatula, drain on paper towels and place in the prepared hot syrup. Add the seasonings and mix everything together.
5. When little cold, make small balls pressing with your fingers and palm. Serve at room temperature.

Makes about 25 servings, 1piece each. Per serving –
Nutritive Value: 262 calories, 4 g protein, 30 g carb, 2.5 g fiber, 15 g fat, 0 mg chol.
Food Group Exchange: 1 Sugar, ½ Grain, 1 Fat.

CARROT BURFI

It is a great dish to make in the winter months when carrots are sweet and juicy. It can be refrigerated for couple of months or frozen. Makes about 48 pieces.

3 lb. carrots, scraped and grated
2½ cups sugar
3 cups nonfat dry milk
½ cup (4 oz.) unsalted butter

<u>Seasonings:</u> 1 teaspoon coarsely crushed cardamom seeds

<u>Garnish:</u>
¼ cup chopped blanched almonds   Varak sheets
¼ cup chopped cashews

1. In a large skillet, cook the grated carrots and sugar, covered, for about an hour until carrots are dry.
2. Add the dry milk; cook, stirring occasionally to avoid sticking at bottom, until no moisture is left (about ½ hour).
3. Stir in the butter. Cook on medium heat until the mixture is of desired consistency that can be spread on a tray and cut into pieces. Add more dry milk as needed.
4. Mix in the cardamoms and spread on a 9x13" greased cookie sheet. Garnish with nuts and varak sheets. Cut into squares when cold.

Variation: May substitute 14 oz. can of condensed milk for most of sugar and dry milk. Cook the carrots and let them dry before adding the condensed milk.

Makes about 24 servings, 2 pieces each. Per serving –
Nutritive Value: 193 calories, 6 g protein, 33.6 g carb, 2 g fiber, 4 g fat, 13 mg chol.
Food Group Exchange: 1 Sugar, ½ Vegetable, ¼ Dairy, 1/3 Fat.

CARROT HALVA

This healthy dessert, served hot, is especially popular in the winter. It can be refrigerated or frozen. Re–warm before serving.

3 lb. carrots, scraped and grated
½ cup milk
2¼ cups sugar
½ cup (4 oz.) unsalted butter
2 lb. Ricotta cheese
1 cup nonfat dry milk

Seasonings:

¼ cup chopped cashews

¼ cup chopped almonds

1 teaspoon coarsely crushed cardamom seeds

1. In a large pot, cook the grated carrots and milk, covered, on medium-high heat. After about 5 minutes, add sugar. Cook, stirring occasionally to avoid sticking at the bottom, until no moisture is left (about 1 hour).
2. In a separate skillet, put half of the butter and Ricotta cheese. Cook on low-medium heat. (Sometimes Ricotta splatters; keep it partially covered at low heat, stirring often to avoid burning.) After about ½ hour, add the dry milk and stir for another 10 minutes at low heat. Ricotta will be of semi-dry consistency. (You may cook Ricotta in the microwave oven, first on high, then on medium heat.)
3. Mix the cooked Ricotta into the cooked carrots. Add the remaining butter. Keep stirring on low heat until it is of semi-dry consistency (few minutes only).
4. Mix in half of the nuts and cardamom. Serve it hot garnished with the remaining nuts.

Variation: Instead of using Ricotta cheese, cook carrots in about ¾ gallon milk for 2–3 hours. Add dry milk as needed to obtain desired consistency. Stir in the sugar and butter. Mix the nuts and serve.

Note: Similar 'halva' can be made from bottle gourd (ghiya or dhudi), or white tender turnips.

Healthy Alternative: Reduce or eliminate the butter.

Makes about 30 servings, ¼ cup each. Per serving –
Nutritive Value: 179 calories, 6 g protein, 23 g carb, 1.6 g fiber, 7 g fat, 20 mg chol.
Food Group Exchange: 1 Sugar, ½ Vegetable, ½ Dairy, 1/8 Fat.

CHUMCHUM (Oval Cheese Balls in Syrup)

Bengal region of India is known for this delicacy. They are served cold. They keep in the refrigerator for 1–2 weeks. To freeze, drain the syrup. Thaw in the refrigerator before serving. Makes about 40 pieces.

1 gallon whole milk
4–6 tablespoons lemon juice (or cream of tartar)
Few drops yellow food color

For syrup:
2 cups sugar   4 cups water

Garnish:
1 tablespoon chopped pistachio   1 tablespoon sweet grated coconut
1 teaspoon crushed cardamom seeds

1. In a 6–8 quart saucepan, boil the water and sugar together for 1 minute, stirring often, to make the syrup.
2. Make fresh cheese (paneer) from milk using lemon juice or cream of tartar (see page 31). Strain in a thin muslin cloth for about an hour. Mash the fresh cheese until it is smooth and fluffy. Mix in the food color to get golden shade. (You may use a food processor to mash the fresh cheese.)
3. Make oval shaped balls, about ½"x1" (approximately 40 pieces) from the mashed cheese. (They increase in size when dipped in syrup.)
4. Bring the syrup to a boil. Put 20-25 balls at one time in the syrup and let them boil in the syrup for about 1 hour until soft and spongy. In between, turn the balls (Chumchum) gently. Also add a little warm water, as needed, making sure that the balls remain immersed in the syrup.
5. When done, remove the 'Chumchum' gently along with little syrup and place in a wide serving container. Cook the remaining balls the same way. Pour the left over syrup over 'Chumchum' when all are cooked.
6. When cold, refrigerate 'Chumchum' in syrup for few hours. To use (or freeze), take 'Chumchum' out of the syrup. Serve cold, garnished as desired.

Pressure cooker method:

In step 4, you may use a pressure cooker (about 6 minutes pressure) to boil 'Chumchum' in the syrup. Boil 6-8 'Chumchum' at a time. To prevent over cooking, immediately put the pressure cooker under cold running water for few seconds, remove the pressure regulator, and open the pressure cooker.

Add a little water to the syrup for next batch to make sure the syrup does not become too concentrated.

Decorated Chumchum Halves:

After 'Chumchum' have soaked for several hours, remove them from syrup and cut into half, lengthwise. Top each half with a mixture of coarsely crushed blanched almonds, some fresh cheese (paneer), and yellow or red food color.

Makes about 20 servings, 2 pieces each. Per serving –
Nutritive Value: 126 calories, 5 g protein, 17 g carb, 0 g fiber, 3.5 g fat, 5 mg chol.
Food Group Exchange: 1 Sugar, ¾ Dairy.

Every man should eat and drink, and enjoy the good of all his labour, it is the gift of God.

Bible Ecclesiastes 3:13

COCONUT BURFI (Fudge)

This is a great dish for coconut lovers; can be refrigerated for couple of months or frozen. Coconut, though a fruit, is treated as half fat and half fruit. Makes about 15 pieces.

2 cups grated un–sweetened coconut
2 cups milk
½ cup (4 oz.) unsalted butter
7 oz. sweetened condensed milk

<u>**Seasonings:**</u> 1 teaspoon coarsely crushed cardamom seeds
<u>**Garnish:**</u> 4 varak sheets (optional)

1. Soak the grated coconut in the milk for 6-8 hours.
2. Stir the butter and soaked coconut in a skillet on medium heat, until the coconut is cooked and fat is separated (about 20 minutes).
3. Add the condensed milk and cardamoms. Keep stirring until the mixture is of desired consistency (soft for serving warm with a spoon, or hard like dough to be spread on a tray and cut into pieces).
4. If desired, spread 'varak' sheets on top for decoration.

Variation: Add 1 lb. Ricotta cheese when cooking coconut (step 2). Can reduce butter.

Makes about 8 servings, 2 pieces each. Per serving –
Nutritive Value: 305 calories, 5.4 g protein, 24 g carb, 2 g fiber, 21.6 g fat, 45 mg chol.
Food Group Exchange: 1 Fat, 1 Sugar, ½ Fruit, ¼ Dairy.

EGGLESS SPONGE CAKE

This cake without eggs is bound to be quite a hit. Serve it cold or at room temperature. Can be refrigerated for several days or frozen.

2 cups self-rising flour
½ cup (4 oz.) unsalted butter, softened
14 oz. sweetened condensed milk
½ cup water

Seasonings:
1 teaspoon baking soda   2 teaspoons vanilla essence
2 teaspoons baking powder

1. Sift the flour, baking soda and baking powder. Add the remaining ingredients and vanilla; beat well.
2. Preheat the oven to 400°F. Grease and dust a 9" round cake pan or a rectangular pan. Bake in the preheated oven for 10 minutes. Then reduce the temperature to 300°F and bake for another 10–15 minutes, until done.

Variation: Add some nuts to the batter if desired. Top the cake with sliced fruit before serving.

Healthy Alternative: Substitute part of flour by whole-wheat flour. Add 1 teaspoon baking powder and ½ teaspoon salt to a cup of whole–wheat flour.

Makes about 10 servings, one medium piece each. Per serving –
Nutritive Value: 329 calories, 6 g protein, 46 g carb, 0.4 g fiber, 14 g fat, 43 mg chol.
Food Group Exchange: 2 Sugar, 1 Grain, 1 Fat.

FALOODA (Vermicelli in Syrup)

Buy rice vermicelli for this dish. It goes well with 'Kulfi' but can be served with ice–cream too. Make it in advance and refrigerate.

1 lb. rice vermicelli (sevia)

Seasonings:

1 tablespoon crushed almonds   ½ teaspoon rose essence

Syrup:

2 cups sugar   ¼ teaspoon saffron mixed with little milk
2 cups water

1. Boil about 5 cups water. Put the vermicelli in boiling water and cook for about 2 minutes until just tender. Drain.
2. Spread the vermicelli in a wide serving dish. Make the syrup by boiling the sugar, water, and saffron mixture together until the sugar is dissolved.
3. Pour the syrup over the vermicelli. Mix in the seasonings and let it soak for about an hour. Refrigerate and serve cold with little syrup.

Makes about 10 servings, ½ cup each. Per serving –
Nutritive Value: 283 calories, 5.6 g protein, 62 g carb, 0 g fiber, 1 g fat, 0 mg chol.
Food Group Exchange: 1 Grain, 1 Sugar.

FIRNI (Cream of Rice Pudding)

A quick dessert to make, it should be made in advance and refrigerated. Serve cold or at room temperature.

½ gallon milk
½ cup cream of rice (or roasted semolina (suji))
½ cup sugar

Seasonings:

¼ cup chopped blanched almonds
¼ cup golden raisins

½ teaspoon crushed cardamom seeds
½ teaspoon rose essence or saffron

Garnish: ¼ cup chopped unsalted pistachios, lightly toasted

1. Heat the milk in a 4-quart heavy pot. (A large pot is needed because milk can easily boil over.)
2. When the milk is about to boil, stir cream of rice (or semolina) slowly into milk, making sure there are no lumps. Cook on medium heat, stirring often, until the pudding thickens (about 30 minutes). Reduce the heat as needed. (Take care that milk does not stick to the bottom of the pot.)
3. Add the sugar and let the mixture cook on low heat for another 10 minutes. It will be semi-liquid.
4. Turn off the heat; stir in the seasonings as desired. Transfer to a serving bowl. The pudding will thicken as it cools. Serve cold or at room temperature garnished with pistachios.

Note: You may cook the pudding in a microwave. Keep for 5 minutes at a time; stir and then cook again as needed.

Variation: Add ¼ cup half–and–half when milk is half-cooked, for creamier taste.

Makes about 8 servings, ½ cup each. Per serving –
Nutritive Value: 214 calories, 10 g protein, 33 g carb, 0.6 g fiber, 4.4 g fat, 10 mg chol.
Food Group Exchange: 1 Dairy, ¾ Sugar, ¼ Grain.

FRUITS in CHEESY CREAM

You may combine fruits to your liking in this low–fat cream. Use apples, bananas, pineapple and oranges. Make the cream in advance and mix with fruits a few hours before serving.

4 cups + ¼ cup milk
1–2 tablespoons lemon juice
1 ripe mango
1 small ripe papaya
1 cup strawberries
1 apple
1 pear
1 banana

Seasonings: ¼ cup sugar (to taste)

1. Make fresh cheese (paneer) from milk using lemon juice or cream of tartar (see page 31). Strain in a thin muslin cloth for a few minutes.
2. Blend the fresh cheese and sugar in a food processor until smooth. Add ¼ cup milk (or evaporated milk) to get the desired consistency.
3. Wash, peel, and chop the fruits in small chunks. Toss with the cheesy mixture. Refrigerate for about 4 hours before serving.

Makes about 15 servings, one cup each. Per serving –
Nutritive Value: 71 calories, 2 g protein, 13 g carb, 1.4 g fiber, 1.4 g fat, 2 mg chol.
Food Group Exchange: 1 Fruit, ¼ Dairy, ¼ Sugar.

FRUIT PUDDING

Use your fancy to choose fruits for this pudding. Litchi fruit can be bought fresh sometimes in the Asian markets. Cans are easily available.

8 oz non-dairy whipped topping
4 tablespoons sweetened condensed milk
¼ cup orange juice
2 cups peeled cut apples
3 bananas sliced
2 oranges peeled in sections
1 lb. seedless grapes
14 oz can litchi, drained (or pineapples)
28 oz can fruit cocktail, drained
¼ cup fresh grated or chopped coconut

1. Blend the whipped topping, condensed milk, and orange juice.
2. Add the desired fruits; refrigerate for 4 hours before serving.

Variation: Use about ½ gallon vanilla ice cream in place of whipped cream and condensed milk. Mix it 1 hour before serving and refrigerate.

Makes about 25 servings, one cup each. Per serving –
Nutritive Value: 109 calories, 1 g protein, 20 g carb, 2 g fiber, 4 g fat, 1 mg chol.
Food Group Exchange: 1 Fruit, 1 Sugar.

GUJIA (Stuffed Sweet Patties)

These patties are filled with a dry mixture of nuts and cheese, and are specially prepared at many holidays. They can be refrigerated for several weeks. You may freeze them and thaw them at room temperature before serving. Makes about 35.

2 cups all-purpose unbleached flour
1 cup whole wheat flour
½ cup milk (or water) to make dough
½ cup oil + oil for frying, 2–3"deep in a wok

For the Filling:

½ cup unsalted butter
1 cup semolina (suji)
1 lb. Ricotta cheese
1½ cups coarsely crushed nuts (almonds & cashews)
2 teaspoons crushed cardamom
2 cups powdered sugar

1. Mix the flours and ½ cup oil together. Knead the dough, adding the milk (or water) as needed, until it becomes smooth and supple.
2. Make little balls (walnut size), press them down, and roll them into thin rounds (about 1/8" thick, 5"diameter).
3. To make the filling, stir the semolina in butter on low-medium heat until golden brown. Cook the Ricotta cheese in the microwave oven until dry. Mix them together. Add nuts and cardamom to make semi–dry mixture. When cold, mix in the sugar.
4. Place the filling in middle of each round and fold to make a patty. Moisten the ends with milk and press together firmly and flute them so that they do not open.
5. Heat the oil in a deep frying pan or wok. Deep-fry the 'Gujia', few at a time, on medium heat, turning as needed, until golden brown on all sides.
6. Drain them on paper towels or brown paper bag. Repeat with the remaining 'Gujia'.

Makes about 35 servings, 1 piece each. Per serving –
Nutritive Value: 305 calories, 5 g protein, 24 g carb, 1 g fiber, 21 g fat, 13 mg chol.
Food Group Exchange: 1.5 Fat, 2/3 Sugar, ½ Grain, ¼ Dairy, 1/6 Legumes/Meat.

GULABJAMUN (Rose Munchkins)

'Gulab' means a rose, and 'jamun' is a berry shaped dark color fruit. These rose–colored munchkin-like sweets are popular with all. They can be refrigerated for about 2 weeks with syrup. You can also drain the syrup and freeze them. Serve warm or at room temperature. Makes about 30.

1 cup baking mix such as Bisquick
2 cups non-fat dry milk
4 tablespoons melted unsalted butter
½ cup + ¼ cup whole-milk
Oil for deep–frying, 2–3" deep in a wok

Syrup:

3 cups sugar

3½ cups water

1 teaspoon coarsely crushed cardamom seeds

1. Make the syrup by mixing the water, sugar and cardamoms in a wide large pot and bringing to a boil on high heat, stirring often. Boil for 1 minute only. Set it aside to cool a little.
2. Stir together the baking mix, dry milk, butter, and ½ cup milk to make a semi thick dough. Add ¼ cup milk as needed. Make small balls (oval or round) with greased hands.
3. Heat the oil in a wok or deep skillet on medium heat. (You may use an electric fryer set at 375°F.) Fry the balls (6–8 at a time that can fit the skillet) on low-medium heat. They should fry slowly, turning reddish brown on all sides as you turn them with a slotted flat spatula. (Test fry a 'Gulabjamun' first; on high heat, it will become dark soon and remain raw inside; on low heat, it will start opening and take longer to cook.)
4. Drain them on paper towel; immerse immediately in the warm syrup in the large pot. When all the 'Gulabjamun' are made, let them soak in the syrup for at least an hour. (You may refrigerate them with syrup.)
5. Serve cold or warm without the syrup.

Variation 1: When making balls, fill each with 2 raisins, and pieces of pistachio and misri (rock sugar). This adds a crunch.

Variation 2: Instead of Bisquick baking mix and butter, use 1 cup self-rising flour, 1 cup non-fat dry milk, and 1 cup heavy cream (whipped well) to make the dough for 'Gulabjamun' balls. There is no change in the syrup or frying.

Makes about 30 servings, one piece each. Per serving –
Nutritive Value: 178 calories, 2.2 g protein, 19 g carb, 0.3 g fiber, 10.3 g fat, 5.5 mg chol.
Food Group Exchange: 1 Sugar, 1 Fat, ¼ Dairy, 1/6 Grain.

JALEBI (Coiled Sweets)

Jalebi are mouth watering delicious. *(Need a bottle – like ketchup bottle – to squeeze the batter).*

1 teaspoon yeast
1 teaspoon sugar
1 cup all-purpose flour
1 tablespoon gram flour (besan)
2 tablespoons plain yogurt
Oil for frying, 2–3" deep

For Syrup:

1½ cups sugar   ½ teaspoon saffron
1¼ cups water   2 teaspoons rose water

Garnish:
8–10 chopped unsalted pistachio   Few rose petals

1. To make the syrup, heat the water, sugar, and saffron together, stirring often, and boil for 2–3 minutes. Stir in the rose water and keep aside.
2. Mix the yeast in 1 cup warm water. Add ½ teaspoon sugar. Let it stand for a few minutes until it rises. Whip the yeast with the flours and yogurt to make a thick batter, adding more water as needed. Let it stand for about an hour and whip it well again.
3. Heat the oil in a deep skillet on medium heat. Put the batter in a plastic bottle with a small hole. Squeeze out the batter into the hot oil in the form of 5–7 small coils (Jalebi) in single layer. Fry on both sides until 'Jalebi' becomes golden and crisp.
4. Drain them on paper towel and immerse in the hot syrup. Dip for a minute and take them out on a plate. Fry and dip the remaining 'Jalebi' the same way.
5. Serve hot garnished with chopped pistachio and rose petals.

Makes about 16 servings, one piece each. Per serving –
Nutritive Value: 149 calories, 1 g protein, 21 g carb, 0 g fiber, 7 g fat, 0 mg chol.
Food Group Exchange: 1 Sugar, ¼ Grain, 1 Fat.

KHEER (Rice Pudding)

This healthy dessert is customarily served at many auspicious occasions. Make it in advance and reheat in the microwave when ready to serve. May be served cold also.

½ gallon 2% or whole milk
2/3 cup Basmati rice
2/3 cup sugar

Seasonings:

¼ cup chopped cashews
¼ cup chopped blanched almonds

1 teaspoon crushed cardamom seeds
½ teaspoon rose essence or saffron (optional)

¼ cup golden raisins (optional)

1. Boil the milk in a 4-quart pot. (A large pot is needed because milk can easily boil over.)
2. Check and rinse the rice. Soak for about 10 minutes; drain. Stir the rice into the milk. Cook on medium heat, stirring often, until the pudding thickens (about 1 hour). It will be semi-liquid. (Reduce the heat if the milk boils out of the pot. Take care because milk tends to burn and stick to the bottom of the pot easily.)
3. Turn off the heat; stir in the sugar and seasonings. Add rose essence if desired. The pudding will thicken as it cools. Serve cold or hot.

Note: You may use a slow cooker (at high temperature) to make 'Kheer'. First add milk. After about ½ hour, add rice. 'Kheer' will be ready in about 5 hours. Turn off the slow cooker and add sugar and nuts as usual. You can also cook rice and milk in a microwave.

Variation: Add ¼ cup half–and–half towards the end of cooking for creamier taste. Or add about 1 cup broken roasted vermicelli (sevia) when rice is almost cooked.

Makes about 10 servings, ¾ cup each. Per serving –
Nutritive Value: 237 calories, 8.5 g protein, 35 g carb, 1 g fiber, 7.4 g fat, 16 mg chol.
Food Group Exchange: 1 Sugar, 1 Dairy, ½ Grain, 1/6 Legumes/Meat.

KULFI (Ice Cream Cakes)

Traditionally, milk is cooked on slow-medium heat for a long time until it thickens. The creamy milk is frozen in special cone–like molds. This recipe is an easy alternative. Make it in advance and freeze. Serve it with 'Falooda'. It is particularly soothing in summer.

14 oz. can sweetened condensed milk
2 12–oz. cans un–sweetened evaporated milk
½ pint half–and–half cream

Seasonings:
1 teaspoon crushed cardamom seeds   1 teaspoon rose water
¼ cup chopped blanched almonds

Garnish: 1 tablespoon chopped pistachios

1. Dilute the condensed milk with evaporated milk and half–and–half cream. (Modify the quantity of evaporated milk to your liking of sweetness.) Mix in the desired seasonings.
2. Freeze in a flat container, individual dishes, or molds, until ready (about 8 hours). Cut and serve garnished with pistachios.

Variation: Cook and reduce some whole milk or half–and–half until thick and creamy. Add that to the mixture.

Healthy Alternative: Mix 1 cup mango pulp or mashed bananas before freezing, to make fruit 'Kulfi'. May not add half–and–half.

Makes about 8 servings, one medium piece each. Per serving –
Nutritive Value: 284 calories, 9 g protein, 33 g carb, 1 g fiber, 13.4 g fat, 32 mg chol.
Food Group Exchange: 1 Sugar, ½ Dairy, 1 Fat.

MANGO MOUSSE

This is a very appealing dessert topped with tropical fruits. Make a lot of it as it goes fast.

6 oz. pkt. peach gelatin
30 oz. can mango pulp
7 oz. sweetened condensed milk
8 oz. non-dairy whipped topping

1. Mix the gelatin in 1 cup boiling water. Add the mango pulp. When cool, whisk in the condensed milk and whipped topping.
2. Chill in the refrigerator for a few hours and serve. You may garnish with fresh mango slices before serving.

Makes about 12 servings, ½ cup each. Per serving –
Nutritive Value: 197 calories, 3 g protein, 35 g carb, 1 g fiber, 5 g fat, 8 mg chol.
Food Group Exchange: 2 Sugar, ¾ Fruit.

MUNG DAL HALVA (Lentil Pudding)

It is a rich delicious dessert, generally made in North India. Make it ahead of time and refrigerate or freeze. Warm it in the microwave before serving.

2 cups peeled split Mung dal
2 cups (1 lb.) unsalted butter or clarified butter (ghee)
4 cups milk
2 cups sugar

Seasonings:
½ teaspoon saffron   1 teaspoon crushed cardamom seeds
½ cup chopped almonds and cashews

1. Check, rinse and soak the 'dal' for minimum 4 hours (or overnight). Drain; grind to a fine paste using minimum water.
2. On medium heat, in a large frying pan, warm half of the 'ghee' (or butter). Add ground 'dal' and stir on low heat until golden brown and dry (about 45 minutes). Keep stirring to avoid sticking at bottom. Add the remaining 'ghee'/butter as needed. Fat should appear separated from 'dal'.
3. Stir in the warm milk and saffron. Turn the heat back to medium. After a few minutes, add the sugar. Cook, stirring as needed, until it is like soft pudding.
4. Serve hot, garnished with the nuts and cardamom.

Variation: Use peeled split Urad dal instead of Mung dal. Add some dry milk if needed.

Healthy Alternative: Reduce the butter and sugar as desired. Brown the ground 'dal' on low heat.

Makes about 20 servings, 2 tablespoons each. Per serving –
Nutritive Value: 338 calories, 6 g protein, 31.4 g carb, 2 g fiber, 21 g fat, 60.4 mg chol.
Food Group Exchange: 1.5 Fat, 1 Sugar, ¾ Legumes/Meat, ¼ Dairy.

PEANUT CHIKKI (Peanut Brittle)

It is a delicious healthy snack, very popular, served anytime. Besides peanuts, you may add roasted chickpeas (chana).

2 cups raw peanuts with inner shell
8 oz. gur (Indian jaggery)
2 tablespoons unsalted butter

Seasonings:
½ teaspoon caraway seeds (ajwain)   1 teaspoon crushed fennel seeds

1. Roast the peanuts in the oven at 350°F for about 5 minutes, until crisp. When cold, rub off the paper–like shell as much as possible. Crush the peanuts lightly.
2. On low–medium heat, in a frying pan, warm the butter. Add 'gur' (jaggery) broken into small pieces. Stir for a few minutes until the 'gur' melts. Sprinkle some water if needed.
3. Mix in the crushed peanuts and seasonings. Spread the mixture on greased cookie sheet. Roll it evenly using a rolling pin. Cut into 1.5" squares and store.

Variation: Use roasted peanuts instead of raw peanuts. Also add some unsalted roasted chickpeas.

Makes about 30 servings, 1.5" square piece each. Per serving –
Nutritive Value: 124 calories, 3 g protein, 16 g carb, 0.8 g fiber, 6 g fat, 4 mg chol.
Food Group Exchange: 2 Sugar, ¼ Legumes/Meat, 1/8 Fat.

PERE (Sweet Patties)

These are similar to 'Ricotta Cheese Burfi' but more decorative and easier to handle. Arrange them in a platter, one layer stacked on another, in beautiful cone–like format. They can be refrigerated or frozen. Use at room temperature. Makes about 20 pieces.

1 lb. Ricotta cheese
4 tablespoons (2 oz.) unsalted butter
1 cup sugar
3 cups nonfat dry milk

Seasonings:
½ teaspoon saffron flakes   2 teaspoons crushed cardamom
½ cup coarsely crushed pistachio

1. Cook the Ricotta cheese and butter on low-medium heat. (Sometimes the Ricotta splatters; keep it half-covered at low-medium heat, stirring often to avoid burning.) **Note**: You may cook the Ricotta in the microwave oven, starting with 5 minutes at high. Stir and continue cooking at medium-high. You can also cook it in the conventional oven, stirring often.
2. After about 15 minutes, stir in the saffron flakes, sugar and dry milk. Cook, while stirring, until the mixture is dry and smooth, like cookie dough. It becomes stiff as it cools.
3. When cold, take about a tablespoon of the mixture, and shape it into a smooth round between your palms. Sprinkle the crushed pistachio and cardamom on top of the round, and press it to make a patty ('pera'). Smooth the edges.
4. Stack and store in the refrigerator.

Healthy Alternative: Add one cup of grated apples or 'ghiya' during cooking. May reduce butter by half. Can also add about ¼ cup slightly roasted and ground sesame seeds towards the end of cooking.

Makes about 20 servings, one medium piece each. Per serving –
Nutritive Value: 115 calories, 3.5 g protein, 11 g carb, 0 g fiber, 6 g fat, 15 mg chol.
Food Group Exchange per piece: 1 Dairy, ¾ Sugar, ½ Fat.

RASMALAI (Milk Cakes in Cream)

This is a delicious dessert and very easy to make using Ricotta cheese. Since it is semi-liquid, serve in small plates or bowls. Makes 25 small pieces.

¾ quart half–and–half
15 oz. Ricotta cheese
1 cup sugar

<u>Garnish:</u> Chopped unsalted pistachio (about 12)

1. Boil the half–and–half in a heavy pan on medium heat, stirring frequently, for about 20 minutes to thicken the cream. Keep aside.
2. Mix the cheese and sugar with a fork. Spread in a un–greased baking dish (9x9" or little smaller).
3. Bake the cheese and sugar mixture uncovered in the oven set at 350°F for 35–40 minutes. (Mixture may become little brownish.)
4. Allow it to cool for about 20 minutes. Cut into about 2" squares. Pour warm thickened half–and–half over the squares. (Loosen some of the squares to allow the liquid to spread all around and cover the pieces entirely.)
5. Cool and refrigerate. Some of the liquid will be absorbed in 1–2 hours. Serve it cold, the cheese pieces along with the liquid, garnished with chopped pistachios.

Healthy Alternative: Substitute the half–and–half by whole or 2% fat milk. Simmer the milk, stirring frequently, for about an hour until slightly thick.

Makes about 12 servings, 2 small pieces each. Per serving –
Nutritive Value: 179 calories, 6 g protein, 18 g carb, 0 g fiber, 9 g fat, 40 mg chol.
Food Group Exchange: 2 Fat, 1 Sugar, ¾ Dairy.

RICOTTA CHEESE BURFI (Fudge)

This is the most popular dessert, made with little variations, and served at different occasions. It can be refrigerated or frozen. Use at room temperature. Makes 48 pieces.

3 lb. Ricotta cheese
½ cup (4 oz.) unsalted butter
2½ cups sugar
2½ cups non-fat dry milk

Seasonings:
1½ cups coarsely crushed almonds   2 teaspoons crushed cardamom

Garnish: 6 Varak sheets (optional)

1. Cook the Ricotta cheese and butter on low-medium heat. (Sometimes the Ricotta splatters; keep it half-covered at low-medium heat, stirring often to avoid burning.) **Note**: You may cook the Ricotta in the microwave oven, starting with 5 minutes at high. Stir and continue cooking at medium-high. You can also cook it in the conventional oven, stirring often.
2. After about ½ hour, stir in the sugar and dry milk. Cook, while stirring, until the Ricotta is of dry consistency, like paste that can be easily spread (10–15 minutes).
3. Mix in the almonds and crushed cardamom. Spread in a non-stick 12x18" cookie sheet, about 1/3" thick. Pat gently with wax paper or spatula to make it even. Cover with the 'varak' sheets for decorative look.
4. Cut into squares or diamond shape when cool. Store in the refrigerator.

Variation: May add about ½ cup cocoa powder along with sugar to give chocolate taste and look.

Healthy Alternative: Add 2 cups of grated apples, 'ghiya', or mashed bananas during cooking. May reduce butter by half. Can also add about 1 cup slightly roasted and ground sesame seeds, along with other nuts, towards the end of cooking.

Makes about 48 servings, one medium piece each. Per serving –
Nutritive Value: 141 calories, 6 g protein, 14 g carb, 1 g fiber, 7 g fat, 16 mg chol.
Food Group Exchange: ¾ Sugar, ¾ Dairy, 1/6 Fat, 1/8 Legumes/Meat.

SAFFRON NANKHATAI (Biscuits)

The taste of saffron is delicious in these biscuits. You can add nuts too, if desired. Make them in advance and refrigerate or freeze. Serve at room temperature. Makes 20.

½ cup unsalted butter
½ cup sugar
1 teaspoon plain yogurt
½ cup all-purpose flour
½ cup semolina (suji)

Seasonings:

½ teaspoon cardamom powder
¼ teaspoon nutmeg powder

¼ teaspoon baking soda
¼ teaspoon saffron (dissolved in a teaspoon of warm milk)

1. Cream the butter and sugar together until light and creamy. Mix in the yogurt and the seasonings. Mix well.
2. Add the flour and semolina; knead to make a smooth dough for cookies.
3. Preheat the oven to 300°F. Break the dough into small rounds (1½" diameter). Arrange on a baking sheet; bake for 30-40 minutes. Cool and store.

Makes about 10 servings, 2 pieces each. Per serving –
Nutritive Value: 168 calories, 2 g protein, 20 g carb, 0 g fiber, 9 g fat, 28 mg chol.
Food Group Exchange: 1 Fat, ½ Sugar, ½ Grain.

SEVIA (Vermicelli Pudding)

This is a delicious dessert that can be made instantly. You may also make it in advance and refrigerate. Serve cold, hot, or at room temperature.

½ gallon whole or 2% milk
2 cups roasted vermicelli (sevia)
½ cup sugar

Seasonings:

¼ cup chopped blanched almonds   ½ tsp. crushed cardamom seeds
¼ cup golden raisins   1/8 teaspoon saffron

Garnish: ¼ cup chopped unsalted pistachios, lightly toasted

1. Heat the milk in a 4-quart heavy pot on medium–high heat. (A large pot is needed because milk can easily boil over.)
2. When the milk is about to boil, stir broken vermicelli slowly into milk, making sure there are no lumps. Cook on medium heat, stirring often, until the pudding thickens (about 15 minutes). Reduce the heat as needed. (Take care that milk does not stick to the bottom of the pot.)
3. Add the sugar and let the mixture cook on low heat for another 10 minutes. It will be semi-liquid.
4. Turn off the heat; stir in the seasonings as desired. The pudding will thicken as it cools. Serve cold or warm garnished with pistachios.

Note: You may cook the pudding in the microwave. Keep for 5 minutes at a time; stir and then cook again as needed.

Variation: Add about 4 cups of vermicelli and let it cook until hard enough to be spread on a wide pan. When it becomes little solid, cut into squares and serve.

Makes about 8 servings, ½ cup each. Per serving –
Nutritive Value: 262 calories, 11 g protein, 43 g carb, 0.6 g fiber, 5 g fat, 18 mg chol.
Food Group Exchange: 1 Dairy, ¾ Sugar, ½ Grain.

SHAHI TUKRA (Royal Bite)

It is an easy dish to make using the packaged 'Rabri mix', i.e., reduced milk with nuts, available from the Indian stores. You may make the 'Rabri' in advance and refrigerate.

150 gr. Rabri mix
8 slices of white or wheat bread
Oil for deep frying, 2–3" deep in a wok

<u>Garnish</u>: 1 tablespoon coarsely crushed unsalted pistachios

1. Prepare the 'Rabri' as per directions on the box; cook until it becomes thick consistency. Let it cool.
2. Cut the bread slices into two, as triangles or rectangles. Heat the oil in a wok or deep skillet on medium heat. Fry the bread pieces, turning couple of times, until golden brown on both sides.
3. Remove and drain the bread pieces on paper towels.
4. Spread a thin layer of 'Rabri' on each piece and let it soak for ½ hour before serving. Garnish as desired. Serve at room temperature.

Healthy Alternative: Pan-fry the bread pieces in a wide skillet instead of deep–frying. Instead of 'Rabri mix', make your own by simmering milk or half–and–half cream until thick. Add sugar and nuts.

Makes about 8 servings, 2 bread pieces each. Per serving –
Nutritive Value: 487 calories, 11 g protein, 38 g carb, 2 g fiber, 35 g fat, 22 mg chol.
Food Group Exchange: 1 Sugar, 1 Grain, 1 Fat, ¼ Dairy.

SHRIKHAND (Grand Sweet Yogurt)

This is considered an auspicious dessert. Mix it with fruit for additional taste. Can be kept in the refrigerator for a week.

4 cups plain yogurt
¾ cup sugar

Seasonings:
½ teaspoon saffron diluted in 1 tablespoon warm milk   1 tablespoon chopped nuts
½ teaspoon crushed cardamom

1. Line a sieve with muslin cloth or cheese–cloth and set over a large bowl. Place the yogurt in the cloth. Cover and refrigerate for about 5 hours and let the yogurt drain. (Makes about 2 cups of yogurt cheese.)
2. Mix the yogurt cheese with the sugar and seasonings. Whisk the mixture to smooth consistency. Chill and serve cold.

Note: Use the drained liquid in soups and breads.

Makes about 8 servings, ½ cup each. Per serving –
Nutritive Value: 149 calories, 6 g protein, 27 g carb, 0 g fiber, 1.7 g fat, 5 mg chol.
Food Group Exchange: 1 Sugar, ½ Dairy.

Tell me what you eat
And
I will tell you who you are.
Anthelme Brillatavarin

SPICY LOAF

This aromatic bread goes well with tea or fruits. You may freeze it for use as needed. Thaw in the refrigerator and warm a little before serving.

½ cup (4 oz.) unsalted butter
1 cup sugar
½ cup water
1 cup raisins
2 cups all-purpose flour
1 teaspoon baking soda
1 teaspoon baking powder
½ teaspoon salt
½ cup plain yogurt
½ cup chopped walnuts (or pecans or almonds)

Seasonings: ½ teaspoon each of crushed nutmeg, cinnamon, cloves, and cardamom

1. Heat the butter, sugar, water, raisins and the seasonings, until bubbly. Let the mixture cool for about an hour.
2. Mix the flour, baking soda, baking powder and salt. Beat the flour mix, yogurt, and the nuts into the cooled down liquid mixture.
3. Grease and flour a large loaf pan or a 9x9" baking dish. Preheat the oven to 350°F. Bake for 35 minutes until done.

Healthy Alternative: Substitute all or part of all-purpose flour by whole-wheat flour and some semolina. Add some pureed fruit like apples or bananas to reduce fat and sugar.

Makes about 12 servings, one medium piece each. Per serving –
Nutritive Value: 263 calories, 4 g protein, 42 g carb, 2 g fiber, 8.5 g fat, 0.4 mg chol.
Food Group Exchange: 1.5 Sugar, 1 Grain, 1 Fat, ½ Fruit, ¼ Legumes/Meat.

STUFFED GULABJAMUN (Rose Munchkins)

A variation of 'Gulabjamun' described earlier in this chapter, these look very festive and taste good too. If you want to freeze them, put in a wide container so that they are not on top of one another. After couple of hours, put them in a freezer bag. Makes about 30 pieces.

15 oval Gulabjamun (from 1 cup baking mix; see page 276)

For Filling:

1 lb. Ricotta cheese
4 tablespoons unsalted butter
¼ cup sugar
½ cup non-fat dry milk

Garnish: ¼ cup chopped pistachio

1. Make 'Gulabjamun' as described on page 276, but make them in large oval shape (about 15). Remove them from the syrup after 24 hours. Cut them into half, lengthwise.
2. Cook the Ricotta cheese with butter on low-medium heat. Cover partially to avoid splattering. Stirring often, cook until the Ricotta is of semi-thick consistency that can be spread (about 20 minutes). Optionally you may cook the Ricotta in the microwave oven.
3. Add the sugar and non-fat dry milk to the Ricotta. Cook together for another 10 minutes on low heat.
4. When cold, spread a teaspoon of stuffing on top of 'Gulabjamun' halves, patting with your fingers to make a smooth topping. Garnish with chopped pistachios before serving.

Variation: Add some crushed almonds to the stuffing to get a nutty taste. May reduce the butter.

Makes about 30 servings, one piece each. Per serving –
Nutritive Value: 226 calories, 4.4 g protein, 22 g carb, 0 g fiber, 13.4 g fat, 16 mg chol.
Food Group Exchange: 1 Sugar, 1 Fat, ½ Dairy, 1/8 Grain.

SUJI HALVA (Semolina Pudding)

It is a tradition to make 'Halva' at auspicious occasions. Try it; you'll love it.

1 cup (½ lb.) unsalted butter or clarified butter (ghee)
2 cups semolina (suji)

Seasonings:

¼ cup chopped almonds
1½ teaspoons crushed cardamom seeds

¼ cup golden raisins (optional)
¼ teaspoon saffron (optional)

For Syrup:

2 cups sugar

6 cups water

1. Make the syrup by heating water and sugar to boiling point, stirring often. Keep separately.
2. On medium heat, in a large frying pan, stir the butter and semolina together until the flour becomes light golden brown (about 20 minutes). Fat appears separated from the flour.
3. Reduce the heat to low; add the almonds, stir for another 5 minutes. Turn the heat back to medium.
4. Stir in the hot syrup and the remaining seasonings; keep stirring until all water is absorbed and it becomes soft pudding like mixture. Turn off the heat, cover for a few minutes and then stir gently to break any lumps. Serve hot.

Variation: Add a little gram-flour (besan) along with semolina. Or make 'Halva' from whole-wheat flour instead of semolina. Whole–wheat requires less sugar (1½ cups), and less water (5–6 cups). It has a different texture and flavor.

Healthy Alternative: Reduce butter and sugar by almost half or as desired. Add some mashed apples along with the syrup.

Makes about 20 servings, 2 tablespoons each. Per serving –
Nutritive Value: 228 calories, 2.4 g protein, 32 g carb, 0.6 g fiber, 10 g fat, 28 mg chol.
Food Group Exchange: 1 Sugar, ¼ Grain, 1 Fat.

SUJI LADDU (Semolina Rounds)

These 'laddu', easy to make, are great for snacking at a picnic or slumber party. They can be kept without refrigeration for several days. They freeze well. Thaw them in the refrigerator or outside. Make the balls 4–5 hours in advance to allow the 'laddu' to become firm.

2 cups semolina (suji)
½ cup (4 oz.) unsalted butter or clarified butter (ghee)
1 tablespoon milk

Seasonings:
½ cup crushed almonds   ½ cup finely grated coconut

For Syrup:
1 cup sugar   ½ cup water

1. To make the syrup, mix the sugar and water, and bring to a boil on high heat, stirring often. Boil for 1 minute only to make it single–thread consistency (see page 257). Keep aside.
2. On medium heat, in a large frying pan, stir the semolina and butter together until it becomes light golden brown (about 15 minutes).
3. Reduce the heat to low; add the almonds and coconut and stir for another 5 minutes. Turn off the heat.
4. Stir in the hot syrup to get cookie dough like mixture that can be shaped into small balls. Add the milk. (The mixture hardens as it cools. If it is too soft, cook on low heat for a few more minutes; keep stirring.)
5. Let the mixture cool for about ½ hour. Make small firm balls pressing with your fingers and palm. Let them rest for couple of hours before serving.

Makes about 15 servings, 1 piece each. Per serving –
Nutritive Value: 224 calories, 4 g protein, 31 g carb, 1 g fiber, 9.7 g fat, 19 mg chol.
Food Group Exchange: 1 Sugar, ½ Grain, ½ Fat, 1/8 Legumes/Meat.

YELLOW SWEET RICE

Sweet Rice is delicious served as a dessert or as a snack with plain yogurt. It is considered an auspicious dish. It is best when freshly made. If you prepare it in advance and refrigerate, reheat covered in the microwave before serving.

2 cups Basmati rice
3 cups water to cook rice
4 tablespoons butter or clarified butter (ghee)
½ cup milk
2 tablespoons plain yogurt
2 cups sugar

Seasonings:
2 teaspoons coarsely crushed cardamom seeds
1 teaspoon yellow food color

½ teaspoon saffron (mixed in 1 teaspoon warm water)

Garnish:
½ cup chopped blanched almonds
1 cup finely chopped coconut

½ cup golden raisins

1. Check the rice for any foreign matter; rinse. Boil the rice in the water; simmer until half-cooked. Strain and rinse in cold water (prevents further cooking of rice) and keep aside.
2. Put the butter (or ghee) in a 4–qt pot on medium heat. When the butter melts, stir in ½ of the crushed cardamoms. Add the milk. As the milk starts boiling, stir in the yogurt slowly. (Milk may separate.) Add the food color and saffron.
3. Add the rice and mix well with a fork. Reduce the heat to low. Sprinkle the sugar evenly over the rice. Cover and let it steam for 10–15 minutes on low heat. When the rice is cooked and the sugar is absorbed, add the remaining crushed cardamom; stir with a fork.
4. Serve hot garnished with the almonds, coconut, and raisins.

Healthy Alternative: Reduce butter as desired. Add about ½ cup of yogurt.

Makes about 12 servings, ½ cup each. Per serving –
Nutritive Value: 268 calories, 2.5 g protein, 55 g carb, 1.3 g fiber, 4.5 g fat, 12.6 mg chol.
Food Group Exchange: 2 Sugar, 1 Grain, 1/4 Fat.

for Young Children   A Daily Guide for 2- to 6-Year-Olds

Cooking by Children
Creative and Appetizing

The motivation for this chapter came from my grand children who love my cooking and help me too. The purpose is to introduce dishes which children can prepare themselves and enjoy or help in preparing. The recipes also indicate fusion of ingredients and cooking techniques used in cuisine of different countries.

This chapter is divided into two parts: Part A: *Grains and Vegetables*, Part B: *For the Sweet Tooth.* Also check some dishes in other sections of the book, e.g., 'Puri' in the chapter *Breads*, and 'Gulabjamun' in the chapter *Desserts*. For details of cooking techniques, refer to the chapter *Preparation Techniques*.

It is a lot of fun to plan the meals and shop for what you need. Look for green and fresh vegetables. Get ingredients for easy and delicious dishes like Cheesy Rice 'n Beans, Lentils Galore, Rice Real, and Vegetable Noodle Soup. It is easy to learn how to mix things, cut vegetables and cook some basic dishes. Another important thing for you to know is that food poisoning bacteria can grow on dirty hands, unclean utensils and

Recipes with a Spice

countertops and on foods left outside the refrigerator. It is essential to keep the kitchen clean and wash your hands before you cook or eat.

Try to learn about nutritive foods that are good for your growth. It is in your childhood when you lay the foundation for your future. Include fresh fruits, vegetables, whole grains, and fish in your diet. Avoid the products that contain hydrogenated oil, a cheap fat used to extend the shelf life of foods. Experiment with new flavors and textures. You'll find new taste in vegetables when you puree them and include in your favorite dishes. Some of the seasonings such as green coriander, parsley, and chives taste good and look great. Use spices such as cumin powder and mustard seeds that are not hot or spicy. A pinch of turmeric powder adds golden color to a dish. Herbs are known to be beneficial and help preserve food. Be imaginative and creative in the use of ingredients. You just may start to like some new things!

To help plan nutritious meals, each recipe gives nutritive value (calories, protein, carbohydrate (carb), fiber, fat, and cholesterol (chol)), and Food Group Exchange for a helping of the dish. Estimate is rounded off for ease of understanding. Garnishes, topping and small amounts of seasoning are not accounted for. (See page 13 for basis of estimating Food Group Exchange and nutritive value.)

Abbreviations:

carb: carbohydrate,	chol: cholesterol,	F: Fahrenheit,
g: gram,	lb: pound,	med: medium,
mg: milligram,	oz: ounce.	

PART A: *Grains and Vegetables*

BAKED ONION RINGS

Onions, known as roots of health, are used in these delicious hors d'oeuvres. Serve them with ketchup or chutney. You may prepare them in advance and bake when ready to eat. They can be reheated in the oven for about 5 minutes at 350°F. Makes about 20 pieces.

4 medium size red onions
½ cup bread crumbs
1 cup crushed corn flakes
¼ cup gram flour (or all–purpose flour)
½ cup milk

Seasonings:

½ teaspoon mango powder   1 teaspoon salt
½ teaspoon red chili powder

1. Cut the onions into about ¼" thick slices. Mix the bread crumbs and corn flakes in a wide bowl and keep aside.
2. Make a thin mixture by whipping together gram flour (or all-purpose flour) and milk. Add the seasonings to taste.
3. Grease a 9x13" baking sheet. Dip the onion slices in the flour solution, roll in the bread crumbs mixture, and place on the baking sheet in single layer.
4. Bake in the oven at 375°F for about 15 minutes. Turn, and bake the other side for another 5–10 minutes.
5. Serve hot with 'Mint–Coriander Chutney' or ketchup.

Variation: Use zucchini or eggplant slices the same way.

Makes about 7 servings, 3 pieces each. Per serving –
Nutritive Value: 121 calories, 3.6 g protein, 26 g carb, 3 g fiber, 1 g fat, 1 mg chol.
Food Group Exchange: ½ Vegetable, ¼ Grain.

BAKED POTATOES

Potato is the most popular vegetable all over the world. The simplest and healthiest way to eat a potato is to bake it. If you cook the potatoes in a microwave before baking in a conventional oven, it expedites the cooking. They are best eaten when freshly baked but leftovers can be refrigerated and re-warmed or used in a stew.

6 baking potatoes

<u>Topping</u>:
Butter, sour cream, yogurt, chutney, or salsa
Salt and black pepper to taste

<u>Garnish:</u> Chopped parsley or dill

1. Wash and scrub the potatoes and remove any blemishes. Cut them into half lengthwise. Microwave them in a covered microwave dish for 8 minutes.
2. Spread the potato halves on a baking pan. Bake at 450°F for 20-25 minutes until light brown.
3. Serve with the desired topping and garnish.

Makes about 6 servings, 2 pieces each. Per serving –
Nutritive Value: 160 calories, 4 g protein, 36 g carb, 3 g fiber, 0 g fat, 0 mg chol.
Food Group Exchange: 1 Grain.

BAKED POTATO WEDGES

Serve them as a snack along with tomato ketchup. If you cook the potatoes in a microwave before baking in a conventional oven, it expedites the cooking.

6 baking potatoes
1 tablespoon oil

Seasonings:
¼ teaspoon garlic powder   ¾ teaspoon salt
¼ teaspoon paprika

1. Wash and scrub the potatoes. Cut them like thick (or thin) french–fries. Half–cook them in a covered microwave dish for about 8 minutes.
2. Mix the oil and the desired seasonings. Toss the potatoes in the mixture and spread on a greased baking pan in single layer. Bake at 450°F for 15-20 minutes until light brown, turning once or twice as needed.

Variation: Sprinkle some Parmesan cheese on the potatoes and then bake.

Makes about 8 servings, 1 cup each. Per serving –
Nutritive Value: 135 calories, 3 g protein, 27 g carb, 2.4 g fiber, 2 g fat, 0 mg chol.
Food Group Exchange: 1 Grain, 1/8 Fat.

BAKED SQUASH

Popular squashes include acorn (round with blue-green rind), and butternut (pear shaped and camel color). You may serve them in their shell and everybody can scoop out what they want.

1 medium size squash — acorn or butternut
1 tablespoon oil

Seasonings:
½ teaspoon garlic powder   ¼ teaspoon paprika
¼ teaspoon salt   ¼ teaspoon black pepper.

Garnish: Chopped parsley, green coriander, or dill

1. Wash the squash. Make small cuts or poke the squash at several places; microwave it covered for 6–8 minutes, until little tender so that it can be easily halved. Cut half lengthwise. Remove seeds and roughage.
2. Sprinkle cut side with half the oil, garlic powder, and salt. Place cut side down on a baking pan; brush top with the remaining oil.
3. Bake at 375°F for about ½ hour until cooked. Serve cut side up sprinkled with black pepper, paprika and chopped green herbs.

Makes about 6 servings, ½ cup each. Per serving –
Nutritive Value: 49 calories, 0.6 g protein, 7.5 g carb, 1 g fiber, 2 g fat, 0 mg chol.
Food Group Exchange: 1 Vegetable, 1/6 Fat.

BEANS 'n BEANS

Use your choice of beans and herbs— one of the favorites is red–kidney beans with a lot of tomatoes. Other beans include black-eyed peas and chickpeas. Use canned, frozen, or dry beans. Depending on your preference, add chopped or pureed vegetables. It should look like chunky soup. Serve it as a main dish with 'Rice Real' or any kind of bread.

2 cups boiled red–kidney beans (or any other beans)
1 cup fresh tomatoes (or ½ cup canned)
½ cup chopped or pureed carrots, celery, or spinach
(or any other veggie)
1 cup water

Seasonings:
1 teaspoon salt   ¼ teaspoon black pepper

1. If using canned beans, drain them. Do not use salt.
2. In a medium size pot, cook everything together on medium heat.
3. When boiling, reduce heat and let it simmer for 20-30 minutes. Add more water as needed to make it like chunky soup. Serve hot. **Note:** To use dry beans, see *Dry Beans– Cooking* on page 30. Add the vegetables when the beans are almost cooked.

Makes about 6 servings, ¾ cup each. Per serving –
Nutritive Value: 85 calories, 5.5 g protein, 16 g carb, 5 g fiber, 0.4 g fat, 0 mg chol.
Food Group Exchange: ¾ Legumes/Meat, ¾ Vegetable.

BROCCOLI-CHEESE CASSEROLE

Broccoli, a queen of vegetables, tastes great in this casserole. You can also use broccoflower, a cross between broccoli and cauliflower. Make it in advance, and refrigerate or freeze it for use when needed.

**8 oz. cream of mushroom soup
½ cup water
1 bunch (about 4 cups) broccoli,
washed, trimmed and chopped
1 small chopped onion
1 tomato sliced
1 cup grated Mozzarella cheese
(or Cheddar cheese)**

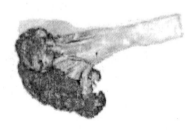

1. Boil the soup and water. Add the chopped broccoli; cook for 5 minutes. Spread in a casserole dish. Top with chopped onions, tomato slices and grated cheese.
2. Bake for 30 minutes at 350°F.

Variation: May add 1–2 cups cooked rice, chopped celery, and celery soup to the casserole before baking. Sauté the onions for a different taste.

Makes about 8 servings, ½ cup each. Per serving –
Nutritive Value: 70 calories, 6.5 g protein, 7 g carb, 2.6 g fiber, 3 g fat, 9 mg chol.
Food Group Exchange: 1 Vegetable, ½ Dairy, 1/8 Fat.

CHEESY RICE 'N BEANS

Make this casserole ahead of time and refrigerate. This one–pot meal combines grains, veggies, legumes, and dairy. Try some of the seasonings, especially green coriander. Add more spices like chili powder if desired. Bake it when ready to serve. Serve with salad, vegetables and yogurt.

1 cup chopped tomatoes (or ½ cup canned)
1 cup chopped carrots and bell pepper
(or any other veggie)
2 cups cooked brown (or white) rice
15 oz can chickpeas or any other beans, drained
1 cup shredded Cheddar cheese, divided
1 tablespoon oil

Seasonings:

1 teaspoon cumin seeds
1 teaspoon minced garlic
½ cup chopped onion

1 teaspoon salt
¼ teaspoon black pepper
1 tablespoon chopped green coriander

1. Heat the oil in a small frying pan. Add cumin seeds, garlic and onion; stir for a few minutes until the onions are translucent.
2. Add the chopped tomatoes and vegetables; cook for about 5 minutes. Mix in the rice, chickpeas, ½ cup of cheese, and the remaining seasonings.
3. Pour everything into a medium size casserole. Sprinkle remaining ½ cup of cheese on top.
4. When ready to serve, bake covered in 350°F oven for 15–20 minutes until nice and hot.

Healthy Alternative: Instead of Cheddar cheese, mix in yogurt cheese. Sprinkle very little cheese for presentation.

Makes about 8 servings, ½ cup each. Per serving –
Nutritive Value: 180 calories, 7.5 g protein, 22 g carb, 1.6 g fiber, 8 g fat, 15 mg chol.
Food Group Exchange: ½ Grain, ½ Vegetable, ½ Legumes/Meat, ½ Dairy, 1/8 Fat.

CURLY CARROT SALAD

Ready for a party! Make this fancy colorful salad. Prepare the carrots 1–2 days in advance and put the salad together the day of the party.

3 medium carrots
2 cups shredded leaf lettuce
1 cup Feta cheese, crumbled

Seasonings:

1 tablespoon lemon juice   ½ teaspoon salt
1 tablespoon olive oil   ¼ teaspoon black pepper

1. Wash and peel the carrots and cut them in pieces 3–4" long. Using a large vegetable peeler, peel the carrot pieces into thin, translucent strips. Place the strips in ice water and let stand until curly, about 20 minutes. Remove the curly carrot strips and paper dry.
2. Combine with lettuce, cheese and the seasonings; serve.

Variation: You can combine any other vegetables such as mushrooms and spinach in this salad. Radishes with 4 cuts on top can also be put in ice water. Wash and trim all vegetables before using.

Makes about 8 servings, ¾ cup each. Per serving –
Nutritive Value: 76 calories, 3 g protein, 3 g carb, 1 g fiber, 6 g fat, 16.7 mg chol.
Food Group Exchange: 1 Vegetable, ¾ Dairy, 1/8 Fat.

DEVILED EGGS

This makes a protein rich snack that can be served after school or work, with salad or vegetables.

6 hard boiled eggs
3 tablespoons mayonnaise

Seasonings:

½ teaspoon paprika
¼ teaspoon black pepper

¼ teaspoon chili powder
¼ teaspoon salt

Garnish: Twigs of green coriander or parsley

1. Peel the boiled eggs; cut them lengthwise in halves. Remove yolk. Mash yolk and mix with mayonnaise and all the seasonings with a fork.
2. Fill the egg–halves with the mixture, heaping it lightly. Arrange on a serving platter and serve. *(Do not refrigerate for more than 24 hours.)*

Variation: Mix grated carrots, sliced cucumbers or anything you like to the mixture to fill the egg halves. Use half–and–half, sour cream, salad dressing or yogurt cheese instead of mayonnaise.

Makes about 6 servings, 1 egg each. Per serving –
Nutritive Value: 111 calories, 6 g protein, 0.6 g carb, 0 g fiber, 9 g fat, 214 mg chol.
Food Group Exchange: 1 Legumes/Meat, ½ Fat.

Experts confirm that
Sharing meals as a family brings
a banquet of benefits.

FINGER SANDWICHES

These are small dainty sandwiches made with a variety of tasty fillings. They are a hit in any party. Be creative in the use of spreads and fillings. Serve extra filling on the side.

**10 slices of whole–wheat, white or pumpernickel
bread, fresh and thinly sliced
4 tablespoons butter (or 8 oz. cream cheese) mixed with salt,
pepper, and chopped herbs like
dill, parsley, watercress
20 thin slices of cucumber
(or 8 oz. sliced smoked salmon)**

<u>Garnish:</u> Sprigs of dill, parsley, or crushed nuts

1. Keep the bread covered so that it remains soft. On a flat work area, roll each slice of bread lightly with a rolling pin. Spread half of the slices with the butter or cream cheese mixture. Layer with the cucumber or salmon slices or both.
2. Place the other piece of bread on top. Trim the crust with a sharp knife. Cut each sandwich into quarters and then into triangles.

Variation: Use mayonnaise or peanut butter as a spread. May use egg salad, grated carrots, hummus, or any pickle or chutney as a filling.

Makes about 10 servings, 1 slice each. Per serving –
Nutritive Value: 112 calories, 3 g protein, 12.4 g carb, 2 g fiber, 5.6 g fat, 12.4 mg chol.
Food Group Exchange: 1 Grain, ½ Fat, ¼ Vegetable.

GOURMET COUSCOUS

Everybody likes couscous. Serve it as a snack or one–pot dish. If you mix it with some sautéed vegetables and serve to your friends or family, you'll be called a gourmet cook who keeps the food from becoming boring. Depending on your preference, add chopped, grated or pureed vegetables. It tastes great at room temperature and is suitable for picnics. Refrigerate (or freeze) the leftovers and reheat when needed. You may have to add some water for re–heating.

2 cups couscous
1 cup chopped (or grated) vegetables such as carrots, zucchini, red cabbage, swiss chard
½ cup boiled beans (chickpeas or red–kidney beans)
2 tablespoons chopped parsley or green coriander
2 teaspoons oil

Seasonings:

½ teaspoon minced garlic
½ cup chopped onion
½ teaspoon salt

¼ teaspoon cumin powder
¼ teaspoon black pepper

1. Put the couscous in a bowl and cover generously with boiling water (about 3 cups). Leave aside, covered, for 10 minutes.
2. Put the oil in a skillet over medium heat. Add the garlic and onions; stir for a couple of minutes. When golden brown, add your choice of vegetables and beans. Sprinkle little water if needed. Add the remaining seasonings to taste. Cook for about 5 minutes until the vegetables are tender.
3. Drain excess water if any from the couscous. Mix the couscous and cooked vegetables and beans; add parsley (or green coriander) and serve.

Makes about 8 servings, ½ cup each. Per serving –
Nutritive Value: 200 calories, 6.7 g protein, 39 g carb, 3.6 g fiber, 1.7 g fat, 0 mg chol.
Food Group Exchange: 1 Grain, ¼ Vegetable, 1/8 Legumes/Meat, 1/8 Fat.

GRAIN-VEGETABLE DELIGHT

Rich in fiber, this casserole can be made in advance and refrigerated or frozen; except do not add cheese. Reheat, covered, until heated through and then sprinkle the cheese. Be creative and change the vegetables or grains, as you like. It is like a complete meal and goes well with any soup.

1 cup boiled black beans or any other beans
½ cup pearl barley
¼ cup bulgur
1 cup corn
1 cup small mushrooms, quartered
2 carrots, thinly sliced in 1–2" long pieces
1 tomato chopped
1 onion chopped
1 cup water (or vegetable stock)

Seasonings:

½ teaspoon crushed ginger   ½ teaspoon red chili powder
1 teaspoon crushed garlic   ½ teaspoon salt

Garnish: ½ cup shredded Cheddar or Mozzarella cheese (optional)

1. Combine all the ingredients and seasonings in a 2 quart casserole. Add more water if needed. Cover and bake at 350°F for about 1 hour until the grains are tender, stirring once halfway through the baking time.
2. When ready to serve, optionally garnish with the cheese, cover, and reheat in the oven until the cheese melts.

Healthy Alternative: Instead of cheese, use a choice of garnishes such as salsa or chutney. You may use hulled barley instead of pearl barley. Soak the barley 4–5 hours or overnight before cooking.

Makes about 8 servings, ½ cup each. Per serving –
Nutritive Value: 123 calories, 5 g protein, 26 g carb, 6 g fiber, 0.7 g fat, 0 mg chol.
Food Group Exchange: 1 Vegetable, 1/3 Grain, ¼ Legumes/Meat.

GRAIN-VEGGIE PUREE

Make this dish for little babies and children who can take only smooth food. It can be smooth enough (and very healthy) to be the first food given to a baby. Start with one or two ingredients and keep on adding others as the baby develops a taste for them. It can be made in advance and refrigerated or frozen. Reheat, covered, in a microwave oven. Be creative and change the vegetables or grains, as you like.

½ cup rice
½ cup peeled (yellow) Mung dal
½ cup chopped potato and carrot
½ cup chopped spinach

<u>Seasonings</u>: 1 teaspoon salt (to taste)

1. Pick over rice and 'dal' for any foreign matter; rinse. Put everything together (except spinach) in a 2–quart pot with 4–5 cups water. Cook on high heat, partially covered. When it starts to boil, lower heat to medium and let it cook until the grains are soft (about 15 minutes).
2. Add the spinach and cook for another 5 minutes at low heat. Add more water if needed. It can be semi-thick or thin consistency.
3. Puree the mixture in a food processor to desired consistency.

Variation: Add a small tomato along with spinach.

Makes about 10 servings, ½ cup each. Per serving –
Nutritive Value: 60 calories, 2.5 g protein, 12 g carb, 1 g fiber, 0 g fat, 0 mg chol.
Food Group Exchange: ½ Grain, 1/3 Legumes/Meat, 1/8 Vegetable.

INSTANT TOMATO SAUCE

Use this sauce on rice, pasta or vegetables. It can be refrigerated for several days or frozen. Thaw it in the refrigerator before serving. Makes about 3 cups.

6 tomatoes, cut
1 cup fresh basil leaves
¼ cup olive oil

Seasonings:

3 garlic cloves
½ diced onion

¼ teaspoon black pepper
½ teaspoon salt

1. Put everything in a food processor; puree for a few seconds to blend it all.
2. Let it sit for 1–2 hours before serving.

Variation: Sauté the garlic and onions before adding tomatoes (fresh or canned). Cook a little before pureeing everything together.

Healthy Alternative: Reduce the quantity of oil. Add vegetables such as mushrooms and spinach to the sauce.

Makes about 6 servings, ½ cup each. Per serving –
Nutritive Value: 107 calories, 1 g protein, 6 g carb, 1.5 g fiber, 10 g fat, 0 mg chol.
Food Group Exchange: 1 Vegetable, ½ Fat.

Skipping meals lowers your metabolic rate.
This is your body's way of trying to store food energy (in the form of fat) in response to what it sees as starvation.

LENTILS GALORE

There is a variety of lentils that you can use. One of the favorites is peeled yellow Mung (yellow lentils) mixed with split reddish Masoor (red lentils). Other lentils include green or yellow split peas and brown lentils. Depending on your preference, add chopped or pureed vegetables. Try brussel sprouts or different types of cabbage. Refrigerate (or freeze) the leftovers and reheat when needed. You may have to add some water for re-heating. Serve it as a main dish with 'Rice Real' or any kind of bread.

2 cups lentils
½ cup rice
7 cups water
1 cup chopped or pureed vegetables such as carrots, squash, spinach, cabbage
½ cup chopped tomatoes (or ¼ cup canned)

Seasonings:
1 teaspoon salt
¼ teaspoon turmeric powder

¼ teaspoon cumin powder
¼ teaspoon black pepper

1. Check the lentils and rice for grit or any foreign matter; rinse a couple of times until water runs clear. In a large (4 quarts) pot, cook the lentils, rice, water, and the desired seasonings on medium heat. When boiling, reduce the heat and let the lentil–rice mixture simmer, half covered, for 15 minutes.
2. Add your choice of chopped (or pureed) vegetables. Add more water if needed to make it like chunky soup.
3. When everything is almost cooked (10–15 minutes), add the tomatoes and let cook for a couple of minutes. Serve hot with a dab of butter on top if preferred.

Healthy Alternative: Use vegetable or chicken stock instead of water for cooking. Also stir in 2 tablespoons of Textured Vegetable Protein (TVP) along with the vegetables for additional protein.

Makes about 10 servings, ½ cup each. Per serving –
Nutritive Value: 135 calories, 7.7 g protein, 26 g carb, 5 g fiber, 0.6 g fat, 0 mg chol.
Food Group Exchange: ¾ Legumes/Meat, 1/3 Grain, 1/3 Vegetable.

LENTIL LOAF

You may make this bread ahead of time and freeze. Warm in the oven before serving with any salad or soup. Use a large loaf pan or 2 small pans to bake.

1 cup brown lentils
1 cup rice
1 cup chopped vegetables such as tomatoes, mushrooms, and green pepper
2 eggs
1/3 cup milk
½ cup bread crumbs
2 tablespoons oil

Seasonings:

1 teaspoon crushed garlic
1 chopped onion
1 teaspoon salt

¼ teaspoon black pepper
3 tablespoons chopped parsley

1. Check the lentils and rice for foreign matter; rinse. In a large (3 quarts) pot, cook the lentils and rice in 4 cups water on high heat. When boiling, reduce the heat and let it simmer, covered, on low–medium heat until all water evaporates (about 15 minutes).
2. Heat the oil in a small skillet. Add the garlic and onions and cook for a minute. Add your choice of chopped vegetables. Cook until golden brown. Turn off the heat.
3. Beat in the eggs and milk. Add the bread crumbs and remaining seasonings. Mix everything with cooked lentils and rice. Mash a little for even consistency.
4. Pour the mixture in a greased loaf pan. Bake at 350°F for 45–50 minutes until the loaf is done. Serve hot.

Healthy Alternative: Use brown rice; they take more water and longer to cook.

Makes about 12 servings, 2 thin slices each. Per serving –
Nutritive Value: 157 calories, 6 g protein, 23 g carb, 2.4 g fiber, 5 g fat, 31 mg chol.
Food Group Exchange: ¾ Grain, ¾ Legumes/Meat, ¼ Vegetable, 1/3 Fat.

LIKE PEANUT BUTTER

This easy to make spread can be used, instead of peanut butter, in sandwiches. Keep some toasted wheat germ handy in the refrigerator or freezer to be used when needed. Makes about 2 cups.

2 ripe bananas
¾ cup toasted wheat germ

Seasonings:

1 tablespoon honey   Pinch of salt

1. Peel the bananas. Mash them along with wheat germ to make a spread.
2. Add the desired seasonings and serve.

Makes about 12 servings, 2 tablespoons each. Per serving –
Nutritive Value: 45 calories, 2.3 g protein, 8 g carb, 1.4 g fiber, 1 g fat, 0 mg chol.
Food Group Exchange: ¼ Grain, ¼ Fruit.

Seven is fine, Nine is Divine
Strive to include plenty of fruits and vegetables in your diet.
Rich in vitamins and minerals,
they help to prevent disease.

MACARONI and CHEESE

The delight of making macaroni and cheese from a scratch is immense. Add any seasonings and cheeses that you may like. You can make it in advance and bake or re–warm when needed.

12 oz. elbow macaroni or any other pasta
1/3 cup all–purpose flour whisked with ½ cup milk
4 cups milk
1 cup shredded Cheddar cheese
3 tablespoons grated Parmesan cheese
1 cup bread crumbs
1 tablespoon oil (or butter)

Seasonings:

½ cup chopped onion
1 teaspoon salt
½ teaspoon black pepper

¼ teaspoon oregano
½ teaspoon chopped basil

1. Cook the pasta according to the directions on the package and drain.
2. Put the oil (or butter) in a skillet over medium heat. Add the onions; stir for a couple of minutes until soft. Stir in the flour whisked with milk. While stirring, add remaining milk and cook on low heat until the mixture thickens, 10–15 minutes.
3. Stir in the cheeses and the seasonings. After a couple of minutes, add the cooked pasta.
4. Heat the oven to 375°F. Pour the mixture in a greased 13x9" baking dish. Top with the bread crumbs. Bake for 35 minutes until bubbly. Serve hot.

Variation: Also stir in ½ cup chopped tomatoes along with the pasta. Or add 1 can of undiluted mushroom soup while the milk and flour are cooking.

Makes about 12 servings, ½ cup each. Per serving –
Nutritive Value: 246 calories, 10.5 g protein, 33.5 g carb, 0.5 g fiber, 7.5 g fat, 18 mg chol.
Food Group Exchange: 1 Dairy, ¾ Grain, 1/8 Fat.

MASHED POTATOES

Potatoes are moistened with warm milk for this dish. It is exciting to try some of the variations. You may make them in advance and refrigerate. Reheat adding little liquid to get the right consistency.

8 medium size boiling potatoes
1 cup warm milk
1 tablespoon butter

Seasonings:
½ teaspoon salt
¼ teaspoon black pepper

¼ teaspoon paprika

1. Wash, scrub or peel, and cut potatoes in 1" pieces. Microwave them in a covered dish for 8–10 minutes until very soft. Or boil them in enough water in a pot until the potatoes are soft. Drain the water.
2. With a potato masher, mash the potatoes when still hot, adding warm milk and butter to get the desired consistency. Mix in the seasonings to your taste.

Variation: Reduce the amount of milk and butter. Instead add ½ cup plain yogurt or ½ cup Ricotta cheese.

Healthy Alternative: Omit butter. Add roasted garlic, chopped chives, parsley or green coriander for flavor. Boil some vegetable or chicken broth and use in place of milk.

Makes about 8 servings, ½ cup each. Per serving –
Nutritive Value: 125 calories, 3.5 g protein, 23.6 g carb, 2 g fiber, 2 g fat, 6.4 mg chol.
Food Group Exchange: 1 Grain, 1/8 Dairy, 1/8 Fat.

PASTA GARDEN

This dish brings out the full flavor of fresh vegetables and pasta. Use any vegetable such as zucchini, scallions, or broccoli. This is a good dish to take to school or a picnic. Refrigerate the leftovers and reheat when needed.

½ lb. pasta (spaghetti, linguini, ziti)
2 chopped tomatoes
10 oz. fresh spinach washed and torn into pieces
2 tablespoons grated Parmesan cheese
1 tablespoon oil

Seasonings:

1 teaspoon minced garlic
½ cup chopped onion

½ teaspoon salt
¼ teaspoon black pepper

1. Cook the pasta according to the directions on the package and drain.
2. Put the oil in a skillet over medium heat. Add the garlic and onions; stir for a couple of minutes. When golden brown, add the tomatoes and spinach. Cook for a few minutes until the spinach is just wilted.
3. Stir in the cooked pasta, salt and pepper. Serve sprinkled with Parmesan cheese.

Makes about 8 servings, ½ cup each. Per serving –
Nutritive Value: 144 calories, 5.4 g protein, 24 g carb, 1.5 g fiber, 3 g fat, 1 mg chol.
Food Group Exchange: ¾ Grain, ½ Vegetable, 1/8 Fat.

PIZZA as you like

If you are a pizza fan, you'll want to make one suited to your taste. Use the flour of your choice and make it thick or thin, with preferred vegetables or pepperoni. You may make the pizza in advance and bake it before serving. Serve with soup and salad.

2 teaspoons dry yeast
2 cups flour (mix of all–purpose & whole–wheat)
1 cup plain yogurt
¼ cup oil

Seasonings:
½ teaspoon sugar   1 teaspoon salt

Topping:
3 cups spaghetti sauce   1 cup grated Mozzarella cheese
2 cups chopped vegetables such as   1 teaspoon garlic powder
onions, bell-peppers, mushrooms
½ cup chopped basil

1. Mix the yeast in ¼ cup warm water. Add sugar. Let it stand for a few minutes until it rises. Mix with the flour, yogurt, oil, and salt in a deep bowl, and knead the dough, adding water as needed, until it becomes smooth and supple.
2. Cover with a kitchen towel and let it rise for at least 3 hours (or overnight) in a warm place like oven. Punch it down, fold over several times and shape into one smooth ball (or 4–5 balls for individualized pizzas).
3. Roll the ball on counter top sprinkled with flour. Spread it evenly with fingers to make into a 14–16" disc. Place the disc on greased pizza pan. Form a ridge around the edges to hold the toppings. Poke with a fork at several places to avoid bubbles when baking.
4. Preheat the oven to 400°F. Bake the pizza disc on the bottom rack for 6–8 minutes until it just begins to brown. (You may freeze the disc at this point.)
5. Take the pizza out and spread the topping — first sauce, then vegetables, herbs and cheese. Sprinkle garlic powder. Put it back in the preheated oven, on top rack, and bake for another 15 minutes, until crispy and cheese is bubbling. Cut and serve.

Variation: Add chopped nuts or any seasoning such as chopped rosemary, basil or garlic to the dough.

Makes about 10 servings, 1 medium piece each. Per serving –
Nutritive Value: 513 calories, 12 g protein, 70 g carb, 12 g fiber, 20 g fat, 7 mg chol.
Food Group Exchange: 1 Grain, ¾ Vegetable, ¾ Dairy, ½ Fat.

POTATO PANCAKES

These pancakes, traditionally made in Jewish homes and called 'latkes', are popular with children (and adults) all over the world. Serve with applesauce, sour cream, yogurt or chutney.

4 potatoes
1 onion chopped finely
2 eggs, whipped
2 tablespoons all-purpose flour (more as needed)
Oil to pan-fry

Seasonings:
¼ teaspoon pepper   ¾ teaspoon salt

1. Wash and scrub the potatoes and grate them. Drain excess water. Mix everything together, except the oil, to make a batter, little thicker than that for pancakes. (Instead of grating potatoes, another way is to chop them and blend everything together in a food processor.)
2. Heat a large skillet on medium heat. Grease with ½ teaspoon oil. Drop 2 tablespoons of batter, 2" apart and let each patty spread into a 3" round. (2–3 pancakes may fit on a large skillet.) As the pancakes start to brown, turn them with a spatula. Put ½ teaspoon oil around the pancakes. Remove when light brown on both sides.
3. Make the remaining pancakes the same way. If cold, wrap in paper towel and warm in the microwave for a minute. Serve hot.

Healthy Alternative: Replace about half of the potatoes by any vegetable such as zucchini, carrots, sweet potato, and spinach. Add fresh basil or green coriander. Finely chop or grate and drain all vegetables before using.

Makes about 8 servings, 2 medium pieces each. Per serving –
Nutritive Value: 108 calories, 3 g protein, 12 g carb, 1.2 g fiber, 5.6 g fat, 47 mg chol.
Food Group Exchange: ½ Grain, ¼ Legumes/Meat, 1/4 Fat.

QUICK GREENS

Fresh looking young greens are generally very mild and tasty. Some of the popular greens are collard, kale, swiss chard, and spinach, rich in vitamins A and C, folic acid, and iron. Wash them carefully because they can be full of grit. Eat them fresh whenever possible. Cooking them is fun; they cook down to ¼–½ of their volume. They make an excellent filling for sandwiches or pita bread. Make them in advance if needed; refrigerate or freeze. Reheat in the microwave.

2 lb. fresh (or frozen) spinach, collard, or kale
1 chopped tomato
1 tablespoon oil

Seasonings:
1 teaspoon minced garlic   ½ teaspoon salt
¼ teaspoon pepper

1. If using fresh greens, pull the leaves from the stems; discard hard stems. Soak the leaves in a colander immersed in a large bowl filled with water; dirt will settle down. Remove the colander and throw the water away. Repeat until water is clear. Tear the leaves into bite-size pieces.
2. Heat a skillet on medium–high heat. Put the oil. Add garlic. Stir for 15–30 seconds; do not let it burn.
3. Add the greens, tomato and seasonings. (Frozen greens take time to thaw.) Cook, stirring frequently, for about 10 minutes until tender. Sprinkle little water if needed. Do not overcook. Spinach cooks faster than other greens. Serve hot.

Variation: Add some cooked potatoes, pasta, or bread crumbs to the greens for a different texture.

Makes about 8 servings, ¼ cup each. Per serving –
Nutritive Value: 43 calories, 3.4 g protein, 5 g carb, 3 g fiber, 2 g fat, 0 mg chol.
Food Group Exchange: 1 Vegetable, 1/8 Fat.

RICE REAL

Rice is extremely popular with everyone. And perhaps it is the first dish that children learn to cook. Left over rice can be refrigerated for 3–4 days. It can be warmed, covered, in the microwave, or used in other dishes. It can be a main dish (no bread is served) or a side dish. Serve with vegetables and soup.

2 cups long grain rice (white or brown)
3¾ cups water to cook (4¼ cups for brown rice)
1 teaspoon butter (optional)

Seasonings: ½ teaspoon salt (to taste)

1. Rinse the rice. Combine everything (except butter) in a 3-quart pot with a tight-fitting lid. When the water starts to boil, lower the heat to low–medium, cover, and let the rice simmer until it is cooked (about 20 minutes for white rice, about 40 minutes for brown). All water should be absorbed.
2. Turn off the heat. Mix in butter if desired, and fluff the rice with a fork. It stays warm in the pot for about ½ hour. Serve hot with any vegetable, lentils, or yogurt.

Variation: Sprinkle 1 teaspoon lemon juice over cooked rice; mix with a fork so that rice does not break.

Healthy Alternative: Replace half or all of the water by vegetable or chicken stock. You can also mix ½ cup of green peas or mixed vegetables when you begin to cook the rice.

Makes about 12 servings, ½ cup each. Per serving –
Nutritive Value: 112 calories, 2 g protein, 25 g carb, 0.4 g fiber, 0 g fat, 0 mg chol.
Food Group Exchange: 1 Grain.

SPINACH CHEESE CASSEROLE

This will be your favorite dish. It looks and tastes great; can be served as a snack after school or work. Make it ahead of time and bake when ready to eat. It can be refrigerated or frozen.

20 oz. frozen (or fresh) chopped spinach
8 oz. cream cheese (softened)
4 tablespoons butter (divided in 2 parts)
3 cups herb–seasoned stuffing

1. Melt half of the butter (2 tablespoons) and cream cheese together in a skillet.
2. Add the spinach and ¼ cup water if using fresh spinach. (Add about 1/8 cup water if using frozen spinach.) Cook for a couple of minutes. Add ½ of the stuffing.
3. Spread the mixture in a greased casserole dish (about 9"x9"). Top with the remaining stuffing and melted butter.
4. Bake at 350°F for 25 minutes. Serve hot.

Healthy Alternative: Replace part of cream cheese and butter by un–sweetened applesauce or grated zucchini. Use low–fat cream cheese.

Makes about 8 servings, ½ cup each. Per serving –
Nutritive Value: 279 calories, 7 g protein, 20 g carb, 3.4 g fiber, 20 g fat, 45 mg chol.
Food Group Exchange: ¾ Vegetable, 1 Dairy, ½ Fat, 1/3 Grain.

SPINACH DIP

Spinach is one of the super foods in terms of nutrition as well as taste. This dip will give your menu a boost of iron and other nutrients. You can make this dip in advance. Serve cold or at room temperature with vegetables or crackers. Makes about 2 cups.

1 lb. chopped spinach, preferably fresh
6 oz. cream cheese

Seasonings:

½ teaspoon minced garlic
½ cup chopped red onion

¼ teaspoon black pepper
½ teaspoon salt

1. Cook the washed chopped spinach, cream cheese, and seasonings for 5–10 minutes. (If using frozen spinach, heat it in the microwave oven for 5 minutes and drain off excess water in a strainer, before mixing with the cheese and seasonings.)
2. Puree in a food processor or blender, until smooth. Cover and refrigerate until serving time.

Variation: Use sour cream instead of cream cheese. Can also add small package of onion soup mix instead of onion.

Healthy Alternative: Use yogurt cheese or silken tofu instead of cream cheese; add more onion and some chopped tomato.

Makes about 16 servings, 2 tablespoons each. Per serving –
Nutritive Value: 42 calories, 2 g protein, 1 g carb, 3 g fiber, 4 g fat, 12 mg chol.
Food Group Exchange: 1/3 Vegetable, 1/3 Dairy.

SOUP PASAND

'Pasand' is a Hindi word which means 'liking'. You make this soup to your liking. High in nutrition and low in fat, you'll be proud of this dish. Select and mix any vegetables and beans. Put more of a particular vegetable such as cauliflower, and call It 'Cauliflower Soup Pasand'. Refrigerate (or freeze) the leftovers and reheat when needed. You may have to add some water for re–heating.

**2 cups chopped vegetables such as carrots, zucchini, cabbage, tomato, celery, mushrooms
2 cups boiled beans such as chickpeas or cannelloni
3 cups water (or vegetable stock)
1 tablespoon oil**

Seasonings:
½ teaspoon minced garlic　　　　　¼ teaspoon cumin powder
½ cup chopped onion　　　　　　　¼ teaspoon black pepper
½ teaspoon salt

Garnish:
1 red pepper or tomato diced　　　　Sprigs of parsley or green coriander

1. In a pot over medium heat, put the oil. Add the garlic and onions; stir until golden brown. Add the desired remaining seasonings and stir for a minute.
2. Add your choice of chopped vegetables and stir. Add half of the beans. Add the liquid and cook for about 10 minutes until the vegetables are tender.
3. When little cold, puree the cooked veggies and beans in a blender. Mix in the remaining beans. Heat the soup, adding more liquid if needed. Garnish as desired and serve.

Variation: Try different veggies such as asparagus and spinach. Garnish with croutons and grated cheese if desired.

Healthy Alternative: Add ½ cup cooked pearl barley or presoaked and cooked hulled barley to the soup.

Makes about 6 servings, ¾ cup each. Per serving –
Nutritive Value: 127 calories, 5.5 g protein, 19 g carb, 5.3 g fiber, 4 g fat, 0 mg chol.
Food Group Exchange: ½ Legumes/Meat, ½ Vegetable, 1/6 Fat.

TANDOORI VEGGIES

Everybody raves about 'Tandoori Chicken' but 'Tandoori Veggies' will be equally appealing. 'Tandoori' is a Hindi word which means 'from the oven'. Select and mix any vegetables and beans for this main dish. Refrigerate (or freeze) the leftovers and reheat when needed.

**3 cups chopped mixed vegetables such as potatoes,
carrots, broccoli, cauliflower, mushrooms
1 chopped tomato + ½ cup tomato sauce
1 cup boiled chickpeas or red kidney beans
2 teaspoons oil**

<u>Seasonings</u>:
½ teaspoon minced garlic
½ cup chopped onion
½ teaspoon salt

¼ teaspoon cumin powder
¼ teaspoon black pepper

<u>Garnish:</u> ½ cup grated Mozzarella or Cheddar cheese

1. In a large roasting pan, combine all the ingredients and seasonings. Bake covered at 400°F until the vegetables are tender (30-40 minutes), stirring twice during baking. Add little water if needed.
2. Bake uncovered at 450°F for another 10 minutes to get a roasted look. Garnish as desired and serve.

Microwave Method: Cook the vegetables in the microwave oven, covered, for 10–12 minutes. Then combine everything else and put in the conventional oven as in step 2, for a roasted look.

Makes about 6 servings, ½ cup each. Per serving –
Nutritive Value: 107 calories, 4.3 g protein, 18 g carb, 4.4 g fiber, 2.4 g fat, 0 mg chol.
Food Group Exchange: 2/3 Vegetable, 1/3 Legumes/Meat, 1/8 Fat.

TOFU-VEGETABLE QUICHE

A complete food in itself, serve it anytime, as a snack or part of a meal. Use any other vegetable such as spinach, swiss chard, scallions and leek. It can be made in advance and refrigerated or frozen. Reheat in the oven before serving.

2 tablespoons cornstarch
½ cup milk
1 large egg
½ cup cottage cheese
½ cup plain yogurt
1 cup (about 8 oz.) soft tofu, drained
1 onion, chopped and sautéed in some oil
½ lb. mushrooms, chopped
9" pie crust shell

Seasonings:

½ teaspoon crushed ginger   ¼ teaspoon ground nutmeg
¼ teaspoon chili powder   1 teaspoon salt (to taste)
½ teaspoon black pepper

1. Beat the cornstarch and milk into a smooth mixture. Put the mixture along with egg, cottage cheese, yogurt, tofu and all the seasonings in a blender; process to a smooth mixture.
2. Stir the sauteed onions and mushrooms into the mixture; pour into the pie shell.
3. Bake at 350°F for about 35 minutes until a fork inserted in the middle comes out clean. If the quiche is not brown, place under a broiler for a few minutes. Let stand for a few minutes before cutting to serve.

Variation: Use Cheddar cheese and chopped spinach instead of onion and mushrooms.

Healthy Alternative: Instead of using a pie shell, bake in a greased 9" pie pan.

Makes about 8 servings, 1 medium piece each. Per serving –
Nutritive Value: 157 calories, 7 g protein, 13 g carb, 1 g fiber, 8.6 g fat, 30 mg chol.
Food Group Exchange: 1/3 Legumes/Meat, 1/3 Vegetable, 1/3 Fat, ¼ Grain, 1/6 Dairy.

VEGETABLE NOODLE SOUP

Use your choice of vegetables and herbs– onions, garlic, cauliflower, broccoli, in this soup. Serve with crackers or bread sticks.

1 cup pasta noodles
11 oz. can Cream of Mushroom soup
¼ cup tomato puree
½ cup chopped carrots
½ cup chopped mushrooms
½ chopped tomato

Seasonings: 4 sprigs of parsley and dill
Garnish: 2 teaspoons Parmesan cheese

1. In a 3–quart pot, boil 4 cups water. Add the noodles and cook, on medium–high heat for about 5 minutes, until little soft.
2. Add the Cream of Mushroom soup. Keep stirring, making sure it does not boil over.
3. Stir in the tomato puree, mushrooms, and carrots (or any other vegetables). Add more water if needed. Reduce the heat, maintaining gentle boil for about 5 minutes until the vegetables are soft.
4. Turn off the heat. Stir in chopped tomato, parsley and dill. Garnish with cheese, if desired, and serve hot.

Healthy Alternative: Cook ½ cup split Mung dal for about 10 minutes before adding the pasta. May also stir in 2 tablespoons of Textured Vegetable Protein (TVP).

Makes about 4 servings, ¾ cup each. Per serving –
Nutritive Value: 155 calories, 4.6 g protein, 21 g carb, 2 g fiber, 6.6 g fat, 16 mg chol.
Food Group Exchange: ½ Grain, ½ Vegetable, ¼ Fat.

VEGGIE BURGERS

These are very popular with all. Surprise your friends by making them or prepare the mixture and let everyone make their own patties adding the vegetable of their choice. Serve with pita bread or buns. They can be refrigerated or frozen. They can be reheated in the microwave oven (1–2 minutes) or in the conventional oven (10 minutes at 400°F) or in a skillet.

1 small onion, finely chopped
1 red (or green) bell pepper
1 lb. mushrooms
1 cup cooked rice
½ cup cooked lentils (or beans)
2 potatoes, boiled, peeled and mashed
½ cup breadcrumbs
1 tablespoon oil + oil to grease pan

Seasonings:

1 teaspoon crushed garlic	¾ teaspoon mango powder
¼ teaspoon grated ginger	½ teaspoon black pepper
1 teaspoon coriander powder	2 tablespoons chopped green coriander or parsley
1 teaspoon cumin powder	1 teaspoon salt

1. Heat 1 tablespoon of oil in a medium skillet. Add chopped garlic and onions and sauté for a few seconds.
2. Chop the bell pepper and mushrooms; add to the skillet. Cook for a few minutes until the vegetables are tender and dry.
3. Add the cooked rice, lentils (or beans), and potatoes. Mix in all the seasonings. Turn off the heat.
4. Blend the mixture in a food processor for a few seconds.
5. Take small balls of the mixture, dip in the bread crumbs, and shape into 2–3" round patties, about ½" thick (makes about 20).
6. Preheat the oven to 400°F. Arrange the patties on a well-greased cookie sheet and bake for about 20 minutes. Turn over, and bake for another 10 minutes until light brown on both sides. Serve hot with any chutney and bread.

Healthy Alternative: Also add ½ lb. tofu to the mixture.

Makes about 10 servings, two pieces each. Per serving –
Nutritive Value: 103 calories, 3 g protein, 16 g carb, 1.5 g fiber, 3 g fat, 0 mg chol.
Food Group Exchange: ¾ Grain, 1/8 Legumes/Meat, 1/8 Fat.

PART B: For the Sweet Tooth

APPLE SQUARES with WALNUTS

A dessert without oil or butter! It can be frozen; or stored in the refrigerator for about a week. Makes about 30 pieces.

2 cups whole–wheat flour
1 cup sugar
1 egg or 2 egg whites
2 cups peeled chopped apples
2½ cups peeled grated apples
1 cup raisins
1 cup chopped walnuts

Seasonings:
2 teaspoons baking soda
2 teaspoons cinnamon
2 teaspoons vanilla

1. Mix the wheat flour, sugar, and the dry seasonings. Beat in the egg. Add chopped and grated apples, raisins, and vanilla; blend well.
2. Preheat the oven to 350°F. Grease a 13x9x2" pan. Spread the mixture in the pan. Sprinkle the walnuts on top.
3. Bake 35–40 minutes until cooked. Cool in the pan. Cut into squares and serve at room temperature.

Makes about 15 servings, 2 medium pieces each. Per serving –
Nutritive Value: 223 calories, 4.7 g protein, 39 g carb, 4 g fiber, 6 g fat, 13 mg chol.
Food Group Exchange: ¾ Sugar, ½ Grain, 1/3 Legumes/Meat, 1/3 Fruit.

BANANA BOAT

Bananas that are over ripe can be used in this dish. Prepare it in front of children to enable them to pick their choice of ingredients.

¼ cup brown sugar
½ cup orange juice
4 bananas, peeled and halved lengthwise
2 tablespoons butter

Seasonings:
2 teaspoons orange zest   ¼ teaspoon cinnamon

Topping: Vanilla frozen yogurt, ice cream or plain yogurt

1. Melt the butter in a skillet on medium heat. Stir in brown sugar, orange juice and seasonings. As soon as the sugar dissolves (about 1 minute), lay bananas, cut side down, in syrup. Drizzle syrup over bananas with a spoon. Cook for 2 minutes until the bananas begin to brown. Turn off the heat.
2. Serve 1 or 2 banana boats on a dessert plate. Top with a scoop of desired topping and drizzle one teaspoon of left over syrup.

Makes 4 servings, 1 banana each. Per serving –
Nutritive Value: 207 calories, 1.4 g protein, 40 g carb, 3 g fiber, 6 g fat, 15.5 mg chol.
Food Group Exchange: 1 Fruit, ¾ Sugar, ½ Fat.

BREAD DELIGHTS

These are best served warm. If made in advance, warm them in the microwave for 1–2 minutes.

8 slices of white or wheat bread
3 tablespoons oil (or clarified butter)

Syrup:
¾ cup sugar
½ cup water
½ teaspoon crushed cardamom

Garnish: 1 tablespoon coarsely crushed almonds and unsalted pistachios or non-dairy whipped cream

1. Use a wide pot to make the syrup so that the bread pieces can be soaked in it. Mix the water, sugar and crushed cardamom on medium heat. Boil for 1 minute only. Set aside.
2. Cut the bread slices into two, as triangles or rectangles. Heat a skillet on medium heat. Spread 1 tablespoon oil. Place bread slices in single layer. When golden brown on one side, turn with a spatula. Put little more oil on edges. Press the slices gently; remove when golden brown on other side too.
3. Put the slices immediately in warm syrup. Let them soak for about 5 minutes, turning once or twice.
4. Lift the bread pieces gently and place on a platter in single layer, garnish with nuts or whipped cream, and serve at room temperature.

Healthy Alternative: Instead of dipping in syrup, top the pan-fried slices with honey or fruit preserve.

Makes about 8 servings, 1 bread slice each. Per serving –
Nutritive Value: 155 calories, 2 g protein, 23 g carb, 1 g fiber, 6.3 g fat, 0 mg chol.
Food Group Exchange: 1 Grain, ¾ Sugar, 1/3 Fat.

CARAMELIZED APPLES

This is a nice way to give a new twist to apples, especially when they are not that sweet. They can be made in advance and refrigerated. Serve warm or at room temperature.

2 tablespoons butter
3 apples, peeled, cored, and cut in long thin slices
¼–½ cup honey

Topping:

Vanilla frozen yogurt or ice cream   Chopped nuts or fine gingersnap crumbs

1. Melt the butter in a skillet on medium heat. Stir in the apples and honey. Cook, partially covered, until the apples are tender and golden.
2. Serve, with the preferred topping.

Variation: You may melt the butter in the oven, mix everything together, and bake at 400°F, covered, for 10–15 minutes until the apples are tender. Bake uncovered for 5 minutes to get caramelized look.

Makes about 4 servings, ½ cup each (without topping). Per serving –
Nutritive Value: 202 calories, 0.3 g protein, 40 g carb, 3 g fiber, 6 g fat, 15.5 mg chol.
Food Group Exchange: 1 Fruit, 1 Sugar, ½ Fat.

CINNAMON CARROT CAKE

Carrots and cinnamon cooking in the oven fill the house with wonderful aroma. The cake can be kept in the refrigerator for about a week or frozen. Makes about 30 pieces.

2 cups sugar
4 eggs
1¼ cups oil
2 cups all–purpose flour
4 cups shredded carrots (about 1½ lb.)
½ cup raisins
½ cup chopped walnuts

<u>Seasonings</u>:

2 teaspoons baking powder
2 teaspoons baking soda
2 teaspoons cinnamon

¼ teaspoon salt
2 teaspoons vanilla

1. Beat sugar and eggs together; beat in the oil gradually.
2. Mix the flour and dry seasonings. Stir into the egg mixture and beat for 2–3 minutes.
3. Add the carrots, raisins, or two small round pans. Bake 35-40 minutes until cooked. Cool walnuts, and vanilla; blend well.
4. Preheat the oven to 350°F. Put the mixture in a greased 13x9x2" pan or a large round cake pan in pan.
5. Cut and serve at room temperature, with a topping, if desired.

Healthy Alternative: Replace all or part of all–purpose flour by whole–wheat flour.

Variation: Make a gingered carrot cake by adding 2 teaspoons grated ginger instead of cinnamon.

Makes about 30 servings, 1 medium piece each. Per serving –
Nutritive Value: 211 calories, 2 g protein, 22 g carb, 1 g fiber, 13 g fat, 25 mg chol.
Food Group Exchange: 1 Sugar, 1 Fat, ¼ Grain, 1/5 Vegetable, 1/5 Legumes/Meat.

CREAMY FRUIT SHAKE

For this hearty colorful beverage, use fresh or frozen fruits that you like. You can also use different fruit juices. If too thick, add some carbonated drink.

2 cups fruit (peeled, chopped mangoes, bananas, strawberries, or blueberries)
½ cup silken tofu
1 cup crushed ice
1 cup fruit juice (apple, grape or orange)

<u>Seasonings:</u> 3 teaspoons sugar or honey (to taste)

<u>Topping:</u> ¼ cup ginger–ale or sparkling water

1. Combine everything in a blender. Blend at high speed for a few seconds until smooth and frothy, taking care not to over–process.
2. Serve immediately with additional ice and topping, as desired.

Variation: May use plain yogurt instead of silken tofu or soy milk instead of fruit juice. You can also add a scoop of ice cream for creamier taste.

Makes about 4 servings, 1 cup each. Per serving –
Nutritive Value: 123 calories, 2 g protein, 28 g carb, 2 g fiber, 1 g fat, 0 mg chol.
Food Group Exchange: 1 Fruit, ¼ Sugar, ¼ Legumes/Meat.

**It is often better to exercise
30 minutes twice a day,
rather than 60 minutes once a day. After exercise, your body burns
calories at a higher-than-normal rate
for a few hours.**

EGGLESS MARBLES

A great snack which you need to plan ahead. When the dough is ready, you may want others to participate, make their own marbles, bake, and roll in sugar. Makes about 30 pieces.

1 cup (½ lb.) butter, softened
½ cup sugar
2 cups all-purpose flour
¾ cup finely chopped pecans or walnuts
½ cup powdered sugar for dusting

Seasonings:

1½ teaspoon vanilla   1/8 teaspoon baking powder
1/8 teaspoon salt

1. In a large bowl, beat butter and sugar together until smooth and creamy.
2. Blend in the flour and seasonings, while stirring. Add nuts and make it into soft dough with your hands.
3. Shape the dough into a ball and wrap in plastic wrap. Refrigerate for 1 hour or more, ready to be used when needed.
4. Take out the dough and make into marble size balls; place on un–greased cookie sheet.
5. Preheat the oven to 375°F. Bake the marbles for 10–12 minutes until firm but not brown.
6. While still warm, roll them in powdered sugar; serve at room temperature.

Makes about 10 servings, 3 pieces each. Per serving –
Nutritive Value: 386 calories, 3 g protein, 38 g carb, 1.5 g fiber, 26 g fat, 50 mg chol.
Food Group Exchange: 1.5 Fat, 1 Sugar, ½ Grain, 1/3 Legumes/Meat.

FROZEN MANGO YOGURT

Mangoes are sweet, healthy and very popular with children and adults! Eat them fresh as a dessert. If mangoes are getting soft, use them to make this frozen yogurt that can be kept for a couple of months.

2 ripe mangoes
1 cup plain yogurt
2 tablespoons orange juice

Seasonings:
2 tablespoons sugar   1 teaspoon vanilla extract

1. Wash, peel and cut the mangoes in chunks. Puree everything together in a blender until smooth. Freeze in an airtight flat container.
2. Take out the container after about an hour and stir to make sure there are no ice crystals. Freeze again for about 2 hours. Cut into squares, garnish with nuts or mango slices, and serve.

Variation: Use any other fruit such as bananas or watermelon.

Makes about 6 servings, ½ cup each. Per serving –
Nutritive Value: 86 calories, 2.4 g protein, 19 g carb, 1 g fiber, 0.5 g fat, 1.7 mg chol.
Food Group Exchange: ½ Fruit, 1/3 Sugar, 1/6 Dairy.

Exercise tends to increase HDL (good cholesterol) that seems to protect you from heart disease.

JELL-O CONFETTI CAKE

This cake is absolutely delicious in summer especially because it does not even have to be baked! Make it in advance, allowing enough time for gelatin to set. Keep it refrigerated until ready to serve.

**4 (3 oz.) packets of gelatin–orange, lime, strawberry, and
lemon (different colors)
1 cup graham cracker crumbs (12 crackers)
1 tablespoon + ¼ cup sugar
2 tablespoons butter melted
8 oz. cream cheese, softened
1 cup whipping cream**

1. Dissolve the orange, lime and strawberry gelatin, separately in small bowls, in 1 cup boiling water each. Add ¾ cup cold water to each and let set in the refrigerator for 4 hours or more.
2. Combine the graham cracker crumbs, 1 tablespoon of sugar, and butter; press into bottom of a spring–foam pan.
3. Beat the cream cheese until smooth.
4. Dissolve the lemon gelatin in 1 cup boiling water. Add ¼ cup sugar. Mix the dissolved lemon gelatin into the cream cheese.
5. Whip the whipping cream and fold it into the mixture.
6. Cut the refrigerated three colors of gelatin into small cubes (like confetti) and fold them into the mixture. Pour everything into the spring–foam pan and let it set in the refrigerator for a couple of hours. Remove from the pan carefully and serve.

*Makes about 15 servings, 1 medium piece each. Per serving –
Nutritive Value: 226 calories, 3.7 g protein, 30 g carb, 0 g fiber, 10.6 g fat, 27 mg chol.
Food Group Exchange: 1 Sugar, 1 Fat, ½ Dairy, 1/8 Grain.*

SPECIAL CHOCOLATE CAKE

Try this cake and surprise everyone. Chickpeas, high in protein, are substituted for flour and give a wonderful taste. The cake can be stored in the refrigerator for about a week or frozen.

**1½ cups semisweet chocolate chips
2 cups cooked chickpeas
4 eggs
1 cup sugar**

Seasonings:
½ teaspoon baking powder   ¼ teaspoon salt

1. Microwave the chocolate chips in a covered bowl until melted, 2–3 minutes.
2. Drain and crush the chickpeas in the food processor. Mix in the eggs. Add the sugar, melted chocolate and the seasonings; process until smooth. **Note:** Do not add salt if using canned chickpeas.
3. Preheat the oven to 350°F. Put the mixture in a greased 9" round pan. Bake about 45 minutes until a fork inserted comes out clean. Cool in pan.
4. Cut and serve at room temperature, with fruit topping, if desired.

Variation: Add ½ cup nuts if desired. For a fancy twist, fill flat bottom ice cream cones with the batter, about half full. Stand the cones in a muffin pan and bake. They may take about 30 minutes to cook. Serve individual cones topped with ice cream.

Makes about 10 servings, 1 medium piece each. Per serving –
Nutritive Value: 290 calories, 6.5 g protein, 47 g carb, 2.5 g fiber, 10 g fat, 76 mg chol.
Food Group Exchange: 1 Sugar, 1 Legumes/Meat.

Appendices

Recipes with a Spice

Food Group Servings

In this book, an estimate at the end of each recipe gives Food Group Exchange for a usual helping of the dish. It is a general guideline that can be used to determine how to combine different dishes and ingredients to ensure that you get the well-rounded nutrition of the USDA's Food Guide Pyramid. For example, if you want to decrease the amount of added sugar or fat, you can change a recipe to substitute sugar and fat by mashed fruit such as apples and prunes.

Food Group Exchange value is rounded off for ease of understanding. Small amounts of ingredients, herbs, and spices are not counted. Only added fat and sugar are accounted for. Analysis of processed foods is not done.

Estimated Servings

Food Group Exchange values are based on the following table that gives estimated Food Group servings in some of the commonly used ingredients in many recipes. The total Food Group servings in a recipe are divided by the estimated number of helpings produced to derive the Food Group Exchange per serving. The estimates are approximate, based on the USDA guidelines for serving sizes.

Recipes with a Spice

Food   Number of Servings

Grains
1 cup bread crumbs   3
1 cup couscous (2 cups cooked)   4
1 cup flour   4
16 oz. pasta (about 4 cups cooked)   8
1 cup pressed parboiled rice (poha)   2
1 potato (medium)   1
1 lb. potatoes   4
1 cup rice (3 cups cooked)   6
1 cup vermicelli (about 2 cups cooked) 3

Legumes/Meat
1 cup dry beans (2 cups cooked)   4
1 cup dal (3–4 cups cooked)   6
1 cup dal flour or soy flour   4
1 egg   1
1 lb. meat or fish   5
1 cup nuts   3
15 oz. tofu   5
1 cup 'wadi' (lentil nuggets)   2

Fruit
1 cup shredded coconut   2
                                  (+ 2 of Fat)
1 med. fruit—apple, orange, …   1
1 lb. grapes, plums, …   3
1 cup lemon juice   4
1 cup raisins or dry fruit   4
1 med. mango   1.5
1 cup mango pulp   2

Vegetable
1 head broccoli (about 4 cups)   4
1 head cauliflower (about 5 cups)   5
1 bunch celery (about 4 cups)   4
10 oz. spinach   3
1 medium eggplant (about 3 cups)   3
1 cup 'makhane' (lotus puffs)   2

Food   <u>Number of Servings</u>

1½ cup green peas (6 oz.)	2
1 cup snow peas	1
1 cup crushed tomato	3
1 medium tomato or onion	1
1 lb. vegetable	4
1 med. size vegetable (zucchini, carrot, …)	1

Dairy

1 cup buttermilk or yogurt	1
1 oz. hard cheese	1
1 oz. cream cheese	1
12 oz. evaporated milk	2
1 cup grated cheese	4
1 cup ice-cream	2
½ gal. milk	8
1 cup nonfat dry milk	3
200 g. (1.3 cups) paneer (cheese) (from ½ gal milk)	4
1 lb. Ricotta cheese	7.5

Fat

½ cup half–and–half	4
½ cup heavy cream	8
8 oz. non-dairy whipped topping	4
½ cup sour cream	4
½ cup oil[1], butter, mayonnaise	8

Sugar

14 oz. condensed sweet milk	12
1 cup sugar (12 tablespoons)	12
1 cup sugar syrup to soak desserts (remainder discarded)	9

[1] It is estimated that a serving of food prepared by pan–frying uses 1 to 1½ teaspoons oil, and that prepared by deep–frying uses ¾ to 1 tablespoon of oil.

Major Nutrients and Vitamins

Major nutrients and some of their benefits and sources are listed below. While each nutrient has its own specific function and relationship to the body, no nutrient acts completely independent of other nutrients. Our body needs all of the nutrients in varying quantities to maintain optimum health. For a 2000 calories diet, it is recommended to take daily 300 grams (g) carbohydrate (25 g fiber), 50 g protein, and less than 65 g fat (20 g saturated fat) and 300 milligrams (mg) cholesterol. Daily values are specified for different vitamins and minerals too.

CARBOHYDRATE (carb): The body metabolizes carb. into glucose, or blood sugar, the body's primary source of fuel. They give energy and endurance. Carb. are classified according to their chemical structure and digestibility. **Simple carb.** are low in nutritional value, promote dental decay, and cause the body to produce insulin and make more fat, cholesterol and uric acid. They are known to have a high glycemic index (GI), that is, they break down fast and convert to glucose to give spurts of energy. They occur in processed sugars. **Complex carb.** comprise of starches and fiber. They are known to have a low GI because the human digestive system breaks down and metabolizes them slowly. It is recommended that 55 to 60% of calories (1 g carb. = 4 calories) come from complex carb. drawn from legumes, whole grains, pasta, rice (brown rice is better than refined rice), fruits, and vegetables; only 10% from processed sugars.

CHOLESTEROL: It is a fatty substance manufactured by the body to build cells and make hormones. But high blood cholesterol is known to increase the chance of heart disease. In general, cholesterol below 200 mg. per deciliter (mg/dl) of blood is considered desirable and should not be higher than 239. LDL (low-density lipoprotein or bad cholesterol) should be below 100 and not more than 160 mg/dl, and HDL (high-density lipoprotein or good cholesterol) should be at least 40 mg/dl, and the higher the better. Cholesterol is present in foods of animal origin. To control it, cut down intake of saturated fat in whole milk and other dairy products, eggs, fatty meats, and tropical oils. Some foods like oat bran, dried beans and green peas, apples and other fruits, and soy products are known to have a cholesterol-lowering effect.

FAT: In small amounts, fats are essential to maintain health but a high-fat diet easily leads to weight gain (1 g fat = 9 calories) and health problems. The general recommendation is to limit fat to 30 % of your calorie intake. *Saturated fat* contained in butter, hard cheese, palm and coconut oils, and fatty meats, is linked to elevated blood cholesterol levels and an increased risk of heart disease and should be avoided. Also avoid *Omega-6* fat found in corn oil and soybean oil; and *trans-fatty acids* found in hard margarine, and partially *hydrogenated vegetable oils* usually contained in commercially baked goods.
Monounsaturated fatty acids contained in olive oil, canola oil, avocados, nuts, either lower cholesterol or have no effect on it. *Omega-3* fat contained in seafood prevent vascular disease and lower **triglycerides**, a kind of fat in the blood that is a recognized factor for heart disease. Omega-3 can also be found in plant food such as flaxseeds and walnuts.

FIBER: It is considered the magic bullet that can prevent or cure everything from cancer to indigestion. It slows down the absorption of sugar, provides bulk, and is low in calories. Fiber falls into 2 broad categories: soluble and insoluble; both are equally important. The *Soluble fiber*, contained in barley, oat bran, oatmeal, rice, wheat bran, flaxseed, fruits, nuts, legumes, and some vegetables, dissolves in water and is absorbed into the bloodstream. *Insoluble fiber*, so called because it passes through the body virtually undigested, promotes the build-up of water in stools, which in turn reduces the time food stays in the colon. It is found in bran, whole wheat bread and cereals, vegetables, and skins of fruits and vegetables. There is no fiber in meats, dairy products or most of the processed foods.

MINERALS: They are considered as essential as vitamins. They include:

Calcium— needed for proper development and maintenance of bones and teeth. The body needs 800–1200 mg daily, depending on age. Sources include milk and milk products, tofu, dark green vegetables, sardines and salmon.

Iron— is present in the red pigment of blood and helps provide energy. The body needs a steady supply of iron, but only in tiny amounts—about 10–15 mg a day. Sources include legumes, brown whole grains, soybean nuts, leafy dark greens specially spinach, fruits, seafood, meat and poultry.

Magnesium— is an important constituent of all soft tissues and bone. Sources are leafy green vegetables, legumes, whole grain products, meat, poultry, fish and eggs.

Phosphorus— works with calcium to form the hard structure of bones and teeth. The body needs about 1000 mg daily. Sources include legumes, dairy products, meat, poultry, fish and egg yolks.

Potassium— maintains an inner balance of body fluids. It is known to lower blood pressure almost as well as drugs do. Is contained in avocados, bananas, citrus fruits, legumes, potatoes, and whole grain products.

Selenium— is an antioxidant that helps to raise level of HDL (good cholesterol). It is found in whole grain products, seeds and nuts, onion, garlic, mushrooms, asparagus, meat, and seafood.

Zinc— is essential for proper immune system function. It is contained in wheat germ, whole wheat, milk, yogurt, and oysters.

PROTEIN: They make up most of our muscles, skin, hair, and other parts and play a vital part in the growth, maintenance, and repair of body tissues, though a poor source of immediate energy for active people. They consist of chains of chemicals called amino acids that are combined and molecularly folded in a unique manner. Complete protein that supply all the amino acids necessary for forming new cells are found in soybeans, meats, eggs and nuts. Legumes are rich in protein but need to be eaten together with whole grains; the amino acids missing from one are made up by the other to supply complete protein. Grains and nuts can also be combined. It is recommended that 10 to 15% of calories (1 g protein = 4 calories) come from sources rich in protein.

VITAMINS: They are known to be essential for energy conversion and other metabolic processes. These are classified according to how they are absorbed and stored in the body. Vitamins A, D, E, and K, the fat-soluble vitamins, require the presence of fat in order to be absorbed from the intestinal tract. Vitamin C and different B vitamins are soluble in water and are more easily absorbed because there is always fluid in the intestines. Some of the vitamins are:

Vitamin A— prevents night blindness and helps maintain healthy skin, hair, nails, and teeth. An antioxidant, it is available from **beta-carotene** in orange and yellow fruits and vegetables such as papaya, mangoes, cantaloupes, carrots, and squash; and leafy green vegetables; and from retinols in fortified milk and dairy products, liver, salmon and other cold-water fish, and egg yolks. It is not easily destroyed in cooking.

Vitamin B— these include:

- **Biotin**: needed for energy metabolism, it is available from soybeans, fortified cereals, yeast, and egg yolks.
- **Folate**: may prevent birth defects and reduce the risk of disease. Sources include broccoli and other cruciferous vegetables, avocados, legumes, oranges, and strawberries. Folic acid is folate's synthetic counterpart and is found in most fortified supplements and foods.
- **Niacin**: promotes normal growth; large doses lower cholesterol. It is found in milk, eggs, legumes, fortified breads and cereal, lean meats, poultry, and seafood.
- **Pantothenic Acid**: aids in energy metabolism; it is contained in almost all foods.
- **Riboflavin**: essential for healthy skin and eyes; it is found in grains and fortified cereals, milk and dairy products, raw mushrooms, lean meat and poultry.
- **Thiamine**: helps maintain digestion, appetite and nerve function. It is obtained from whole grains, legumes, nuts and seeds, and pork.
- **B6**: promotes protein and carbohydrates metabolism. It is available from grains, legumes, green leafy vegetables, potatoes, soybeans, meat, fish, and poultry.
- **B12**: needed to make red blood cells, DNA, RNA, and myelin, it is found in all animal products.

Vitamin C— is needed in higher quantity (recommended daily allowance (RDA) is 60 mg). It strengthens blood vessel walls, promotes iron absorption, and helps control cholesterol. An antioxidant, it is available in all citrus fruits, melons, berries, peppers, broccoli, potatoes, and many other fruits and vegetables. Vitamin C is heat sensitive and is easily destroyed by over-cooking or processing.

Vitamin D— is necessary for calcium absorption, and helps to build and maintain strong bones and teeth. It is obtained from fortified milk and butter, egg yolks, and fish and is also made by the body when exposed to sun.

Vitamin E— maintains muscles and red blood cells. An antioxidant, it is available from whole grains, wheat germ, soybeans, green leafy vegetables, nuts and seeds, vegetable oils, margarine, and eggs.

Vitamin K— is essential for blood clotting; it also strengthens bones significantly. Sources include green and dark green vegetables such as spinach, collard and cabbage, green tea, pork, and liver.

Eliminating one soda a day (160 calories) means a reduction of 58,400 calories in a year.

NUTRITION TABLE

This table is based on the information given on food labels. Get into the habit of checking the ingredients and nutrition information on all foods, especially, the processed foods that you buy.

Abbreviations:
cal: calcium   carb: carbohydrate   chol: cholesterol   iro: iron
mag: magnesium   nia: niacin   pho: phosphorus
pot: potassium   sod: sodium   thi: thiamine

Food (1 serving)	Calories (G)	Protein (G)	Carb (G)	Fiber (G)	Fat (G)	Chol (MG)	Minerals	Vitamins
Bread (1 piece)								
White	80	2.0	16.0	0.5	1.5	0	Cal, iro	Nia, thi
Wholewheat	60	3.0	11.4	2.0	1.0	0	Iro	Thi
Chapati	100	4.0	19.0	2.0	2.0	0	Iro	Thi
Butter (1 tbls)	100	0	0	0	11.0	30.0	-	A
Cheese (1 oz)								
Cheddar	114	7.1	0.4	0	9.4	29.8	Cal,pho sod	A
Cottage 2%	25.5	3.9	1.0	0	0.5	2.4	Cal,pho iro, sod	A
Cream	100	2.2	0.8	0	10.0	31.0	-	A
Mozzarella	80	6.0	0.4	0	6.0	20.0	-	-
Parmesan	110	9.0	1.0	0	7.6	22.4	Cal	-
Ricotta (¼ cup)	110	7.0	2.0	0	8.0	25.0	Cal	A

Food (1 serving)	Calories (G)	Protein (G)	Carb (G)	Fiber (G)	Fat (G)	Chol (MG)	Minerals	Vitamins
Coconut (shelled 1oz.)	100	0.9	4.3	2.6	9.5	0	-	-
Cream								
Half-&-Half (2 tbls)	40	1.0	1.0	0	3.0	15.0	-	-
Heavy (1 tbls)	50	1.0	1.0	0	5.0	20.0	-	-
Sour (2 tbls)	60	0.9	1.2	0	5.0	20.0	-	-
Egg (1)	70	6.0	1.0	0	4.5	215	Pho	A
Fish (raw, 3 oz.)								
Cod	70	15.2	0	0	0.5	31.0	Cal, pho	-
Lobster	77	16.0	0	0	0.8	81.0	Cal, iro	-
White	114	16.2	0	0	5.0	51.0	Cal, pot	A
Flour (1 oz dry about ¼ cup)								
Corn	102	2.0	21.8	3.8	1.1	0	Thi	-
Gram (besan)	110	7.0	17.0	3.0	1.9	0	Iro	B
Soy	125	10.0	9.0	4.0	5.5	0	Mag, pho,pot	B
White unbleached	100	3.0	22.0	0.6	0	0	Iro, thi	-
Whole-wheat	100	3.7	20.0	2.5	2.0	0	Iro, pho pot	B, E
Fruits								
Apple(med)	81	0.3	21.0	3.8	0.5	0	Cal	A
Banana (med.)	105	1.2	26.7	2.7	0.6	0	Cal, pot	A, B
Grapefruit (1 cup)	69	1.3	17.3	2.5	0.2	0	Pot	A, B, C
Mango (1 cup)	107	0.8	28.1	3.0	0.5	0	-	-
Papaya (1 cup)	55	0.9	13.7	2.5	0.2	0	Cal, pot	-
Strawberry (1 cup)	45	0.9	10.5	3.9	0.6	0	Pot	-

Food (1 serving)	Calories (G)	Protein (G)	Carb (G)	Fiber (G)	Fat (G)	Chol (MG)	Minerals	Vitamins
Legumes (1/4cup,40-50g, uncooked)								
Chickpeas	170	10.0	29.0	6.0	2.0	0	Iro, cal	B
Kidney beans	160	11.0	29.0	10.0	0.5	0	Iro, cal	A, B
Lentils	150	11.0	27.0	7.0	0.5	0	Iro, cal	B
Mung beans	160	11.0	28.8	9.0	0.5	0	Cal, pot	B
Margarine (1 tbls)	90	0.1	0	0	11.0	0	-	A, D
Milk (1 cup)								
Skim	80	8.0	11.0	0	0	0	Cal	A, D
Lowfat (1%)	110	8.0	13.0	0	2.5	10.0	Cal	A, D
Lowfat (2%)	130	8.0	13.0	0	5.0	20.0	Cal	A, D
Whole	150	8.0	12.0	0	8.0	35.0	Cal	A, D
Nuts (shelled, 1 oz.)								
Almonds	160	6.0	6.0	3.0	15.0	0	Iro, cal	E
Cashews	160	5.0	8.0	0.5	14.0	0	Iro, pho	B
Pistachio	164	5.8	7.1	3.1	13.7	0	Iro, cal	-
Onion (med.)	42	1.3	9.5	2.0	0.2	0	Cal, pot	B
Oil (1 tbls.)	120	0	0	0	14.0	0	-	-
Pasta (uncooked, dry)								
Macaroni (1.8 oz.)	185	6.2	37.6	0	0.6	1.2	-	-
Spaghetti (1.3 oz.)	140	4.8	29.6	0	0.5	1.2	-	-
Rice (1/4 cup dry, uncooked)								
Basmati white	180	4.0	38.0	1.0	0.5	0	Iro	-
Basmati brown	150	3.0	32.0	2.0	1.0	0	Thi	-
White long Grain	160	3.0	35.0	0	0	0	Iro, thi, nia	-

Food (1 serving)	Calo-ries (G)	Prot-ein (G)	Carb (G)	Fib-er (G)	Fat (G)	Chol (MG)	Mine-rals	Vita-mins
Sprouts (1 cup raw)								
Mung bean	30	3.0	4.0	0.5	0.1	0	Iro	A, C
Soy Bean	100	11.0	8.0	2.0	6.0	0	Cal, iro	C
Sugar (1 tbls.)	48	0	12.0	0	0	0	-	-
Tofu (3 oz.)	50	6.0	2.0	0	2.5	0	Cal	-
Tomato (med.)	26	1.0	5.7	1.4	0.4	0	Pot, nia	-
Vegetables (raw)								
Broccoli (1cup, 88 g)	25	2.6	4.6	2.6	0.3	0	Cal, pot	A, C, E
Cauliflower (1cup, 100 g)	25	1.9	5.2	2.5	0.2	0	Pot	B
Green Beans (2/3 cup, 81 g)	25	1.0	4.0	2.0	0.2	0	Cal, iro	A, C
Green Peas (2/3 cup, 89 g)	70	5.0	12.0	4.0	0.5	0	Iro	A, C
Spinach 2 cups, 60 g)	13	1.6	2.0	1.6	0.2	0	Iro	A
Yogurt, Plain (1 cup, 2% fat)	140	11.0	16.0	0	3.0	15.0	Cal	A
Whole Grains (uncooked, ½ cup, about 2 oz)								
Barley, pearl	352	9.9	77.7	15.6	1.2	0	Iro, pot, pho	B
Bulgur wheat	282	8.5	60.7	7.6	1.4	0	Iro	B
Oatmeal	150	5.0	27.0	4.0	3.0	0	Iro	B
Wheat Germ	216	16.4	28.0	7.3	6.0	0	Mag, pho,pot	B, E

Index

This includes all recipes and other ingredients that are used. First letter of the recipe name is capitalized.

ABOUT THE AUTHOR

Kusum Gupta, a graduate from Delhi University, India, has thirty-six years of successful professional career. She worked in International Business Machines (IBM) in USA for nearly twenty-five years and retired as Advisory Programmer in 1992. Since then, she has been involved in several community activities:

- Teaches Indian cooking, a part of Continuing Education Program in schools.
- Is member of Interfaith Council. Gives classes and presentations on Hindu spirituality.
- Organizes India Festival every year, in collaboration with local organizations, to promote multiculturalism.
- Served on the board of 'Community Family Development' for several years. Acted as President for two terms.

Her prime interest is finding new ways to cook and promoting a healthy way to live, physically and spiritually. She teaches Indian cooking and also gives classes on Hindu spirituality. She has also published:

1. *Recipes with a Spice - From Asian Indian Kitchens*
2. *Hindu Spirituality - A Practical Approach Based on the Bhagavad Gita.*